THE LETTERS OF ST. JEROME

ANCIENT CHRISTIAN WRITERS

THE WORKS OF THE FATHERS IN TRANSLATION

EDITED BY

JOHANNES QUASTEN
Catholic University of America
Washington, D.C.

WALTER J. BURGHARDT, S.J.
Woodstock College
Woodstock, Md.

No. 33

THE LETTERS OF
ST. JEROME

TRANSLATED

BY

CHARLES CHRISTOPHER MIEROW, Ph.D.

INTRODUCTION AND NOTES

BY

THOMAS COMERFORD LAWLER

VOLUME I

Letters 1-22

NEWMAN PRESS

New York, N.Y./Ramsey, N.J.

De Licentia Superioris
  Nihil Obstat
          J. Quasten
              Cens. Dep.

Imprimatur:

          Patricius A. O'Boyle, D.D.
              Archiep. Washingtonen.
                  die 21 Aprilis 1963

Library of Congress
Catalog Card Number: 63-22028

ISBN: 0-8091-0087-8

PUBLISHED BY PAULIST PRESS
Editorial Office: 1865 Broadway, New York, N.Y. 10023
Business Office: 545 Island Road, Ramsey, N.J. 07446

PRINTED AND BOUND IN THE UNITED STATES OF AMERICA

CONTENTS

v

THE LETTERS OF ST. JEROME

INTRODUCTION

The letters of St. Jerome comprise one of the most important collections of epistles in all Latin literature. It is a large collection—over 150 items, some 120 by the Saint himself and the remainder including a number by other notables of the day. Indispensable to the biographer and to the student of Jerome's work, this body of correspondence is also a significant source of information on the world of Jerome and the people in it, on the general social and ecclesiastical life of his time. Jerome's letters are, moreover, stylistically the best of his works.

It is, of course, for his work on Scripture, and especially for his production of the Latin Vulgate version of the Bible, that Jerome is best known; but it is from his letters that he himself is known best. No other source gives such an intimate picture of this Saint, one of the four great doctors of the Western Church and generally regarded as the most learned of the Latin Fathers. Here we can see the tireless scholar, the gifted translator and exegete; here we have the great ascetic and promoter of the ascetic life, albeit himself impatient at times and irascible, strong-minded and intransigent, given to exaggeration and free with vituperation; here an uncompromising and outspoken critic of contemporary morals, firm and insistent in his spiritual direction, yet also a man of kindliness and sympathy; here an adviser to the Chair of Peter, strong champion of the primacy of the papacy, staunchly orthodox, frequently in controversy, a powerful and devastating polemicist. Here also are precious details of his life not otherwise known. Jerome was one of the leading figures of his day, widely acquainted as well as widely known, and a man of considerable travel before his settlement for good at the monastery in Bethlehem. Deeply versed in both sacred and profane literature, he was himself a fluent writer, a superb Latin stylist, and he has preserved for us vivid descriptions of personalities and events of his day, of, for example, monastic life, doctrinal dispute, social custom. The correspondence which has survived is a veritable treasure-trove for the hagiographer, but also for the theologian, the scriptural scholar, the historian of the period.

Not all of the letters are of equal interest or importance. Some are only brief notes, running but a few lines; others amount to pamphlet-length tracts. This one will be little more than a few complaining words from Jerome taking a correspondent to task for not writing; that one will be an exegetical treatise; another will be a long exhortation to the ascetic life; another still will amount to a funeral oration on a departed soul; this one will be an essay on virginity; that one will impart advice on the rearing of children. Jerome's addressees will range from contemporary luminaries such as the Pope in Rome and the illustrious Augustine of Hippo all the way down to persons unknown to history except for the fact that Jerome wrote to them.

How extensive St. Jerome's total correspondence may have been, we can only guess. But we must make our estimate a high one, judging from what has survived and bearing in mind the extraordinary reputation he had, the number of persons who sought his advice and knowledge, the controversies in which he was involved, the caustic criticism he attracted as well as ardent admiration. We know that he was an indefatigable writer, and he himself asserts at one point that he does not know how many letters there had been to Paula and Eustochium "because they are written every day."[1]

The correspondence corpus as it has come down to us consists of 154 items. One of these, No. 18, seems clearly to be composed of two separate documents,[2] and the total thus may be given as 155. Thirty-two of the lot have authors other than Jerome (about half of these are letters *to* Jerome; some are translations; one, No. 150, is of a later era and does not properly belong in the collection; one, No. 46, is from Paula and Eustochium to Marcella but may actually have been drafted or at least rewritten by Jerome[3]); and two additional ones, Nos. 148 and 149, are considered spurious. Thus, the number we have certainly written by Jerome is 120 or 121, depending on whether Letter 18 is counted as a single document or as two. Four of the epistles actually written by Jerome have been added to the corpus only within this century, and it is by no means unreasonable to expect that further discoveries will be made of new letters, or perhaps of evidence to permit the inclusion in the corpus of certain letters now known but considered spurious or of doubtful authenticity.[4]

JEROME'S LIFE AND THE LETTERS

The time span of Jerome's extant correspondence covers most of his life, the big exception being his early years. Jerome was born in Stridon in or about the year 347 of fairly well-to-do parents.[5] Having received his initial education locally, he spent his teens as a student in Rome, and it was there that he was baptized, perhaps by Pope Liberius. Jerome's parents were Catholics, but infant baptism was not then so general a custom as it is today, and there was nothing particularly unusual in the timing of his reception of the sacrament. About the year 367 he set out from Rome, ac-

companied by his childhood friend and fellow student
Bonosus, and traveled to Gaul, to Treves, to the "semibarbarous banks of the Rhine."[6]   At Treves he made copies of
some commentaries of Hilary of Poitiers, and there also he
seems to have learned something of the hermits of Egypt. It
was following his return to home territory that he became
associated with the famous group of young ascetics at
Aquileia grouped around Bishop Valerian—"a choir of the
blessed" is the term Jerome himself would use later.[7]   He
renewed contact with Rufinus of Aquileia, whom he had met
earlier in Rome. Names we find in this period include
Chromatius, Jovinus, Eusebius, Julian, Heliodorus of Altinum, Evagrius of Antioch, and others.   Unfortunately, there
are no letters extant from all these early years, with the possible exception of Letter 1, which may have been written at
Aquileia.[8]   Letters written later include a number of references to his childhood and youth; the biographer will find
much of interest on the young Jerome, but at the same time
will find the facts and details on this period frustratingly
sparse.

Letter 1, while possibly to be dated earlier, may have been
composed only after Jerome's arrival at Antioch, probably in
the fall of 374, on his first trip to the East.   Jerome's departure from Aquileia was evidently an abrupt one—in a
letter to Rufinus, for example, he mentions a "sudden tornado," *subitus turbo*, which took him from Rufinus' side[9]—
but the full reasons for it are not known.   Letters 2–9 and
11–17 date from Jerome's stay at Antioch and the time he
spent as a hermit in the desert of Chalcis.   Letter 10 may
belong to the same period, but also may with Letter 18A
(and possibly 18B) have been written at Constantinople.
Jerome went to Constantinople around 379—which is also
the likely year of his ordination as a priest—and was there at

the time of the General Council of 381. He was a disciple of Gregory of Nazianzus, and it was also in Constantinople that he came to know Gregory of Nyssa.

In 382 he left the imperial capital of the East and went with Bishops Paulinus and Epiphanius to Rome. The next couple of years were likely one of the happiest periods of his life. He served as secretary to Pope Damasus, and devoted hours also to scholarly work on Scripture and to promotion of the ascetic life. It is during this period that we find him giving spiritual direction on the Aventine to a number of noble Roman ladies, holy women interested in the ascetic life, Marcella, Asella, Paula, Eustochium, and the rest. Near the end of 384, however, Pope Damasus died; and Jerome, his friend and protector gone and himself the target of much open criticism and abuse from those who resented his criticism of the clergy, envied his influence, considered the way of life he fostered extreme, or misunderstood his work on the Bible, left the city in the fall of 385. Letters dating from these few years are Nos. 19–45 (and possibly 18B).

Again Jerome went to the East, never to return in his lifetime, and the remainder of his correspondence, Letters 46–154, belong to the last thirty-odd years of his life. In 385/386 we have the trip, together with a group under the guidance of Paula, in Palestine and in Egypt; then came the final settlement at Bethlehem, where Jerome supervised a religious community and Paula, later Eustochium, headed a convent for women. The following years were marked by controversies and quarrels, with his former friend Rufinus, with John of Jerusalem, with the distant correspondent Augustine. They also saw the completion of his work on the Vulgate as well as an outflow of scriptural commentaries and other writings, including his correspondence. In all, it was a period of work and prayer and study and teaching to the end. The date of death of this controversial figure is itself controversial: 419 or 420.[10]

PUBLICATION AND EDITIONS

Jerome's letters seem in many cases to have been greatly admired and esteemed from the start, and there was no waiting for his death for publication and circulation. In fact, as first editor and publisher of his letters it would seem that we can name the Saint himself. Writing in the year 392 or 393 in his *De viris illustribus*,[11] he mentions among the works he had produced thus far one book of letters to various addressees as well as one of epistles to Marcella. Certainly a number of his letters seem clearly to have been composed with care and stylistically adorned with an audience in mind far wider than those to whom they were immediately addressed. Through the years Jerome's letters have been prized for their literary excellence as well as for their content.[12] Their popularity in the Middle Ages is attested by the many manuscript copies of various epistles or collections which have survived —some of the manuscripts go back beyond the year 600— and indeed by the numerous references to the letters or quotations from them found in the literature of the Middle Ages. "It was Saint Jerome," writes Dom Leclercq of medieval monastics, "they consulted on the philological interpretation of Holy Scripture, though he seems to have exerted influence above all through his letters: here were at the same time models of the art of letter writing and a source, as well, for ideas on monastic asceticism."[13]

The first printed editions of Jerome's works appeared in the third quarter of the fifteenth century. Important among the editions of following years were those of Erasmus (1516–

20), M. Victorius (1565–72), and I. Martianay and A. Pouget (1693–1706). A landmark in the field, superseding all previous editions, was the monumental work of D. Vallarsi (two editions: Verona 1734–42 and Venice 1766–72). It is the Vallarsi text which is reprinted in Migne's *Patrologia latina* (Vols. 22–30; the letters are in Vol. 22). So far as the letters are concerned, the Vallarsi text was superseded by the definitive edition of I. Hilberg in the Vienna Academy's *Corpus scriptorum ecclesiasticorum latinorum*: Vol. 54 (1910), Letters 1–70; Vol. 55 (1912), Letters 71–120; Vol. 56 (1918), Letters 121–54. The present translation is based upon the Hilberg edition. It is to be regretted that Hilberg was not able to crown his work with the indexes and prolegomena he had intended. More recent is the edition, together with a French translation, of J. Labourt (*Saint Jerome: Lettres*, 8 vols., Paris 1949 ff.).[14] There have, in addition, been a number of editions of selected epistles from the total correspondence.[15]

The mixed character of the letters of St. Jerome has been alluded to above. In publishing a translation of the complete collection, as is projected in the present series, there is little alternative to offering the letters in the traditional sequence, in which, as has been indicated, the letters are for the most part in general chronological order. Unfortunately, this order in some cases separates letters on the same or similar subjects which it is interesting to read and study together; it also keeps apart, for example, the letters making up the historic exchange between Jerome and Augustine. The number of ways in which the letters might be grouped or classified—some of the letters, of course, falling into more than one category—is almost limitless. In order to give a better picture of the collection as a whole and of what it contains, some of the possible general categories are noted in the following paragraphs. The lists of examples given of the various types are not in all cases exhaustive. Questions on the identification of personalities, as well as on the times and places of composition and other matters, are discussed in the notes to the individual letters.

TYPES OF LETTERS BY JEROME

A number of the letters Jerome wrote were virtually essays in letter form, and some were referred to by the Saint himself as *libelli*, "little books," "pamphlets." The term *libelli* could in truth be fittingly applied to many of his longer epistles. As examples of his essay-letter form might be mentioned Letters 14 (to Heliodorus, an exhortation to the ascetic life), 22 (to Eustochium, on virginity), 52 (to Nepotian, on the duties of the clergy), 53 (to Paulinus, on zeal for learning), 57 (to Pammachius, on the best method of translating), 58 (to Paulinus, on how a priest should live), 130 (to Demetrias, on virginity). There are other letters on moral or ethical questions, such as Nos. 54 (to Furia, on widowhood), 107 and 128 (the first to Laeta, the other to Pacatula, on the training and education of a daughter), 117 (to a mother and daughter in Gaul, on widowhood and virginity and the avoidance of scandal and temptation), 122 and 147 (the first to Rusticus, the other to Sabinian, on penitence), 123 (to Geruchia, on widowhood), 145 (to Exuperantius, on the monastic life).

Many of Jerome's letters deal with matters of scriptural interpretation, a hardly surprising fact in view of the many questions addressed to him as a pre-eminent biblical authority. These letters are of especial interest in forming an estimate of Jerome as a philologist and exegete. As examples of this group might be cited Letters 18A–18B (to Pope Dama-

sus, a commentary on Isa. 6.1–9, Isaias' vision of the seraphim and of the Lord sitting on a throne), 20 (to Damasus,
on the word "hosanna"), 21 (to Damasus, a commentary on
Luke 15.11–32, the parable of the prodigal son), 25 (to
Marcella, on the ten names used by the Hebrews in referring
to God), 26 and 29 (to Marcella, explaining certain Hebrew
words), 30 (to Paula, on the Hebrew letters inserted in Ps.
118), 36 (to Damasus, replying to several scriptural questions), 55 (to Amandus, answering three questions on the
New Testament), 65 (to Principia, a commentary on Ps.
65), 140 (to Cyprian, an exposition of Ps. 89).

Another grouping could be compiled of letters from
Jerome dealing with doctrinal matters and refutations of
heterodoxy. Examples are Letters 15 and 16 (to Pope Damasus, regarding the dispute involving three claimants to the
bishopric of Antioch and on whether there is one or three
hypostases in God), 41 (to Marcella, against the Montanists),
42 (to Marcella, against Novatian), 48 (to Pammachius,
against Jovinian), 61 (to Vigilantius, repudiating his charge
of Origenism), 84 (to Pammachius and Oceanus, defining
and justifying his attitude toward Origen), 85 (to Paulinus,
in reply to questions on the problem of free will and on why
the children of believers are said to be holy), 109 (to Riparius, against Vigilantius), 126 (to Marcellinus and Anapsychia, replying to a query on the origin of the soul), 133
(to Ctesiphon, on some points in the teaching of Pelagius).

Jerome wrote a number of epitaphic and consolatory letters occasioned by deaths among his friends. Here we may
note his Letters 23 (to Marcella, on the death of Lea),
39 (to Paula, on Blesilla), 60 (to Heliodorus, on Nepotian),
66 (to Pammachius, on Paulina), 75 (to Theodora, on Lucinus), 77 (to Oceanus, on Fabiola), 79 (to Salvina, on Neb-
ridius), 108 (to Eustochium, on Paula), 118 (to Julian, on

Julian's wife and daughters), 127 (to Principia, on Marcella).

The collection includes a number of letters from Jerome which might be classified simply as personal notes. As examples of this group might be cited Letters 8, 9, 11, and 12 (to various addressees, largely devoted to complaints of their failure to write), 13 (to his Aunt Castorina, urging a reconciliation), 31 and 34 (the first to Eustochium, the other to Marcella, acknowledging some gifts), 45 (to Asella, a letter of farewell as Jerome was about to leave Italy forever), 71 (to Lucinus, praising this wealthy Spaniard's virtues and urging him to visit the Holy Land).

Letters addressed to women add up to around a third of all the extant letters from Jerome. Marcella is by far the woman most frequently addressed, quite likely because of her leading position in that celebrated circle of religious-minded women that met at her house on the Aventine. Of the other female addressees, most are addressed but once, and none is addressed more than three times. Jerome's previously noted reference to frequent writing to Paula and Eustochium is evidence of the loss of additional epistles. In content, the extant letters addressed to women deal largely with doctrinal matters and scriptural interpretation. Strangely enough, the collection does not include a single letter addressed to Jerome by any of these female addressees.

Correspondence with Pope Damasus

Of Jerome's correspondence with Pope Damasus, we have today eight letters (or nine, again depending on whether No. 18 is to be counted once or twice). Except for the two from Damasus, these have all been mentioned above. It is only reasonable to assume there were others, particularly in the period between Jerome's return to Rome in 382 and the death of the Pontiff near the end of 384.

The first of Jerome's extant letters to Damasus, No. 15, was written from the desert of Chalcis; it speaks of the controversy then dividing the Church in the East and asks the Pope for guidance. It is not known whether Jerome knew Damasus personally at this time. Letter 16, also written from the desert, is on the same theme; in it Jerome notes that he has written the Pope before and he renews his request for a judgment. We have no answer to either of these letters, whether because of nondelivery or perhaps because of a failure of the Pope to reply. In 18A–18B we have a commentary by Jerome—more like a treatise than an epistle, but apparently addressed or dedicated to Damasus—on the vision of Isaias. Letter 19 is a short note from Damasus asking Jerome for the meaning in Hebrew of the word "hosanna"; Jerome's lengthy reply on the meaning and origin of the word is his Letter 20. Letter 21 contains a long commentary by Jerome on the parable of the prodigal son. Letter 35 is from Damasus with five scriptural questions; No. 36 is Jerome's response.

THE JEROME-AUGUSTINE EXCHANGE

The Jerome-Augustine correspondence accounts for some seventeen epistles among the letters of St. Jerome: eight addressed to Jerome by Augustine (Nos. 56, 67, 101, 104, 110, 116, 131, 132) and nine addressed to Augustine by Jerome (Nos. 102, 103, 105, 112, 115, 134, 141, 142, 143; this last, No. 143, is to both Alypius and Augustine). The collection also includes two other letters of Augustine: No. 111, to Praesidius, to whom Augustine was entrusting a letter (No. 110) for Jerome, and No. 144, to Optatus of Milevis, dealing with a discussion between Jerome and Augustine on the origin of the soul. All of these letters appear, of course, also among the letters of St. Augustine.[16]

The number of letters addressed to each other by these two giants of the early Church, Jerome and Augustine, is actually quite small when it is considered that the exchange spanned altogether approximately a quarter of a century. Their correspondence, undoubtedly one of the most interesting such exchanges in all patrology, had its tragic aspects in the misunderstandings that arose between the two, differences that could easily have been reduced more quickly had they been able to meet and talk face to face, or even if the mail in those days had traveled more swiftly and reliably. Each knew the other only by reputation and through letters. There is nothing to suggest that their paths ever crossed when both were in Rome; when Augustine left Africa for Rome in 383, he had not yet broken with Manicheanism, whereas Jerome at the time was not only a Catholic and a priest, but was a friend and confidant of the Pope. Their letters to each other start with one from Augustine about the year 394 or 395; Augustine had by then been ordained and was settled at Hippo, but was not yet a bishop, and Jerome had long since been established at Bethlehem.

The exchange got off to a bad start. It seems that Augustine entrusted his first letter to Jerome to one Profuturus, who never reached the Orient. A second letter from Augustine, written some time later, also went astray. Word eventually reached Jerome, however, that Augustine had written—but with the unfortunate impression being gained by Jerome that Augustine had written a "book" against him. It can be questioned, of course, whether Jerome, already a recognized scholar and certainly a more qualified linguist than Augustine, would have received that first letter from Hippo with complete good grace even if it had reached him directly and promptly; he might in any event have considered it some-thing of an impertinent "challenge" from a relatively un-known priest of Africa. Augustine, not convinced by argu-ments for a new translation of the Old Testament directly from the Hebrew, had written Jerome asking him to continue his translation of the Bible on the same lines he had em-ployed in his edition of Job, wherein signs had been used to show where the Latin text differed from the Septuagint; quite frankly, Augustine would like Jerome's translation to be made from the Septuagint. Here was a clash between Augustine's emphasis on the authority of that Greek version and Jerome's pursuit instead of the *veritas hebraica*. More-over, Augustine had disputed a point in Jerome's commen-tary on the Epistle to the Galatians, and in fact in his second letter urged a recantation by Jerome of his suggestion that St. Paul was guilty of a polite fiction or falsehood when recount-ing, in chapter 2 of Galatians, St. Peter's accommodation to Jewish prejudices and his own stand against Peter on this. In his second letter to Jerome, Augustine also mentioned that he had seen a copy of a certain book by Jerome, and that while the copy he had seen had no title on it, someone had suggested that it be called *Epitaphium*. Augustine felt that Jerome might not agree with this title, since the book con-tained accounts of the lives and writings of some persons who were still living. The book in question was the *De viris illustribus*, with Jerome himself (though not Augustine) among the "famous men."

The irascible Jerome proved his irascibility. Some of his lines to Hippo drip with biting sarcasm and irony; he sug-gests that Augustine is trying to show off his learning and might better keep to his own business; and for good measure he has virtually sneering remarks for some of Augustine's work, the *Enarrationes in psalmos*. Augustine meanwhile assured Jerome that he had not written a "book" against him, and explained how the first letters had gone astray. Jerome finally had in Bethlehem authenticated copies of the first two letters from Augustine—this was about a decade after the first had been sent—and he wrote an exhaustive reply to the questions raised. He explained the title of *De viris illustribus;* he defended his position on the interpretation of Galatians and cited other authors in support; he expounded his views on the Septuagint. Then there is another letter from Jerome, a short but very friendly one. Augustine's next letter contains an effective rebuttal of the view about a "lie" in Galatians—the request for a "recantation" is not withdrawn, but this point is not now pressed; at the same time Augustine recognizes Jerome's argument for translating the Old Testament directly from the Hebrew instead of merely correcting the Latin text by the Septuagint.

There was now a break of around five years in the exchange. Later letters, however, show the reconciliation between the two men to be complete (though Augustine did keep his views on the authority of the Septuagint[17]), with sincere respect and admiration on the part of each for the other, and the two were as one in the common fight against the Pelagian heresy. Jerome's letters to Augustine never contained the "recantation" which had been asked; but in his *Dialogus adversus Pelagianos* Jerome not only had warm words of praise for the "holy and eloquent Bishop Augustine,"[18] but also had evidently come around to Augustine's view in the Galatians dispute.[19] Augustine had been throughout the much more patient and understanding of the two, never losing his temper; if either is to be said to have come off best in the exchange, the nod would go to Hippo.

OTHER NON-JEROME LETTERS

There are three letters from Pope Innocent I among the

letters of St. Jerome: Nos. 135 (to Bishop Aurelius, enclosing a letter, No. 136, to Jerome), 136 (to Jerome, expressing sympathy following the pillaging and partial burning of Jerome's monasteries by the Pelagians and offering to take action if Jerome will make specific charges), 137 (to Bishop John of Jerusalem, taking him to task for allowing such havoc to be wreaked in Bethlehem).

Three of the Easter letters of Theophilus of Alexandria are preserved, in Latin translation, in the collection: Nos. 96, 98, 100 (these letters, the first two of which are especially rich in theological content, deal with the errors of Origen and of Apollinaris of Laodicea). There is also a synodical letter of Theophilus directed to the bishops of Palestine and of Cyprus (No. 92, reporting on a gathering in Alexandria against the adherents of Origen), as well as a reply (No. 93) to this synodical letter from the Council of Jerusalem. There are four other letters of Theophilus among Jerome's letters: Nos. 87 and 89 (to Jerome, brief epistles in connection with moves against Origenists), 113 (a fragment of a letter to Jerome which contained a long invective against John of Jerusalem), 90 (to Epiphanius of Salamis, urging this metropolitan of Cyprus to call a synod which would condemn Origenism).

Two letters of Epiphanius of Salamis are preserved, also in Latin translation, in the collection: Nos. 51 and 91 (the first to John of Jerusalem, the second to Jerome, both pertaining to Epiphanius' fight against Origenism).

Up to this point mention has been made of two letters of Pope Damasus, ten of St. Augustine, three of Pope Innocent I, eight of Theophilus of Alexandria, one of the Council of Jerusalem, and two of Epiphanius of Salamis, as well as of Letters 46 (from Paula and Eustochium to Marcella, though possibly actually drafted by Jerome), 148 and 149 (considered spurious), and 150 (a Latin version of a letter from

Procopius of Gaza to a Jerome later than our Jerome of Stridon; Hilberg does not give the text of this letter). The remaining four non-Jerome items among the letters are Nos. 80 (from Rufinus to Macarius, a preface to Rufinus' Latin translation of Origen's *First Principles*), 83 (from Pammachius and Oceanus to Jerome, dealing with the translation of Origen's *First Principles*), 94 (from Dionysius, bishop of Lydda, to Theophilus, praising the latter's victories over Origenism), 95 (from Pope Anastasius I to Simplicianus, on the condemnation of Origenism).

*   *   *

The present volume contains the first twenty-two of the letters of St. Jerome. A majority of these twenty-two have been referred to in the foregoing section.

Letter 1, addressed to Jerome's priest friend Innocent and apparently written at Innocent's suggestion, contains an account of a woman who was accused of adultery but who survived seven attempts to execute her with the sword; composed somewhere in the period 369–75, it is of interest largely as perhaps the oldest of Jerome's extant writings, and also as an illustration of the Saint's early style.

Letter 2 is from Jerome asking some monks to pray that he may have both the will and the power to withdraw from the world; it was written perhaps in the fall of 374 at Antioch. Letter 3 is from Jerome to Rufinus and is clear testimony to the close friendship that existed between the two men before their later estrangement. Nos. 4 and 5 are from Jerome to Florentinus, the first asking Florentinus to give a letter to Rufinus, the second evidently written after receipt of news from Florentinus that Rufinus had not by then arrived in Jerusalem as Jerome had heard; Letter 5 shows that Jerome by this time had actually entered the desert of Chalcis. Nos.

6–13 are miscellaneous letters from Jerome to various addressees: he asks forgiveness because this one has not heard
from him, and he complains to others because he has not
heard from them; he writes to an aunt urging a reconciliation, but does not tell us what their difference was about;
there are references to his present life in the desert as well as
allusions to earlier days.   Letter 10, to Paul of Concordia,
may actually have been written somewhat later, after Jerome
had left the desert and Antioch.   Letter 14 is from Jerome
to Heliodorus with a long exhortation to the ascetic life; it is
written in a highly rhetorical style, and Jerome himself referred to it later somewhat disparagingly as the product of a
youth, but nonetheless it won considerable admiration.   Nos.
15 and 16 are the first of Jerome's extant letters to Pope
Damasus; these deal with a doctrinal (and semantic) dispute
then dividing the Church in the East, and they show
Jerome's strong support for the primacy of Rome.   Letter 17
is to a priest of Chalcis indicating that Jerome will soon be
leaving the desert.   In 18A–18B, likely composed in whole
or in part in or about the year 381 at Constantinople, we
have a commentary on the vision of Isaias; this appears to be
the oldest, exclusive of translations, of Jerome's extant biblical works.

The remaining four epistles in the present volume date
from the period of Jerome's stay in Rome following his first
trip to the East.   Letter 19 is a brief request from Pope
Damasus regarding the meaning of the word "hosanna"; No.
20 is Jerome's reply to this letter.   Letter 21 contains a long
exegesis of the parable of the prodigal son.   Letter 22, one
of the most famous of the entire collection, is addressed to
the young Eustochium and amounts to a lengthy treatise on
motivations and rules of conduct for a life of virginity; it is
this *libellus* which contains Jerome's celebrated account of

the dream or vision he had in which he was accused of being a "Ciceronian" and not a "Christian."

The text followed in the translation of these letters is that provided by I. Hilberg, *Sancti Eusebii Hieronymi epistulae* (Corpus scriptorum ecclesiasticorum latinorum 54 [Vienna-Leipzig 1910] 1–211). An earlier English translation of Letters 1–17 and 22 was given by W. H. Fremantle, with the assistance of G. Lewis and W. G. Martley, in *The Principal Works of Saint Jerome* (A Select Library of Nicene and Post-Nicene Fathers of the Christian Church, Second Series, Vol. 6 [Grand Rapids 1954] 1–41). An English translation of Letters 1, 7, 14, and 22 also appears in F. A. Wright, *Select Letters of St. Jerome* (Loeb Classical Library [London 1933] 3–159). An English translation of Letters 9, 10, 14, and 22 is included in P. Carroll, *The Satirical Letters of St. Jerome* (Chicago 1956) 1–2, 129–31, 2–15, 17–68.

*   *   *

Dr. Charles Christopher Mierow, who prepared for Ancient Christian Writers a translation of almost a third of St. Jerome's Letters, unfortunately died before completing preparation for publication of an introduction and notes to the letters. Following Dr. Mierow's death, the present writer, who never had the pleasure of knowing Dr. Mierow personally but knew of his work for Ancient Christian Writers, was asked by the Editors of the series to prepare an introduction and to annotate these letters. While taking, of course, full responsibility for the introduction and notes as here published, the present writer wishes to acknowledge that his task was considerably eased by the many helpful notes left by the late Dr. Mierow.

*   *   *

LETTER 1

To the priest Innocent
Concerning the woman seven times struck by the sword[1]

1. You have often charged me, dearest Innocent, not to keep silent about the miraculous event that occurred in our time. I kept refusing through modesty and, as I now learn by experience, with good reason. I mistrusted my ability to do your bidding, both because all that man can say is inadequate to extol what is heavenly, and because inactivity, like a sort of rust upon the intellect, had dried up what little power of expression I once possessed.[2] You, however, kept urging that in the affairs of God it is not our limitations that must be considered, but the spirit which we apply to them, and that words cannot fail him who places his trust in the Word.[3]

2. What am I to do, then? The task is beyond me, yet I dare not decline it. An unskilled passenger, I am placed in charge of a merchantman.[4] A man who has never so much as pulled an oar on a lake, I am made to shift for myself on the roaring Euxine Sea.[5] Now the shores are vanishing from my sight, "sky there is everywhere and everywhere sea."[6] Now the crest of the waves bristles in the darkness,[7] and the foaming floods show white against the black night of the storm clouds.

2 You urge me to hoist the bellying sails to the masthead, loosen the sheets, and take the tiller. And so I am acting in obedience to your command, and because love can do all things, I feel confident that with the Holy Spirit prospering my course I shall find solace whatever the event. If the surf bears me to the desired haven, I shall be regarded as a navi-

gator. If my rude speech falters on the rough quicksands of the tale, you may question my ability, but certainly you will not be able to doubt my good intentions.

3. Well, then, Vercelli[8] is a city of Liguria, situated not far from the foothills of the Alps. Once prosperous, it is now half-destroyed and has but few inhabitants. When the governor was making his visitation there, a certain woman and a man accused by her husband of being her paramour were brought before him. He consigned them to the horrors of punishment in prison. 2 Not long afterwards the infliction of pain was used to discover the truth. As the blood-stained hook kept furrowing his sides and his flesh became black and blue, the unhappy youth sought to avoid prolonged torture by the short cut of death. But while speaking falsely against his own passions, he brought accusation against another's also, and thus it appeared that among all men he was the most miserable and deserving of execution, because he left an innocent woman no chance to deny the accusation.

3 But, as a matter of fact, the woman was more courageous than her sex. Her body lay stretched upon the rack, and her hands, stained with the filth of the prison, were tied behind her back; yet she looked up to heaven with her eyes, which alone the executioner had no power to coerce, and with tears streaming down her cheeks she said: "Thou, Lord Jesus, from whom nothing is hidden, who art a searcher of the reins and of the heart,[9] thou art my witness that it is not to save myself from death that I persist in denying the charge, but to avoid sin that I refuse to lie. 4 But you, O most wretched man, if you are in haste to die, why must you destroy two innocent lives? As for myself, I too desire to die. I desire to lay aside this hateful body—but not as being an adulteress. Here is my throat—I welcome the shining sword unafraid—but I shall take my innocence with me! He does not die who is slain to live again."

4. Then the governor, who had been feasting his eyes on the gory sight, like a wild beast that after once tasting blood always thirsts for more, ordered the tortures to be doubled. Savagely gnashing his teeth, he threatened the executioner with like punishment if the weaker sex did not confess what a man's strength had not been able to refuse to confess.

5. Help, Lord Jesus! For this one creature of thine how many torments have been devised![10] Her hair is tied to a stake, her whole body is bound more tightly to the rack, and fire is brought close to her feet. The executioner stabs both her sides, nor are her breasts spared. The woman remains unshaken. Her spirit remains untouched by her bodily pain. At peace with her conscience, she kept the raging torments from having any effect on her. 2 The cruel judge rises, frustrated. She continues in prayer to the Lord. Her limbs are wrenched from their sockets, but she only raises her eyes to heaven. Another confesses guilt charged to both; she denies it for him who confesses it; in peril of her own life, she vindicates one who is in peril of his.

6. Meanwhile she is always saying: "Beat me, burn me, tear me to pieces, I did not do it. If you will not believe my words, the day will come when this charge will be scrutinized with care. I shall have a Judge to do me justice!"

2 Tired now, the tormentor was sighing and groaning. There was no place for a new wound. His ferocity vanquished, he shuddered to behold the body he had mangled. Straightway the governor was aroused to anger. "Why are you surprised, you onlookers," he said, "if the woman prefers torture to death? Surely, it takes two to commit adultery, and I find it easier to believe that a guilty woman should deny the charge when accused than that an innocent youth should make a confession."

7. Accordingly, a like sentence was pronounced on both, and the executioner dragged the condemned pair away. The

entire populace poured forth to see the sight; in fact, it might have been supposed that the city was emigrating, so dense was the throng rushing out through the crowded gates. As for the wretched young man, his head was cut off by the very first stroke of the sword, and his headless trunk rolled over in its blood. 2 When they came to the woman, she knelt down upon the ground. The gleaming sword was raised above her trembling neck, the executioner brought down his trained right arm with all his strength. But the moment it came in contact with her body, the deadly sword was stayed: it lightly grazed the skin, enough to draw a little blood. The man who had struck the blow was terrified by the failure of his hand, and marveling at his drooping sword, he whirled his vanquished right arm aloft for a second blow. 3 Again the sword lost its force as it fell upon the woman, and, as though the steel feared to touch the accused, it rested harmlessly on her neck. Thereupon the headsman, enraged and panting, threw his cloak back across his shoulder. As he was exerting all his strength, he shook to the ground a clasp pin which held the edges of his mantle. Unaware of this, he brandished his sword for the stroke. "Look," said the woman, "a gold pin has fallen from your shoulder. Pick it up. It has cost you much labor. You will lose it."

8. I ask you, how do you explain such composure? She has no fear of impending death. She that is smitten is full of joy; the executioner turns pale. Her eyes fail to see the sword—they behold only the clasp. And as though to have no fear of death were not enough, she bestowed a kindness on her fierce assailant.

2 And now came the third stroke: it too the mystery of the Trinity had rendered naught.[11] Then the executioner, thoroughly terrified and no longer trusting his blade, put the point to her throat, in order that the sword which could not

cut her body might at least be buried in her body by the pressure of his hand. But the sword—a startling fact, unheard of through the ages—bent back to the hilt and, as though vanquished and looking to its master, confessed that it could not give her the death blow.

9.   Here let me bring to mind the instance of the three young men who amid the chilled, swirling flames sang hymns instead of weeping, about whose turbans and holy locks the fire played harmlessly.[12] Now let us recall the story of the blessed Daniel, before whom the lions lay down with fawning tails, afraid to touch the prey offered them.[13] 2 Let the minds of all turn also to Susanna in the nobility of her faith, who when condemned by an unjust judgment was saved by a youth filled with the Holy Spirit.[14] Note that the mercy of the Lord is the same in both cases: Susanna of old was freed by the judge that she might not die by the sword; this woman, who had been condemned by the judge, was absolved by the sword.[15]

10.   At last the people take up arms to rescue the woman. Young and old, men and women drive the executioner away. The crowd forms a circle about her, and they all can scarcely believe their eyes. The news throws the city nearby into an uproar, and the governor's entire constabulary is assembled. 2 From their midst the man charged with the responsibility for condemned persons burst forth, "staining his snowy locks with dust that he poured upon them,"[16] and exclaimed: "Fellow citizens, is it my life you are seeking? Are you making me a substitute for her? You may be compassionate, you may be merciful, you may wish to save the condemned woman, but surely I, who am innocent, ought not to perish."

3 The throng being cut to the heart by this plea, a gloomy sense of frustration descended upon all, and their purpose underwent a remarkable change. Whereas their previous

defense of her had seemed the path of duty, it now seemed to be a sort of duty to permit her to be executed.

11.   Accordingly a new sword is produced; likewise a new executioner.   There stands the victim, with Christ's favor her only strength.   The first time she is struck she is shaken; at the second blow she totters; wounded by the third,[17] she falls on her face and—oh the majesty of the divine power to be exalted!—she who previously had been smitten by four strokes without injury, appears—for the moment—to die that an innocent man need not die in her stead.

12.   Those of the clergy whose duty it was wrapped her bloodstained body in a linen cloth.   They dug a grave and prepared a tomb, building it of stones in the customary fashion.   Hastening its course, the sun sets in the west, and the night comes on to permit the Lord's mercy to work in secret.   2 Suddenly the woman's bosom quivers, her eyes seek the light, her body is restored to life.   Now she breathes, she sees, she raises herself and speaks.   At last she is able to cry: *The Lord is my helper: I will not fear what man can do unto me.*[18]

13.   Meanwhile an aged woman, supported by alms given by the church, rendered back to heaven her soul which was owed thereto.   And as though the course of events had designedly taken this turn, her body was buried in the tomb in place of the other.   When it was yet scarcely light, the devil[19] came up in the person of the headsman, looked for the corpse of the woman executed, and asked to have her grave pointed out to him.   Surprised that she could have died, he suspects that she is still alive.   2 The clergy show him the fresh turf and the earth that had just now been heaped up.   They rebuke his demands as follows: "Go ahead, dig up the bones just laid to rest!   Bring war upon her anew in her tomb!   And if that is not enough, tear her limb from limb to be hacked by birds and beasts!   A woman struck

seven times by the sword ought to endure something more than mere death."

14. The while the executioner was being thrown into confusion by such show of hostility, the woman was secretly revived in the house.[20] And that the frequent calls of the physician at the church might not open the way for suspicion, they cut her hair short and removed her in the company of some virgins to a secluded country house. There she changed her garb to male attire, and the wound gradually healed and became a scar. And—how true it is that "Law too rigidly enforced will bring grave injustice"[21]—after such miracles the laws still raged against her!

15. And now witness the climax of this my whole story! We now come to the name of our friend Evagrius.[22] If I were to imagine that I could give adequate expression to his labors for Christ, I would only betray my folly. And if I decided to say nothing about them, I could not do so: my voice would cry out in joy. 2 Who, for instance, could worthily eulogize the man who by his vigilance practically buried Auxentius,[23] the incubus of Milan, even before he was dead, and enabled the bishop of Rome,[24] when all but enmeshed by the snares of faction, to vanquish his adversaries and yet spare them when he had overcome them? 3 But myself

> Unfriendly time forbids to treat of these:
> I leave them here for later lips to sing.[25]

I am content merely to give you the conclusion of the present account. Evagrius loses no time to seek an audience with the emperor,[26] importunes him with his entreaties, gains his sympathy for the merits of the case. His earnest pleading is successful: the emperor restored to freedom the woman who had been restored to life.

LETTER 2

*To Theodosius and the other anchorites
living in residence with him*[1]

1 Oh how I wish I were now present in your community
and—though these eyes of mine are unworthy to behold—
to share with all enthusiasm your wonderful fellowship! I
would then be gazing upon the desert, the fairest city of all.
I would be seeing places deserted by their inhabitants
thronged by bands of saints—a veritable paradise.

2 But since my sins[2] keep my person, beset by every form
of transgression, from becoming a member of your blessed
society, therefore I beseech you—and I have no doubt that
you can do it—that by your prayers you set me free from the
darkness of this world. I have told you this before when I
was with you, and now by way of letter I mention to you
again my ardent desire; for my mind and heart are unaltera-
bly set on its achievement. It is for you, then, to see that
success follows my resolve. My part is to show the will; it
is that of your prayers that I have the power as well as the
will.

3 I am like the sick sheep that strays from the rest of the
flock.[3] Unless the Good Shepherd takes me on His shoulders
and carries me back to His fold, my steps will falter, and in
the very effort of rising my feet will give way. I am that
prodigal son who wasted all the portion entrusted to me by
my father.[4] But I have not yet fallen at my father's knees.
I have not yet begun to put away from me the enticements
of my former riotous living.

4 And because I have not so much given up my sins as
begun to wish a little to give them up, now the devil is trying

to ensnare me in new nets.   He puts new stumbling blocks in
my way, he encompasses me on every side with the ocean's
waters and on every side with the ocean's deep.[5]   I find myself in the midst of the element,[6] unwilling to retreat and
unable to advance.   It remains that through your prayers the
breath of the Holy Spirit waft me onward and bring me to the
haven of the longed-for shore.

LETTER 3

To Rufinus[1]

1. God grants more than He is asked, and He often bestows things *that eye hath not seen, nor ear heard, neither hath it entered into the heart of man.*[2] This, my dearest Rufinus, I have long known from the teaching of Holy Scripture, but now I have had proof of it in my own case. For I who used to think that I was quite audacious in my desires if I counterfeited the likeness of your presence with me through the interchange of letters, hear that you are penetrating the hidden places of Egypt, visiting the bands of monks, and going the rounds of heaven's family on earth. 2 Oh, if only the Lord Jesus Christ would suddenly grant me the swift passage of Philip to the eunuch or of Habacuc to Daniel,[3] how tightly would I clasp your neck with my embraces! How fervently I would kiss that mouth that has sometimes erred with me, sometimes uttered wisdom! But because I do not deserve it, and frequent illnesses have weakened my poor body, frail even when it is well, I send you this letter to meet you in my stead: may it bring you to me bound by the tie of love.

2. It was Heliodorus who first brought me the happy tidings and this unexpected joy.[4] I could not believe to be certain what I desired to be certain. This the more as he said he had heard it from someone else; and as the news came unexpected, I could not believe his story. Then while my mind was in longing suspense and uncertainty, an Alexandrine monk, whom the pious devotion of the people had sent over to the Egyptian confessors[5]—in will they are already martyrs—by his firsthand account impelled me to believe. 2

I must admit that not even this convinced me fully. For since he was ignorant of both your native country and your name, this appeared to be the only contribution he made, that he affirmed what another had already intimated. At last the full weight of the truth burst upon me: Rufinus is in Nitria and has reached the blessed Macarius;[6] so persisted the report of a steady stream of people passing through.

3 Now indeed I gave free rein to credulity. Then I really grieved that I was sick. And had not my attenuated physical strength put shackles, as it were, on my feet, neither the heat of midsummer nor the perennial risks of a sea voyage would have prevailed to prevent my setting forth in loving haste. Do believe me, my brother, no storm-tossed sailor so looks for the harbor, no parched fields so long for rain, no anxious mother sitting on the curving shore so eagerly awaits her son.[7]

3. After that sudden tornado tore me from your side,[8] after that impious severance wrenched me, cleaving to you with tenacious affection, from your side,

Then a black raincloud settled o'er my head.

There were seas on all sides, and on all sides sky.[9] Finally, as I wandered on uncertain peregrinations, when Thrace, Pontus and Bithynia, and all my journeyings through Galatia and Cappadocia, yes, and the land of Cilicia with its burning heat had shattered my health, Syria offered itself to me as a safe harbor for a shipwrecked mariner. There I experienced all possible maladies and lost one of my two eyes.[10] For Innocent, the half of my soul,[11] was carried off by a sudden burning fever.

2 Now my one remaining eye, my all, my joy, is our dear Evagrius.[12] Always weak of health, I have come to him as a burden added to his labors. Hylas, the servant of the holy Melania,[13] was with us. By the purity of his character he

had wiped out the stain of servile condition.[14] And he reopened a wound not yet entirely reduced to a scar. But as we
are forbidden by the Apostle's saying[15] to be sorrowful concerning them that are asleep, and the exceeding weight of
sorrow has been lightened by the glad tidings that have since
reached me, I am recounting this to you, that, if you are not
informed, you may learn it; and if you have heard it already,
we may rejoice together.

4. Bonosus,[16] your good friend, rather—he is my friend
too—our good friend, is now climbing the ladder foreshown
in Jacob's dream.[17] He is bearing his cross.[18] He takes no
thought for the morrow.[19] He does not look back.[20] He is
sowing in tears, that he may reap in joy.[21] Adopting the
symbol of Moses, he has hung up the serpent in the wilderness.[22]

This is a true story. Let the miracles invented by lying
Greek and Roman pens pall before it. 2 Here you have a
young man, educated in the world with us in the liberal arts.
He had ample means, was of high station among his peers.
He has given up his mother, his sisters, and his brother whom
he loved dearly. Like a new colonist of Paradise, he has
settled upon an island ruinous to ships because of the sea
that roars about it, whose sharp reefs and bare rocks and
solitude make it a terrifying place.[23] No farmer is there, no
monk, not even the little Onesimus you know of, in whom
he used to take delight as in a little brother, is there in that
awful desolation to offer him companionship.

3 Alone there—no, in the companionship of Christ he is
not alone—he beholds the glory of God, which even the
apostles beheld only in the wilderness.[24] He does not,
indeed, behold towered cities, but he has inscribed himself in
the citizenry of a new city. His limbs are a sorry sight in
their ugly sackcloth, but thus he will be the better taken up

in the clouds to meet Christ.[25]   There are no charming water-
ways for him to enjoy, but from the Lord's side he drinks the
water of life.[26]   Picture this to yourself, my dear friend, and
with all your mind's reflection concentrate upon the scene;
when you realize the effort put forth by this warrior, then
you will be able to applaud his victory.   4 The sea rages
madly about the entire island, while the towering crags along
its winding shores resound as the waves pound against them.[27]
There is no grass, no green earth, no fruitful field dotted with
shady copses.   Sheer cliffs shut in as it were a prison of
horror.   But he, carefree, unafraid, and wearing the Apostle's
armor,[28] now hears God speaking to him as he reads Sacred
Scripture, now speaks with God as he calls on the Lord in
prayer; and perhaps while he tarries in the isle he has some
visions like those seen by John.[29]

5.   What wiles do you think the devil is now devising,
what snares do you suppose he is preparing?   Perhaps, remembering his ancient guile, he will seek to tempt him with
hunger.   But he already has his answer—that *not in bread
alone doth man live*.[30]   It may be that he will offer him
wealth and fame, but he will be told: *They that will become
rich fall into the trap of temptation*,[31] and, *All my glorying is
in Christ*.[32]   He may strike his limbs wearied by fasting with
oppressing illness but will be struck back by the Apostle's
word, *When I am weak, then am I powerful,* and, *Power is
made perfect in infirmity*.[33]   He may threaten death but will
hear: *I have a desire to be dissolved and to be with Christ*.[34]
He may brandish fiery darts, but they will be received upon
the shield of faith.[35]   In short, Satan will assail him, but
Christ will protect him.

2 Thanks be to thee, Lord Jesus, that in thy day I shall
have one who can entreat thee for me.   To thee all hearts are
open, thou scrutinizest the secrets of the heart,[36] thou seest

in the deep the prophet shut up in the belly of the great monster.[37]   Thou knowest well how he and I grew up together from tender infancy even to the flower of manhood, how the bosoms of the same nurses, the embraces of the same servants that carried us, cherished us.   When after our school days at Rome we ate the same food and shared the same lodgings by the semibarbarous banks of the Rhine, it was I who first began to wish to worship thee. Remember, I pray, that this thy warrior was once a raw recruit with me.   I have the promise of thy Majesty: *He that shall teach and not do shall be called the least in the kingdom of heaven; but he that shall do and teach, he shall be called great in the kingdom of heaven.*[38]

3 May he enjoy the crown of virtue and in return for his daily martyrdom follow the Lamb, robed in white.[39]   As for me—*there are many mansions in my Father's house*[40] and *star differeth from star in glory*[41]—grant that I may lift up my head among the heels of the saints.[42]   While I merely resolved, he accomplished.   Forgive me that I did not have the strength to carry out my resolve,[43] and bestow upon him the reward he deserves.

6.   I may perhaps have been diffuse and made a longer story of this than the limits of a letter warrant.   This always happens to me when I have to say anything in praise of our good Bonosus.   Now to return to the point with which I began.   A friend is long sought, is rarely come upon, and is hard to keep: I plead with you, do not let your mind lose sight of me, as have your eyes.   Anyone who will can shine resplendent with gold, and gleaming gold and silver may glitter from the trappings of showy litters; love cannot be purchased, and affection has no price.   Friendship that can cease was never real.

LETTER 4

To Florentinus
On the origin of friendship[1]

1. How much Your Grace's name is mentioned in the conversation of people everywhere, you may judge from the fact that I begin to love you before I know you. For as the Apostle says, *Some men's sins are manifest, going before to judgment,*[2] so by contrast the renown of your charity is so widespread that a man is considered not so much praiseworthy if he loves you, as a villain if he does not love you.

2 I pass over the countless instances in which you have supported Christ, given Him to eat, clothed Him, visited Him.[3] The way you helped our brother Heliodorus in his need might bring speech even to the dumb. With what gratitude, with what enthusiastic praise he would relate the story of how you assisted him through the troubles of his journey! Thus I myself, that notoriously slow person (my sickness is beyond endurance), come to you with winged feet, as they say, and by way of letter express my desire to greet you and to embrace you in advance. I give you my compliments and pray that the Lord may deign to establish our nascent friendship.

2. Our brother Rufinus, who is reported to have come with the holy Melania from Egypt to Jerusalem, is bound to me by the closest bonds of brotherly love. I beg you, therefore, to favor me by giving to him the enclosed letter. Do not judge of me by his own good qualities. In him you will perceive the express marks of sanctity, whereas I am but ashes and a bit of common dirt[4] and with only a spark of life

35

in me. I am satisfied if my weak eyes can endure the bright light of his character.

2 He has but now bathed, he is clean and made white as snow.[5] I, defiled by all the stains of sin, wait day and night with trembling the command to pay the last farthing.[6] But nevertheless, since *the Lord looseth them that are fettered,*[7] and *hath respect to the humble and meek and him that trembleth at His words,*[8] perhaps he may say even to me lying in the tomb of my sins: "Jerome, come forth!"[9]

The holy priest Evagrius[10] sends you hearty greetings. We both with united esteem greet brother Martinianus.[11] I would like very much to see him, but I am tied down by the chain of illness.

LETTER 5

To Florentinus[1]

1.   Here where I am staying in that part of the desert which adjoins the Saracens, near Syria,[2] your letter, my dear friend,[3] reached me. Upon reading it my desire to set out for Jerusalem[4] was so aroused anew that I all but sacrificed my vows[5] to satisfy my affection. Wherefore, under the circumstances I am doing the best I can: I am sending you a letter in my stead. Though absent in person, I do come to you in love and in spirit, earnestly beseeching you that no extent of time or space may tear asunder our growing friendship, cemented as it is in Christ. No, let us rather give it stability by our mutual correspondence. Let letters travel between us; let them meet each other on the way; let them speak with us. Our affection will not lose much if it keeps up talking and chatting in this manner.

2.   Well, as you say in your letter, brother Rufinus has not yet come.[6] Even if he does come, my desire to see him will scarcely profit, for I shall not be able to see him at this time. The distance separating him from me is so great that he cannot come here; and as for myself, I am so hindered by the bounds of the desert I have so eagerly made my own, that it has become impossible for me to do what I have decided not to do.

2 Thence I beseech you and earnestly beg that you ask him to provide you the commentaries of Bishop Reticius of Autun to have them copied. In them he has discussed the Song of Songs in eloquent style.[7] Further, I have a letter from a certain Paul,[8] an aged compatriot of the aforesaid Rufinus, stating that he has his manuscript of Tertullian: he

37

urgently asks for its return. And next I request that you have a copyist transcribe on papyrus the books which the enclosed list[9] will indicate that I do not have. 3 I pray you also to have sent to me St. Hilary's commentary on the Psalms of David and his very comprehensive book on synods, which works I transcribed for him with my own hand at Treves.[10] You know that this is the food of the Christian soul—to meditate on the law of the Lord day and night.[11] You receive others in hospitality, comfort them with consolation, help them to meet their expenses; as for myself, you will be most generous to me if you grant my requests.

4 And since, by the Lord's grace, I have an abundance of manuscripts of the Holy Bible, command me in your turn. I shall send you whatever you want. And you must not be afraid that a request from you will inconvenience me: I have pupils who devote themselves to the scribe's art.[12] Nor do I merely promise a favor in return for the one I am asking. Brother Heliodorus[13] informs me that you are looking for many parts of the Scriptures and are not entirely successful in finding them. But even if you have them all, our devotion will surely assert its rights and ask for itself more than it already has.

3. While I was still at Antioch, the priest Evagrius[14] frequently reproved, in my presence, the present master of your slave[15] concerning whom you have thought fit to write—the man who was undoubtedly his kidnaper. His answer to Evagrius was: "I have nothing to fear." He says he was dismissed by his master; and, if you want him, he is here. Send him wherever you like. I think I am not doing wrong in not permitting a vagrant to flee farther. Settled here as I am in this desert, I cannot do your bidding personally. I have therefore asked my dear friend Evagrius to attend to the matter immediately, for your sake as well as my own.

LETTER 6

To the deacon Julian of Aquileia[1]

1. It is an old saying: "Liars achieve that they are not believed even when they tell the truth."[2] That is what I see has happened to me, judging by your reproof of my failure to write. Shall I say, "I have written often, but the fault lies with the letter carriers"? You will reply, "That is the standard excuse of all who fail to write." Shall I say, "I found no one to take my letters"? You will say that a great many have gone from here to where you are. Shall I insist that I gave them letters too? No, they simply have not delivered any and will deny having received; and, living away from each other, we shall not know where we stand. 2 What shall I do, then? Though not to blame, I am going to ask you to pardon me, thinking it better to yield my position and make overtures for peace than to hold my ground and stir up strife. As a matter of fact, continued physical illness and mental affliction have so exhausted me that I was near death and scarcely knew what I was doing. And now, lest you think this to be mere fiction, I shall take my cue from the attorney and call in witnesses to prove my arguments for the case.

2. Our holy brother Heliodorus was here; he wished to live in the desert with me, but my sins put him to flight—he left. But my present talkativeness will make amends for all my past neglect; for, as Flaccus says in the satire:

> This fault is common to all singers: among friends
> They can never make up their mind to sing when asked;
> But unasked they cannot stop.[3]

The next thing I shall do, I shall so bury you under reams of letters that you will turn about and begin to beg me not to write.

I rejoice that my sister, your daughter in Christ, is persisting in her resolve;[4] you are the first to report this to me. 2 For here where I now am, I am not only unaware of what is going on in my native land, but even whether it still exists. And although the Spanish viper[5] may rend me with the fangs of baleful rumors, I shall not fear the judgment of men, for I shall have my own judge.

> If the world were to fall in ruins about me,
> Its fragments would strike me unafraid.[6]

Wherefore I entreat you to be mindful of the Apostle's admonition,[7] wherein he teaches us that our work should be abiding: prepare for yourself a reward from the Lord in my sister's salvation, and by your frequent reports make me happier in our common glorying in Christ.

LETTER 7

To Chromatius, Jovinus, and Eusebius[1]

1. The written page should not divide those whom mutual affection has united, nor, therefore, ought I to portion out to you individually these my attentions and thoughts. For you so love each other that the bonds of affection binding the three of you are no less close than nature has provided for two of your number.[2] Indeed, did circumstances permit, I would include your names without division under a single caption. What is more, your own letter challenges me to recognize in each of you all three and each in all.

2 The letter was brought to me through the instrumentality of the holy Evagrius in that part of the desert[3] which draws a vast line of demarcation between the Syrians and the Saracens. I rejoiced even more than did the Romans on that happy day when, in the battle fought by Marcellus at Nola, Hannibal's proud troops were defeated for the first time since the battle of Cannae.[4] The aforesaid brother often pays me a visit and cherishes me in Christ like his own flesh and blood, yet he is separated from me by many miles,[5] so that his departure always leaves me with as great regret as his coming brings me joy.

2. I am now having a chat with your letter, I embrace it, it speaks to me. It is the only thing here that understands Latin. Here in your aging days you must either learn to talk a barbarous language or else remain silent.[6] As often as the familiar handwriting brings back to me your dear faces, so often am I no longer here, or else you are here. Do believe my love, that it is speaking the truth: in this case too, as I write this letter, you are here with me.

2 In this present letter I first of all have this complaint to make: Why did you send me so short a letter, when so great an expanse of sea and land lies in-between? It can only be because, as you state in your own letter, I had not written before. I do not suppose that paper was lacking, with Egypt supplying the market. Even if a Ptolemy had blockaded the seas, yet King Attalus would still have sent parchments from Pergamum, so that the shortage of paper would have been offset by his skins. It was because of such shortage that the word "parchment" has been preserved to this very day, handed down from one age to the next.[7] 3 So, what next? Am I to assume that the postman was in haste to be on his way? But one night is sufficient for a letter, however long. Or were you hindered by some matter of business? There is no more urgent exigency than love. Two explanations remain: either you were not inclined to write, or I did not deserve a letter. Of the two, I prefer to charge you with procrastination than to condemn myself for lack of merit. Obviously it is easier to remedy neglect than to procreate love.[8]

3. Bonosus, as you say in your letter, like a true son of the Fish, has taken to the water.[9] As for me, being still impure from my guilt of long standing, like the basilisks and the scorpions I seek out all the dry places. Bonosus already has his heel set upon the head of the serpent, whereas I am still serving as food for the same serpent that by divine decree eats earth.[10] He can now ascend to the very summit of the Gradual Psalms,[11] while I, still weeping over the first step, do not know whether it shall ever be given me to say: *I have lifted up my eyes to the mountains, from whence help shall come to me*.[12] He, amid the threatening waves of this world, is sitting in the shelter of his island—that is, in the bosom of

the Church—and is perhaps even now, following John's example, eating the book.[13]   But I lie in the sepulchre of my wicked deeds, bound with the chains of my sins, awaiting the Lord's cry in the Gospel: "Jerome, come forth!"[14]   2 Bonosus, moreover, with the prophet saying that all the devil's strength is in his loins,[15] has carried his loincloth across the Euphrates, hiding it there in a hole in the rock;[16] and afterwards, finding it torn, he has sung: Lord, *thou hast possessed my reins; thou hast broken my bonds; I will sacrifice to thee the sacrifice of praise.*[17]   But a real Nabuchodonosor has led me in chains to Babylon,[18] that is, to the babel of a mind confused.   There he has placed the yoke of captivity upon me, there he has fastened a ring of iron in my nose and has bidden me sing a hymn of the songs of Sion.[19]   To him I have said: *The Lord looseth them that are fettered; the Lord enlighteneth the blind.*[20]   In short—to terminate the contrast I have drawn— while I seek for pardon he is hoping for a crown.

4.   My sister is the fruit in Christ of the holy Julian.   He has done the planting, do you care for the watering; the Lord will give the increase.[21]   Jesus has given her to me to compensate me for the wound which the devil inflicted.   He restored her to life, from the dead.   For her, in the words of the pagan poet,

I am fearful even when all is safety.[22]

You yourselves know how slippery is the path of youth, a path on which I have myself fallen,[23] and one you have gone not without fear.   2 As she enters upon this path, she must above all be helped by the advice of all, must be sustained by the encouragement of all.   She must draw strength from frequent letters coming from you, my holy brethren.   And because charity *endureth all things,*[24] I beseech you that you also obtain from Father Valerian[25] a letter to hearten her. As you know, a girl's courage is often made firm by the knowledge that she is an object of concern to her superiors.

5. You see, my native land is a slave of heathenism, men's *god is their belly,*[26] and they live only for the present. The richer a man, the holier. What is more, to use a well-worn popular dictum, the dish has a cover to fit it: Lupicinus is their priest![27] Here the saying also applies—one at which, so Lucilius tells us, Crassus laughed for the one and only time in his life: "Like lips, like lettuce," the reference being to an ass eating thistles.[28] Obviously, here we have the case of an infirm pilot steering a leaky ship, of the blind leading the blind into a pit,[29] and of a ruler adapted to the ruled.

6. My greetings to the mother of you two, with all the respect which, as you know, I hold for her. She is your companion in the practice of sanctity; but she has this pre-eminence over you: she is *your* mother, and thus we truly have cause to term her womb golden. With her I salute your sisters. They are deserving of the respect of all: they have triumphed over our sex and the world, they await the Bridegroom's coming, their lamps well filled with oil.[30] 2 O happy household, where dwells a widowed Anna, virgin prophetesses, and twin Samuels reared in the temple![31] O blessed rooftree, beneath which we see a mother encircled with the crowns of the Maccabean martyrs, herself a martyr.[32] For though you daily confess Christ by keeping His commandments, yet to this private glory there is added for you this public and open confession: the fact that it was through you that the poison of the Arian teaching was once banished from your city.[33]

And perhaps you will be surprised that now at the end of my letter I am beginning all over again. What am I to do? I cannot forbid my heart to speak. The brief compass of a

letter compels me to be silent; my yearning for you forces me
to speak.   Words come to me in precipitate haste, my speech
is disordered and confused; but love knows nothing about
order.

LETTER 8

To Niceas, subdeacon of Aquileia[1]

1 The comic poet Turpilius,[2] speaking of the exchange of letters, says: "It is the only thing which makes the absent present." Though made in a bit of fiction, the remark is not untrue. For what is there so present, to put it that way, when we are absent from each other, as to be able to speak to and to hear those you love through correspondence? Take even those primitive Italian people whom Ennius calls the *casci*,[3] who, as Cicero states in his books on rhetoric,[4] hunted their food like wild animals: before papyrus and parchment came into use, they used to exchange conversation through notes hewed into wood or the bark of trees. Hence men called the bearers of these "board-bearers," and the writers of them "bark-users," from their use of the bark of trees.[5] 2 Under how great obligation then are we, living in a world civilized by the arts, not to discontinue a practice afforded themselves by men living in a state of stark savagery and, to an extent, ignorant of human ways!

Look, here we have the blessed Chromatius and the holy Eusebius, his brother in sameness of character as well as by birth: they have roused my conscience in the matter of letter writing.[6] But you, who have but recently left me, are rending our new-made friendship asunder rather than unstitching it—a process which Laelius wisely says should be left alone.[7] Or is it that you hate the Orient so much that you dread to have even your letters come this way?

3 Wake up, wake up, arouse yourself from sleep! Let me have just one sheet of paper as evidence of fond remembrance

46

of the joys we experienced at home, and of the sighs too we sometimes heaved on the journey we took together. If you love me, answer this. If you are angry, at least write in your anger. This too will mean real solace to my longing desire, if I receive a letter from my friend, even though he be angry.

LETTER 9

To Chrysocomas, monk of Aquileia[1]

1 Heliodorus,[2] whom we both regard very highly and who is as devoted to you as I am, has been able to give you a good account of my sentiments toward you; and perhaps he has—of how I always have your name on my lips, how at our every conversation I first hark back to my pleasant association with you, and how I admire you for your humility and sing the praises of your good qualities and proclaim your affectionate nature. 2 But you—and that is a natural trait with lynxes, that when they look behind them they forget what they have just seen and their mind loses what their eyes have ceased to see—you are so utterly forgetful of our bond of friendship that you have obliterated, not by a casual erasure, but, as the saying goes, erasing wax and all, that epistle which the Apostle speaks of as written in the hearts of Christians.[3]

3 Now the beasts I have mentioned lurk on the low-hanging leafy bough of a tree for fleet roes or stags—a timid creature. They pounce upon them, and the while the victim, carrying its enemy on its back, vainly tries to flee, they mangle it with ravenous fangs; and they remain preoccupied with their prey as long as an empty belly provokes the gullet parched with hunger. But when their ferocity has been sated with blood and they have stuffed their inwards to satiety, oblivion overtakes them. They have no further concern for prey until hunger once more brings it to their attention.

4 You, if you are not yet bored with me to satiety, why do you write finis to what you have just begun? Why do you let go before you have taken a good hold? Perhaps you have

48

the excuse that always goes with negligence and claim that you had nothing to write.   But then you should have written this very thing: that there was nothing else to write.

LETTER 10

To Paul, an old man of Concordia[1]

1.   The brevity of human life is a punishment for our sins, and the fact that frequently on the very threshold of life the newborn child is overtaken by death is clear proof that the times are lapsing daily into wickedness.[2]   For when the serpent had dragged down to earth the first inhabitant of Paradise, entangled in its snaky coils, eternity was exchanged for mortality, but one of nine hundred and more years:[3] the sentence of man's curse had been deferred for so long that it amounted to a quasi-immortality.   Then, as sin gradually burst out anew, the impiety of the giants brought on the shipwreck of the entire world.[4]   2 After that baptism—if I may so call it—of the world thus cleansed, the life of man was contracted into a brief span of time.   This span we have again all but lost, as our iniquities are ever in conflict with the divine.   For how few pass beyond the age of a hundred years, or attain to it without regretting the attainment—even as Scripture bears witness in the book of Psalms: *The days of our life are threescore years and ten, and if it is long, fourscore; what is more of them is labor and sorrow!*[5]

2.   Why, you say, all this harking back to our noble origin, and why reach back so far?   One might quite properly make sport of me with that quip of Horace:

He begins the Trojan War from the twin egg.[6]

My purpose is, of course, to extol with fitting words your great age and your head snow-white like Christ's.[7]

2 Here we have your years circling their orbits for the hundredth time, and you, ever observing the precepts of the

Lord, bear in mind the blessings of the future life as you
enjoy a foretaste of them in this life. Your eyes clear and
full of life, your steps steady, your hearing unimpaired, your
teeth white, your voice is resonant, your body robust and
full of energy. Your ruddy cheeks give the lie to your white
hairs, your physique protests your age. Extreme old age has
not (as we commonly see) impaired the tenacity of your
memory, nor has cooling blood blunted the sharp edge of
your warm spirit. There is no furrowed brow to give a for-
bidding look to a face contracted by wrinkles, and there is no
trembling hand to cause an errant stylus to trace out crooked
paths over the writing wax. 3 The Lord shows us in you the
flowering of the resurrection to come: He wants us to know
that while it is by reason of sin that the rest of us, though still
alive, die prematurely in the flesh, it is an evidence of virtue
practiced that you counterfeit youth at an age alien to it.
And though we see such health of body given to many—even
sinners—yet in their case the devil supplies it to them that
they may sin, while in your case the Lord bestows it that you
may rejoice.

3. The greatest scholars among the Greeks—and concerning them Tully in his plea on behalf of Flaccus uses the
brilliant words, "congenital frivolity and accomplished
vanity"[8]—used to sing the praises of their kings or princes
and received pay for it. Doing the same here, I ask pay for
my praise.

2 And you must not imagine that what I ask is a modest
return: you are asked for the pearl[9] in the Gospel, *the words
of the Lord, pure words, as silver of the earth tried by the fire,
refined seven times*.[10] To be explicit, I ask for the commentaries of Fortunatian[11] and—for its information on the per-
secutors—the history of Aurelius Victor,[12] and also the letters
of Novatian,[13] so that as we become acquainted with the

poisons of the schismatic, we may the more gladly drink of the antidote of the holy martyr Cyprian.[14]

3 Meanwhile I am sending to you, to Paul the aged, a still older Paul,[15] on whom, to accommodate the less erudite readers, I have labored much to bring down the style to a more ordinary level. But somehow or other, though it be filled with water, the flask preserves the same odor which it acquired when first used.[16] If this little token pleases you, I have others also in store which, if the Holy Spirit will swell the sails, will make the voyage to you with an abundance of Oriental goods.

LETTER 11

To the virgins of Haemona[1]

1 The scantiness of my writing paper is an indication of my hermit's life. And this is why I have compressed a long discourse in a small space—because I not only wanted to speak with you at some length, but the limitations of this bit of paper compelled me to hold my peace. So, under such circumstances, poverty was overcome by ingenuity. To be sure, it *is* a small letter, but actually a long discourse. But in the grip of this necessity, do observe my devotion, since even the scarcity of materials could not keep me from writing.

2 But now, I beg you, pardon me for having a grievance. I am saying it because I am hurt. I say it in tears and in anger: you have not addressed a single syllable to one who so often bestows his affection on you. Yes, I know, there is no fellowship between light and darkness,[2] handmaidens of the Lord do not associate with sinners. And yet even a harlot washed the Lord's feet with her tears,[3] and dogs eat of their masters' crumbs,[4] and the Saviour Himself came not to call the just but sinners,[5] for *they that are whole need not the physician.*[6] 3 And He wishes the repentance of a sinner rather than his death,[7] and He brings home the poor lost sheep on His own shoulders,[8] and when the prodigal son returned, his father received him with joy.[9] No indeed rather the Apostle says: *Judge not before the time!* [10] For *who art thou that judgest another man's servant? To his own lord he standeth or falleth.*[11] And *let him that standeth take heed lest he fall;*[12] and *bear ye one another's burdens.*[13]

4 Dearest sisters, man in his spitefulness judges in one way, Christ in another. The verdict of His tribunal is not the

same as that of the backstairs gossipers. Many ways seem right to men and will later be found to be wrong,[14] and a treasure is often stored in earthen vessels.[15] Bitter tears restored to his place Peter, who thrice made denial.[16] He to whom more is forgiven loves the more.[17] Regarding the flock as a whole there is silence, and at the same time the angels in heaven rejoice over the safety of one sick sheep.[18] And if anyone thinks this is not right, let him listen to this coming from the Lord: *Friend, if I am good, why is thy eye evil?*[19]

LETTER 12

To Antonius, monk of Haemona[1]

1 When the disciples were arguing about greatness, our Lord, that master of humility, took a little child, saying: *Whosoever of you shall not have been converted and become as a little child cannot enter the kingdom of heaven.*[2] And that He might not seem merely to teach this and not do it, He fulfilled the precept by example when He washed the disciples' feet,[3] when He received His betrayer with a kiss,[4] when He spoke with the Samaritan woman,[5] when He discussed the kingdom of heaven as Mary sat at His feet,[6] when He rose from the dead and appeared first to mere women.[7]

2 Moreover, Satan fell from the height of the archangels for no other reason save pride—the opposite of humility.[8] And the Jewish people, because they claimed for themselves the chief seats and greetings in the market place,[9] was destroyed and succeeded by the people of the Gentiles, who had previously been accounted as a drop of a bucket.[10] Likewise Peter and James, the fishermen, were sent to oppose the sophists of their time and the wise men of this world, wherefore the Scripture says: *God resisteth the proud, but to the humble He giveth grace.*[11]

3 See, brother, what a sin it is that makes God a rival. Therefore in the Gospel the proud Pharisee is rejected and the humble publican is heard.[12] Ten times already, if I am not mistaken, have I sent you letters full of kindness and entreaties. But you do not deign to utter even a grunt, and though the Lord spoke with His slaves, you, a brother, do not speak with your brother.

4 You will say: "You speak too insultingly." Believe you

me, if respect for my pen did not forbid, in my annoyance I would be showering such rebukes upon you that you would begin to answer my letters—indignantly. But as it is human to become angry and Christian to abstain from harm, I return to my old way: I entreat you once more to love me as I love you and, as a fellow servant [of Christ], speak to your fellow servant.

LETTER 13

To Castorina, my mother's sister[1]

1 John the apostle and evangelist says in his Epistle: *Whosoever hateth his brother is a murderer.*[2] And he is right. Since murder has its origin in hatred, whosoever hates, even though he has not yet struck a blow with the sword, is nevertheless a murderer at heart. "Why such a beginning?" you say. Of course, in order that putting aside old animosities we may prepare for God the dwelling place of a clean heart. *Be ye angry,* said David, *and sin not.*[3] The Apostle explains at greater length how he would have this understood: *Let not the sun go down upon your anger.*[4]

2 What shall we do upon the day of judgment, we upon whose anger the sun—not of a single day but of many years —has gone down as a witness? The Lord says in the Gospel: *If thou offer thy gift at the altar, and there thou remember that thy brother hath anything against thee, leave there thy offering before the altar, and go first to be reconciled to thy brother, and then coming thou shalt offer thy gift.*[5]

3 Woe is me, poor wretch! Not to mention you also, who in so long a time either have not offered a gift at the altar or have offered it vainly, since my anger continued. How have we ever been able to say in our daily prayer: *forgive us our debts as we also forgive our debtors,*[6] while the heart is not in accord with the words, the prayer at variance with our deeds?

4 I beseech you, therefore, as I asked you in a previous letter a year ago, that we hold fast the peace which the Lord left us.[7] May Christ behold both my desire and your thought! Soon before His tribunal shall our reconciliation

receive its reward or our discord its penalty. But if you are unwilling (which I hope is far from being the case), I shall be blameless: this letter when read shall absolve me.

LETTER 14

To Heliodorus the monk[1]

1. With how great eagerness and love I urged that we should remain together in the desert, your heart, conscious of our affection for each other, fully realizes. With what lamentations, with what grief, with what groaning I pursued your departure, even this letter to you is a witness; you see it is blotted with tears. But you, like a spoiled child, softened with flattering words your contemptuous refusal of my request. And I in my abstraction did not know at the time what to do.

2 Should I have kept still? But because of my burning eagerness I could not hide my feelings and control myself. Should I have besought you more earnestly? But you were unwilling to listen, because you did not love me as I loved you. My spurned affection has done the one thing it could. Unable to keep you when you were present, it seeks you when absent. So, since you yourself when on the point of departure asked me to send you a letter of invitation after I had moved to the desert,[2] I promised that I would do so. I'm inviting you. Now make haste.

3 I don't want you to remember old privations: the desert loves the naked. I don't want the difficulty of our pilgrimage of other days to dismay you. Since you believe in Christ, believe also in His words: *Seek ye first the kingdom of God, and all these things shall be added unto you.*[3] You need not take wallet or staff.[4] He is rich enough who is poor with Christ.

2. But what am I about? Am I again rashly entreating you? Away with prayers. An end to persuasion. Slighted

love should become angry. You who ignored me when I importuned will perhaps give ear to my reproof. What are you doing in your ancestral home, luxury-loving soldier?[5] Where is the wall, the ditch, the winter spent under tents of skins? Lo, the trumpet sounds from heaven. Lo, our commander, fully armed, comes forth, surrounded by clouds, to conquer the world. Lo, a sharp two-edged sword goes forth from the king's mouth and cuts down all that stands in its way.[6] And do you come forth, pray, from bedchamber to battle, from the shade to the sunlight?

2 A body accustomed to a tunic cannot bear the weight of a coat of mail. A head covered with a linen cap refuses a helmet. A hard sword hilt chafes a hand soft from idleness. Hear the pronouncement of your king: *He that is not with me is against me; and he that gathereth not with me scattereth.*[7] Remember the day of your enlistment when, buried with Christ in baptism,[8] you took the oath of allegiance: that for His name's sake you would spare neither mother nor father.

3 Lo, the adversary within your very breast is attempting to kill Christ. Lo, the camp of the enemy pants for the donative which you received when about to set forth on military service. Even if your little nephew[9] is clinging to your neck, although your mother with disheveled hair and torn garments is displaying the breasts with which she nurtured you, although your father lies on the threshold, trample your father underfoot and set forth. Fly with dry eyes[10] to the standard of the cross. Cruelty is a kind of dutiful conduct in these circumstances.

3. Later the day will come on which you will return to your own country, on which you will walk about the heavenly Jerusalem,[11] crowned as a brave man. Then you will take up your citizenship with Paul; then you will seek rights in

that same city for your parents; then you will make intercession on my behalf, since I incited you to conquer. Nor, indeed, am I ignorant of the fetters by which you are now impeded.

2 I have no breast of iron, no heart of stone, I was not born of flint, nor did Hyrcanian tigers suckle me.[12] I, too, have passed through all this. Now your widowed sister clings to you with caressing arms. Now those house slaves with whom you grew up say: "To whom will you leave us as servants?"[13] Now, too, your onetime nurse, already old, and her spouse— second only to your own father in claims on your affection— exclaim: "Wait a little for us to die, and then bury us."

3 Perhaps your foster mother, with pendulous breasts, her brow furrowed with wrinkles, recalling an old lullaby,[14] may repeat it for you. Your teachers of grammar, if they wish, may say:

On you the whole house turns and leans.[15]

The love of Christ and the fear of hell can easily burst these bonds.

4 But (you say) the Scriptures teach that we must obey our parents.[16] But whosoever loves parents more than Christ loses his own soul.[17] The enemy grasps his sword to slay me —and shall I think of my mother's tears? Shall I desert the ranks for the sake of my father, to whom for Christ's sake I do not owe burial, although for His sake I owe it to all men? Peter, by his cowardly advice, was a scandal unto the Lord before His passion.[18]

5 When his brethren sought to prevent Paul from going to Jerusalem, he replied: *What do you mean weeping and afflicting my heart? For I am ready not only to be bound but to die also in Jerusalem for the name of our Lord Jesus Christ.*[19]

6 That battering-ram of affection, by which faith is shaken, must be beaten back by the wall of the Gospel: *My mother and my brethren are they who do the will of my Father that is in heaven.*[20]   If they believe in Christ, they should support me when I am about to fight for His name; if they do not believe, *let the dead bury their dead.*[21]

4.   "But this," you say, "holds true only of martyrdom." You are greatly mistaken, brother, if you think a Christian is ever free from persecution.   Even now you are being fiercely attacked if you are not aware of being attacked.   Our adversary, as a roaring lion, goes about seeking someone to devour,[22] and do you think this is peace? *He sitteth in ambush with the rich in private places, that he may kill the innocent; his eyes are upon the poor man; he lieth in wait as a lion in his den.   He lieth in ambush that he may catch the poor man.*[23]   And do you, destined to be his prey, enjoy soft slumbers, protected by the shade of a leafy tree?[24]

2 On this side luxury assails me, on that avarice seeks to burst in, on another my belly desires to be my god instead of Christ.[25]   Lust constrains me to drive away the Holy Spirit that dwells within me, to violate His temple.[26]   An enemy *who has a thousand names, a thousand deadly arts,*[27] pursues me, I say.   And shall I, poor wretch, deem myself the victor even while I am being taken captive?

5.   I would not, my dearest brother, have you weigh transgressions against each other and judge these which I have mentioned to be less than the sin of idolatry.   Nay, give heed to the opinion of the Apostle, who says: *For know you this and understand, that no fornicator, or unclean, or covetous person (which is a serving of idols), hath inheritance in the kingdom of God and of Christ.*[28]   2 And although in general whatever is of the devil savors of hostility to God, and what is of the devil is idolatry, for all idols are subject to him, yet in

another passage he makes a definite statement, saying specifi-cally: *Mortify your members which are upon the earth: forni-cation, uncleanness, evil concupiscence, and covetousness, which are the service of idols, for which things the wrath of God cometh.*[29]

3 The service of an idol consists not merely in this, that one takes a pinch of incense between two fingers and casts this upon an altar fire, or pours a libation of wine from a saucer.   Let him deny that avarice is idolatry who can describe as justice the selling of the Lord for thirty pieces of silver.[30]   Let him deny that there is sacrilege in lust who has polluted the members of Christ and the living sacrifice pleas-ing to God[31] by shameful intercourse with the victims of public vice.   Let him not admit that they who in the Acts of the Apostles kept back part of their inheritance—perishing by an immediate punishment[32]—are idolaters; but only in case he is like them.

4 Observe, brother, it is not permitted you to keep any of your possessions. *Everyone that doth not renounce all that he possesseth,* says the Lord, *cannot be my disciple.*[33]

6.   Why are you a Christian so lacking in spirit? Remem-ber him who left his father as well as his nets;[34] remember the publican who arose from the custom house, becoming an apostle at once.[35]   *The Son of Man hath not where to lay his head,*[36] and do you measure out wide porticoes and build-ings of great extent?[37]   Do you, *a joint heir with Christ,*[38] expect an inheritance in this world?   Translate the word "monk": that's your proper title.   What are you, a "solitary," doing in a crowd?[39]

2 I am no experienced sailor, with ship and cargo intact, addressing warnings suited to those unacquainted with the waves.   But as one lately cast ashore after shipwreck, I give advice, with timid voice, to those about to set sail.   In that

boiling flood the Charybdis of luxury swallows up our salvation. There lust, with a smile like that of Scylla on her girlish lips, by flattery seeks to lure us to make shipwreck of our chastity. Here is a savage shore, here the pirate devil with his comrades carries fetters for his captives-to-be.

3 Don't be credulous. Don't be unconcerned. Although the smooth surface of the sea, spread out like a pond, smiles at you, this great plain contains mountains within it. Danger is concealed within it. The enemy is within. Let out the sheets, raise the sails. Let the cross fashioned by the yard-arm be set up in front. This stillness portends a storm.[40]

4 But you say: "What do you mean? Are not all in the city Christians?" Your case is not the same as that of the rest. Give ear to the Lord when He says: *If thou wilt be perfect, go, sell what thou hast, and give to the poor . . . and come follow me.*[41] Now you have promised to be perfect. For when you forsook military service and made yourself a eunuch for the kingdom of heaven's sake,[42] what else did you seek to achieve than the perfect life? But the perfect servant of Christ has nothing but Christ; or, if he has anything but Christ, he is not perfect. And if he is not perfect, he lied in the first place when he promised God that he would be perfect. *And the mouth that belieth, killeth the soul.*[43]

5 Therefore, to conclude, if you are perfect, why do you long for your hereditary goods? If you are not perfect, you have deceived the Lord. The Gospel thunders in divine accents: *You cannot serve two masters;*[44] and does anyone dare make Christ a liar by serving mammon and the Lord? He often cries: *If any man will come after me, let him deny himself, and take up his cross, and follow me.*[45] Do I, when laden with gold, think I am following Christ? *He that saith he abideth in Christ ought himself also to walk even as he walked.*[46]

7. But if you have nothing (as I know you will say in reply), as you are so well prepared for war, why do you not start your campaign? Unless perhaps you think you can do so in your own country, although the Lord did no signs in His. And why was this? Take this explanation on His own authority: *No prophet has honor in his own country.*[47] "I do not seek honor," you will say; "my conscience is enough for me." Neither did the Lord seek it; for He fled lest He be made a king by the crowds.[48]

2 But where there is no honor, there is contempt; where there is contempt, there violence is frequent; and where there is violence, there also is indignation, there is no rest; where there is no rest, there the mind is often diverted from its purpose. Moreover, where something is taken away from enthusiasm by restlessness, enthusiasm is made less by as much as is taken away, and when anything is made less, it cannot be called perfect. From this course of reasoning the conclusion is that a monk cannot be perfect in his own country. And not to wish to be perfect is a sin.

8. But when driven from this position you will appeal to the clergy. How can I presume to say anything of these who surely remain in their cities? Far be it from me to say anything unfavorable of these who, succeeding to the status of the apostles, partake of Christ's body with holy lips, through whom we too are Christians, who hold the keys of the kingdom of heaven.[49] They judge us, in a certain measure, before the Day of Judgment, who in sober chastity guard the Lord's bride. But as I have previously set forth, the status of a monk is one thing, that of the clergy another.

2 The clergy feed the sheep; I am fed. They get their living from the altar; if I bring no gift to the altar, the axe is laid to my roots as a barren tree.[50] I cannot make poverty my excuse, since in the Gospel I see the old woman giving the

two copper coins which were all she had left.[51] For me to sit in the presence of a priest is not permitted. He, if I have sinned, is permitted to deliver me to Satan for the destruction of the flesh, that my soul may be saved.[52]

3 And, indeed, under the Old Law, whosoever was disobedient to the priests was either thrust outside the camp and stoned by the people, or else a sword was put to his throat and he expiated his contempt with his blood.[53] But now the disobedient is either cut off by the sword of the spirit or he is cast out of the Church and torn asunder by the jaws of infuriated demons.

4 But if the pious flatteries of the brethren invite you to take holy orders, I shall rejoice at your elevation—and shall fear a fall. *If a man desire the office of a bishop, he desireth a good work.*[54] We know that; but add to the statement the words that follow: *It behooveth, therefore, a man of this station to be blameless, the husband of one wife, sober, chaste, prudent, of good behavior, given to hospitality, teachable, not given to wine, no striker, but modest.*[55]

5 And after setting forth other points that follow from this, he used no less care in speaking of clergy of the third degree,[56] saying: *Deacons in like manner chaste, not double-tongued, not given to much wine, not greedy of filthy lucre, holding the mystery of faith in a pure conscience. And let these also first be proved; and so let them minister, having no crime.*[57]

6 Woe to that man who enters the feast not having a wedding garment![58] Nothing remains for him but that he hear straightway: *Friend, how camest thou in hither?* And when he is speechless, the servants will be told: *Lift him by his hands and feet, and cast him into the exterior darkness; there shall be weeping and gnashing of teeth.*[59]

7 Woe unto him who having received a talent ties it in a napkin, merely keeping what he had received, while others

make a profit! Straightway he shall be assailed by the cry of his angry lord: *Thou wicked servant, why didst thou not give my money into the bank, that at my coming I might have exacted it with usury?*[60] That is, "You might have laid down at the altar what you could not use. For while you, a poor businessman, held on to the money, you took the place of another man who might have doubled his principal." Therefore, just as he that ministers well purchases to himself a good degree,[61] so he who approaches the chalice of the Lord unworthily shall be guilty of the body and of the blood of the Lord.[62]

9. Not all bishops are bishops. You observe Peter, but consider Judas also. You regard Stephen, but note Nicholas also, whom the Lord in His Apocalypse hates.[63] He devised such base and impious things that from this root grew the heresy of the Ophitae.[64] Let every man prove himself and so draw near.[65] Ecclesiastical rank does not make a Christian. Cornelius the centurion, while still a pagan, is filled with the gift of the Holy Ghost.[66] Daniel, a young boy, judges the elders.[67] Amos, while plucking blackberries, is suddenly a prophet.[68] David, a shepherd, is chosen king.[69] Jesus loves most the least of His disciples.[70]

2 Sit down in a lower place, brother, that when a lesser person comes you may be bidden to go up higher.[71] Upon whom does our Lord lean save on the lowly and the quiet and on him that trembleth at His words?[72] To whom more is entrusted, from him more is demanded. *The mighty shall be mightily tormented.*[73] Nor let anyone applaud himself for the chastity of a body only that is pure, since every idle word that men shall speak, they shall render an account for it in the Day of Judgment,[74] because even a reproach against a brother is an offense of murder.[75]

3 It is not easy to stand in Paul's place, to hold the rank of

those already reigning with Christ, lest perchance an angel come to rend the veil of thy temple,[76] who shall move thy candlestick out of its place.[77]   If you have a mind to build a tower, reckon the charges of the future work.[78]   Salt that has lost its savor is good for nothing but to be cast out and to be trodden on by swine.[79]   If a monk has fallen, a priest will pray for him; but who will pray over the fall of a priest?

10.   But as my speech has sailed out from the rocky places,[80] and my frail boat has proceeded into the deep from among rocks hollowed out by the foaming breakers, my sails must be spread to the winds.   Having passed beyond the reefs of controversy, I must now, like rejoicing sailors, sing out a glad word of command as epilogue.

2 O desert of Christ, burgeoning with flowers!   O solitude, in which those stones are produced of which in the Apocalypse[81] the city of the great king is constructed!   O wilderness that rejoices in intimacy with God!   What are you doing in the world, brother, you who are greater than the world? How long will the shadows of houses oppress you?   How long will the smoky prison of these cities close you in? Believe me, I behold a little more light.   It is a delight to cast aside the burden of the flesh and to fly to the sheer glory of the ether.

3 Do you fear poverty?   But Christ calls the poor blessed.[82] Are you afraid to work?   But no athlete is crowned without exertion.[83]   Are you thinking of food?   But faith perceives not famine.   Do you dread bruising on the ground your limbs made lean by fasting?   But the Lord lies at your side. Does the unkempt hair of a neglected head cause you to shudder?   But Christ is your head.[84]   Does the boundless expanse of the wasteland terrify you?   Then do you walk in paradise in your imagination.   As often as you ascend thither in thought, so often shall you not be in the desert.   Is your

skin made scabrous without baths? But he who is once washed in Christ need not wash again.[85]

4 And, that you may hear the Apostle replying concisely to all these things: *the sufferings of this time are not worthy to be compared with the glory to come, that shall be revealed in us.*[86] You are a voluptuary, my dearest, if you wish both to rejoice with the world and afterwards to reign with Christ.

11. It will come, that day will come, on which this corruptible and mortal will put on incorruption and immortality.[87] Blessed is the servant whom his Lord shall find watching.[88] Then at the sound of the trumpet the earth with its peoples shall quake with fear; you shall rejoice. The universe will groan mournfully when the Lord is about to judge; tribe by tribe, men will beat their breasts. Kings once most mighty will tremble with naked flanks. Then Jupiter with his offspring will be displayed truly on fire. Foolish Plato will be brought forward also with his disciples. The reasoning of Aristotle will not avail.

2 Then you, the illiterate and the poor, shall exult. You shall laugh and say: "Behold my God, who was crucified, behold the Judge. This is He who whimpered as a babe wrapped in swaddling clothes, in a manger. This is that son of a laboring man and a workingwoman.[89] It was He who, carried in His mother's bosom, fled into Egypt, a God from a man. This is He that was clothed in scarlet, He it is that was crowned with thorns.[90] This is the magician, the man possessed of a devil, the Samaritan.[91] Behold, O Jew, the hands which you nailed. Behold, O Roman, the side that you pierced.[92] Look at this body, whether it is the same as that you said the disciples carried off secretly by night."[93]

O my brother, what labor now can be too hard, that it may fall to your lot to say these words and to be present on that occasion?

LETTER 15

To Damasus[1]

1. Inasmuch as the Orient, set at variance by the inveterate rage of its peoples against each other, has torn to pieces, little by little, the seamless robe of our Lord that was woven from the top [throughout],[2] and the foxes are destroying the vines,[3] so that amid the broken cisterns that can hold no water[4] it is hard to discover where the fountain sealed and the garden enclosed is,[5] therefore I have decided that I must consult the chair of Peter and the faith that was praised by the lips of the Apostle. I now crave food for my soul from that source whence I originally obtained the vestments of Christ.[6]

2 Nor, indeed, could the vast expanse of the watery element and the intervening stretch of land keep me from my quest for the pearl of great price.[7] *Wheresoever the body shall be, thither will the eagles also be gathered together.*[8] While a wicked progeny wasted their patrimony, by you alone is the inheritance of the fathers preserved intact. There the land with fertile soil gives back the purity of the Lord's seed in a hundredfold crop. Here the grain that is buried in furrows degenerates into tares and wild oats.

3 Now the Sun of Justice is rising in the West; but in the East that notorious Lucifer, who had fallen, has exalted his throne above the stars.[9] *You are the light of the world.*[10] *You are the salt of the earth.*[11] You are vessels of gold and of silver.[12] Here are vessels of clay or of wood that await the rod of iron and the eternal burning.[13]

2. Therefore, although Your Eminence terrifies me, yet does Your Humanity invite.[14] From the priest I, a victim, seek

safety; from the shepherd I, a sheep, claim protection. Let envy be off, let flattery of the eminence of Rome recede. I speak with the successor of the fisherman and the disciple of the cross. Following none but Christ as my primate, I am united in communion with Your Beatitude—that is, with the chair of Peter. Upon that rock I know the Church is built. Whosoever eats a lamb outside this house is profane.[15] Whoever is not in Noe's ark will perish when the flood prevails.[16]

2 And because for my sins I exiled myself in that desert which bounds Syria by its adjacent border of wasteland, and because of the vast space that intervenes I cannot always seek from Your Sanctity[17] the sanction of the Lord, therefore I follow here your colleagues the Egyptian confessors[18] and—myself but a little skiff—lie hid beneath these ships of burden. I do not know Vitalis.[19] I spurn Meletius. I am unacquainted with Paulinus. Whosoever gathereth not with thee scattereth,[20] that is, he that is not of Christ is of Antichrist.

3. Accordingly, now—O woe!—after the Nicene creed, after the Alexandrine decree with the West equally in accord, I, a Roman, am importuned by the Campenses, that offspring of Arians, to accept a newfangled term, "three *hypostases*."[21] What apostles, pray tell me, authorized it? What new Paul, teacher of the Gentiles, has promulgated this doctrine? We ask what three *hypostases* may be supposed to signify. "Three subsistent persons," they say. 3 We reply that this is what we believe. The meaning is not enough for them; they demand the word itself, because some bane lies hid in its syllables. We exclaim: "Whosoever does not confess three *hypostases* as three *enhypostata*, that is, in the sense of three subsistent persons, let him be anathema!" And because we have not uttered the specific terms we are adjudged heretics. Furthermore, whosoever interprets

hypostasis as *ousia* and does not say that there is one *hypo-stasis* [= substance] in three persons, he is a stranger to Christ.   By reason of this confession you and I are alike marked with the brand of union.²²

4.   Make a decree, I pray.   If it is your pleasure, I shall not fear to say "three *hypostases*."   If it is your bidding, let a new creed be established succeeding the Nicene, and let us be declared orthodox while using the same terms as the Arians.   The entire school of secular literature recognizes *hypostasis* as no different than *ousia*.   And will anyone, I ask, declare with sacrilegious mouth that there are three sub-stances?   2 The unique nature of God is the only thing that really exists; for, as to that which is subsistent, it has no other source, it is His own.   All other things, which have been created, although they seem to exist, do not, because there was a time when they were not; and that which did not exist may again cease to be.   God alone, who is eternal, that is, who has no beginning, truly possesses the name of "being." Therefore also He speaks to Moses from the bush: *I am who am*, and again: *He who is hath sent me*.²³   Assuredly there were then angels, heaven, the earth, and the sea: and how does God claim the common name of "being" as peculiar to Himself?

3 But inasmuch as that is merely unfinished nature, and the one divine essence consists of three persons, *that which truly is* is one nature.   And whosoever says there are three— that is, three *hypostases*—attempts under the name of piety to assert that there are three natures.   And if this is so, why are we separated by walls from Arius, being united with him in perfidy?   Let Ursinus be coupled with Your Beatitude, let Auxentius be associated with Ambrose.²⁴

4 Far be it from our Roman faith.   Let not the pious hearts of the peoples imbibe so great a sacrilege.   Suffice it for us

to say that there is one substance; there are three subsistent persons: perfect, equal, coeternal. Let nothing be said, if it please you, concerning three *hypostases* and let there be held to be but one. It is a suspicious circumstance when different words are used with the same meaning.

5 Let us rest content with the aforesaid article of faith or, if you think it right, write in reply that we ought to use the term "three *hypostases*" with the necessary interpretations. I do not object, but believe me, poison lies concealed under the honey. An angel of Satan has transformed himself into an angel of light.[25] They put a fair interpretation on *hypostasis*, and when I say I hold the belief that they themselves set forth, I am adjudged a heretic. Why do they so carefully cling to one word? What lies concealed beneath their ambiguous language? If their faith is in accord with their interpretation, I do not condemn them for holding it. If I believe what they themselves pretend they think, let them allow me to express their thought in my own words.

5. Wherefore I implore Your Beatitude by the Crucified, the Salvation of the world, by the consubstantial Trinity, that I may be authorized by your letters either to refrain from saying *hypostases* or to say it. And lest the obscurity of the place in which I dwell should baffle the letter carriers, deign to direct your epistle to the priest Evagrius, whom you know very well.[26]

2 At the same time also indicate with whom I should communicate at Antioch, because the Campenses are united with the heretics of Tarsus. They strive for nothing else than to publish abroad the three *hypostases* in the ancient sense of the word, relying upon the authority of communion with you.

LETTER 16

To Damasus[1]

1.   The importunate woman in the Gospel finally earned the right to be heard,[2] and although the door was shut and the slaves within—even at midnight—a friend received bread from his friend.[3] God Himself, who can be overcome by no strength, is vanquished by the publican's petitions.[4] The city of Ninive, doomed by its sins, survived by reason of its entreaties.[5] Why do I recall these things in so long a prologue?   Of course, that you, who are great, may have regard for the insignificant; that you, the affluent shepherd, may not despise the ailing sheep.

2 Christ bore the thief from the cross to paradise,[6] and lest any man should suppose that conversion is ever too late, the punishment for murder produced martyrdom.   Christ, I say, rejoicing, embraces the prodigal son on his return[7] and, leaving the ninety-nine sound creatures, carries upon His shoulders, as a good shepherd, the one small lamb that had strayed.[8]   Paul the persecutor becomes a preacher;[9] he is blinded in the eyes of his body that he may see more with his mind, and he who used to bring the servants of Christ bound to the council of the Jews afterwards boasts of his bonds in Christ.[10]

2.   To come to the point: as I have told you before, I who received the garment of Christ in the city of Rome, am now held within the limits of Syria, a barbarian land.   And lest you suppose this to have been another's sentence upon me, I myself decided my fate.   But as the pagan poet says:

He changes the scene, not his feelings, who speeds across the seas.[11]

So has the unwearying foe pursued and followed after me that I am now enduring greater onslaughts in solitude.

2 From one side the Arian madness enters upon its frenzied course, supported by assistance from the world.[12] From another the Church, rent into three parts, is hastening to do herself violence. The ancient authority of the monks who dwell hereabout rises up against me. Meanwhile I exclaim: "Whosoever is united with the chair of Peter is my ally." Meletius, Vitalis, and Paulinus say they are on your side. I might believe it if one of them made the claim. As it is, either two of them are lying or they all are.

3 Therefore, I beseech Your Beatitude by the cross of our Lord, by the Passion, the indispensable glory of our faith: so may you who are the successor to the apostles in your office be their successor also in merit; so may you sit upon the throne with the twelve that shall be the judges;[13] so may another gird thee, like Peter, when thou shalt be old;[14] so may you, with Paul, attain citizenship in heaven[15] as you indicate to me by letter with whom I ought to hold communion in Syria. Do not despise a soul for whom Christ died.[16]

LETTER 17

To Mark, a priest at Chalcis[1]

1. I had decided that I must accept the statement of the Psalmist, who says: *When the sinner stood against me, I was dumb, and was humbled, and kept silence from good things;*[2] and again: *But I, as a deaf man, heard not; and as a dumb man not opening his mouth. And I became as a man that heareth not.*[3] But since love overcometh all things[4] and affection prevails over determination, I do not so much render a return to those that have done me an injury as reply to you at your request. For among Christians, as someone puts it, not the man who suffers insult, but he who inflicts it, is wretched.[5]

2. And now, first of all, before I speak to you about my faith, which you know very well, I am obliged to cry out against the barbarism of that place of yours, using the familiar lines: "What race of men is this? Or what land permits so barbarous a custom? We are kept from the hospitality of the shore. They start a war and forbid us to land on the coast," etc.[6]

It is on this account that we have borrowed these words from the pagan poet, that he who does not keep Christ's peace[7] may at least learn peace from a heathen.

2 I am called a heretic for preaching that the Trinity is consubstantial. I am accused of the Sabellian heresy for proclaiming with unwearied voice that there are three subsistent persons, true, undiminished, and perfect. If I am accused by Arians, it is deserved. If by the orthodox, who criticize a faith of this kind, they have ceased to be orthodox. Or, if they please, let them condemn me as a heretic with

76

the West, a heretic with Egypt, that it to say, with Damasus and Peter.

3 Why do they condemn one man, passing over his associates? If a brook flows with a slight stream, that is not the fault of its bed but of its source. I'm ashamed to say it: out of the caves of our [hermits'] cells we condemn the world if, while wallowing in sackcloth and ashes,[8] we pass judgment on bishops. Why this regal attitude under a garb of penitence? A chain and squalid hair are evidence, not of a diadem, but of weeping.

4 Let them permit me, I pray, to say nothing. Why do they rend him who does not deserve ill will? I'm a heretic? What is that to you? Be still, it has already been said. You are evidently afraid that I, a most eloquent man in the Syrian tongue or in Greek, may go about to the churches, seduce the people, bring about a schism.[9] I have taken nothing from anyone. I accept nothing as an idler. It is by the sweat of our brow that we daily seek our food, knowing what was written by the Apostle: *if any man will not work, neither let him eat.*[10]

3. These words, holy and venerable father, with what groaning, with what grief I have written them Jesus is witness. *I have kept silent. Shall I always hold my peace?*[11] saith the Lord. Not one corner of the desert is granted me. Daily I am asked my faith as though I had been born again without faith.[12] I make confession as they wish: it does not please them. I sign their formula: they do not believe me. 2 There is only one thing that does please them: that I should leave this place. Soon, soon I shall leave. They have taken from me part of my very soul: my dearest brothers.[13] Lo, they are eager to depart—nay, they are departing, saying it is better to dwell amid wild beasts than with such Christians. And I myself, did not bodily infirmity and the rigors of winter

keep me here, would be fleeing right now.   However, until the springtime arrives, I beseech you that for a few months the hospitality of the desert may be granted me.   Or, if even this seems too slow, I am leaving.

3 *The earth is the Lord's and the fulness thereof.*[14]   Let them alone ascend into heaven.   It is for them alone that Christ died.   Let them have it, possess it, boast of it.   *But God forbid that I should glory save in the cross of our Lord Jesus Christ, by whom the world is crucified to me, and I to the world.*[15]

4 Now concerning the faith about which you did me the honor of writing to me, I gave a statement of my faith to the holy Cyril,[16] in writing.   Whosoever does not believe thus is a stranger to Christ.   But I have as witnesses of my faith your own ears and those of blessed brother Zenobius,[17] to whom—with you—all of us who are here send hearty greetings.

LETTER 18A

To Damasus[1]

And it came to pass in the year that King Ozias died:[2] *I saw the Lord sitting upon a throne high and elevated, and the house was filled by His glory.*[3] *2 And seraphim stood about Him: the one had six wings, and the other had six wings; with two they covered His face, and with two they covered His feet, and with two they flew. 3 And they cried one to the other and said: Holy, holy, holy, the Lord of Sabaoth, all the earth is full of His glory. 4 And the lintel of the door was lifted up at the voice of them that cried, and the house was filled with smoke. 5 And I said: Woe is me (because I felt remorse), because I am a man of unclean lips, and I dwell in the midst of a people that hath unclean lips, and I have seen with my eyes the King the Lord of Sabaoth. 6 And one of the seraphim was sent to me, and in his hand he had a live coal, which he had taken with the tongs off the altar. 7 And he touched my mouth and said: Behold, this hath touched thy lips, and it shall take away thy iniquities and shall cleanse thy sins. 8 And I heard the voice of the Lord saying: Whom shall I send? and who will go to that people? And I said: Lo, here am I, send me. 9 And He said: Go and say to this people: Ye shall hear with the ear and not understand, and perceiving ye shall behold and shall not see.*[4]

1. AND IT CAME TO PASS IN THE YEAR THAT KING OZIAS DIED: I SAW THE LORD SITTING UPON A THRONE HIGH AND ELEVATED.[5] Before we speak of the vision, it seems that we must set forth who this Ozias was, how many years he had reigned, who among the other kings were his contemporaries. 2 And indeed, as regards his character, as we read in the

books of Kings[6] and of the Chronicles,[7] he was a just man and *did that which was right in the eyes of the Lord*,[8] building a temple and an aqueduct, providing the instruments of warfare, and deservedly overcoming his adversaries and— what is the greatest indication of his piety—having many prophets in his realm. As long as Zacharias the priest, surnamed the Understanding, was alive, Ozias pleased God and entered His sanctuary with all reverence.[9]

3 But after Zacharias died, desiring to make the religious offerings himself, he infringed upon the priestly office, not so much piously as rashly. And when the Levites and the other priests exclaimed against him: "Are you not Ozias, a king and not a priest?" he would not heed them, and straightway he was smitten with leprosy in his forehead, in accordance with the word of the priest, who said: *Lord, fill their faces with shame*.[10] That is the part of the body which the priest used to cover with a plate of gold,[11] which in Ezechiel the Lord orders to be marked by the imprint of the letter tav.[12] David exults over it, saying: *The light of thy countenance, O Lord, is signed upon us*.[13] It was here also that the insolent alien[14] was smitten by a stone from the sling and died.

4 Now Ozias reigned fifty-two years,[15] at the time when Amulius reigned among the Latins and Agamestor, the eleventh king, among the Athenians. After his death the prophet Isaias saw the vision which we are now endeavoring to explain; that is, in the year in which Romulus, the founder of the Roman empire, was born, as will be evident to those who shall be willing to read the book of the Chronicles which we have translated from the Greek speech into the Latin tongue.[16]

2. AND IT CAME TO PASS IN THE YEAR THAT KING OZIAS DIED: I SAW THE LORD SITTING UPON A THRONE HIGH AND ELEVATED. After the story has been set forth, there follows

the spiritual significance, for the sake of which the story itself has been set forth. While the leprous king lived and, so far as was in his power, was destroying the priesthood, Isaias could not see the vision. 2 As long as he reigned in Judea, the prophet did not lift his eyes to heaven; celestial matters were not revealed to him; the Lord of Sabaoth did not appear, nor was the word "holy" thrice heard in the mystery of the faith.[17] But when he died, all the things which the following discourse will point out made themselves known in clear light. Something analagous to this is written also in Exodus: while Pharaoh lived, the people of Israel did not turn from their work with mud and brick and straws and aspire unto the Lord.[18] While he reigned, no one sought the God of their fathers, Abraham, Isaac, and Jacob.

3 But when he died, the sons of Israel aspired, as the Scripture says: *and their cry went up unto the Lord,*[19] whereas according to history they should then particularly have rejoiced and previously have aspired, while he was alive. Also while Ezechiel was prophesying, Pheltias, the son of Banaias, died, and after the death of that most evil ruler he said: *I fell down upon my face, and cried with a loud voice, and said: Alas, alas, O Lord God: wilt thou make an end of all the remnant of Israel?*[20]

4 If, therefore, you understand in Ozias and Pharaoh and Pheltias and all others of this sort forces opposed to godly living, you will see how none of us can see and aspire and fall repentant while they live. *Let not sin,* says the Apostle, *reign in your mortal body.*[21] While sin reigns, we build cities for the Egyptians, we go about in dust and ashes, we seek chaff instead of grain and structures of mud instead of solid rock.

3. Next: I SAW THE LORD SITTING UPON A THRONE HIGH AND ELEVATED. Daniel, too, saw the Lord seated, but not

upon a throne high and elevated.[22]   Elsewhere also the divine voice makes a promise, saying: *I will come and will judge the people in the valley of Josaphat,* which is by interpretation *the judgment of the Lord.*[23]

2 He that is a sinner—like me—sees the Lord sitting in the valley of Josaphat, not on a hill, not on a mountain, but in a valley, and in the valley of judgment.   But whosoever is righteous—like Isaias—sees Him sitting upon a throne high and elevated.   Again (to make a further suggestion), when I view Him with my mind's eye, reigning over thrones, dominions, angels, and all other virtues,[24] I see His lofty throne.   But when I consider how He deals with the human race and is said frequently to descend to earth for our salvation, I see His throne low and very near the earth.

4.   Next: I saw the Lord sitting upon a throne high and elevated: and the house was filled by His glory, and seraphim stood about Him.   Certain ones who have interpreted this passage before me, Greeks as well as Romans, have declared that the Lord sitting upon a throne is God the Father, and the two seraphim which are said to be standing one at each side are our Lord Jesus Christ and the Holy Spirit.

2 I do not agree with their opinion, though they are very learned men.[25]   Indeed, it is far better to set forth the truth in uncouth fashion than to declare falsehood in learned style.[26] I dissent especially because John the Evangelist wrote that it was not God the Father but Christ who had been seen in this vision.   For when he was speaking of the unbelief of the Jews, straightway he set forth the reasons for their unbelief: *Therefore they could not believe in Him, because Isaias said: "Ye shall hear with the ear and not understand, and perceiving ye shall behold and shall not see." And he said these things when he saw the glory of the Only-begotten and bore witness concerning Him.*[27]

3 In the present roll of Isaias[28] he is bidden by Him who sits on the throne to say: *Ye shall hear with the ear and not understand.* Now He who gives this command, as the Evangelist understands it, is Christ. Whence we comprehend that the seraphim cannot be interpreted as Christ, since Christ is He who is seated.

4 And although in the Acts of the Apostles Paul says to the Jews that agreed not among themselves: *Well did the Holy Ghost speak to our fathers by Isaias the prophet, saying: Go to this people and say: With the ear you shall hear and shall not understand, and seeing you shall see and shall not perceive. For the heart of this people is grown gross, and with their ears have they heard heavily, and their eyes they have shut, lest perhaps they should see with their eyes, and hear with their ears, and understand with their heart, and should be converted, and I should heal them*[29]—for me, however, the diversity of the person does not raise a question, since I know that both Christ and the Holy Spirit are of one substance, and that the words of the Spirit are not other than those of the Son, and that the Son has not given a command other than the Spirit.

5. Next: AND THE HOUSE WAS FILLED BY HIS GLORY. The house of God which is above is seen to be full of glory. But I do not know whether this house which is below is full of glory—save perhaps in the sense of the Psalmist when he says: *The earth is the Lord's and the fulness thereof.*[30] Thus we, too, may say that those persons on earth are full of glory who can say: *of His fulness we all have received.*[31]

2 That house wise women build and the foolish pulls it down with her hands;[32] it is that of which Isaias also speaks: *And in the last days the mountain of the Lord shall be manifest, and the house of God on the tops of the mountains, and it shall be exalted above the hills.*[33]

3 This is the house of which the aforesaid Paul elsewhere bears witness with inspired voice: *And Moses indeed was faithful in all his house as a servant, for a testimony of those things which were to be said; but Christ as the Son over His own house, of which house are we, if only we hold fast the first principle of His substance firm unto the end.*[34] Of this he speaks also to Timothy: *These things I write to thee . . . that thou mayest know how thou oughtest to behave thyself in the house of God, which is the church.*[35]

6. Next: AND SERAPHIM STOOD ABOUT HIM: THE ONE HAD SIX WINGS AND THE OTHER HAD SIX WINGS. WITH TWO THEY COVERED HIS FACE AND WITH TWO THEY COVERED HIS FEET, AND WITH TWO THEY FLEW. AND THEY CRIED ONE TO THE OTHER AND SAID: HOLY, HOLY, HOLY, THE LORD OF SABAOTH, ALL THE EARTH IS FULL OF HIS GLORY.

2 We wish to know what the seraphim are that are standing about God. What are the six wings of (each) one, and the twelve when they are joined together? How do they cover His face with two and His feet with two and fly with two—since they are said to be standing about God? Or how do they stand about Him when they are but two in number? What is that which they cry, the one to the other, and thrice repeat the word "holy"? How is it that above the house is said to be full of glory, and now the earth is said to be?[36]

3 Since these questions raise no small cloud of dust[37] and at the very outset interpose a difficulty of interpretation, let us pray the Lord together that to me also a coal may be sent from the altar, and that, when all the uncleanness of my sins has been swept away, I may be enabled first to contemplate the mysteries of God and then to tell what I have seen.

4 *Seraphim,* as we have found in the *Translation of Hebrew Words,* may be rendered either "fire" or "the beginning of speech."[38] We ask what this fire may be. The

Saviour says: *I am come to cast fire on the earth, and how I wish that it may burn!*[39] The two disciples to whom the Lord opened the Scriptures in the way, beginning at Moses and all the prophets, after their eyes were opened knew Him and said: *Did not our heart burn within us in the way while He opened to us the Scriptures?*[40] 5 And in Deuteronomy God Himself is described as a consuming fire.[41] In Ezechiel also His likeness from His loins to His feet is as the appearance of fire.[42] *And the words of the Lord are pure words, as silver of the earth tried by the fire, refined seven times.*[43] And there are many other passages: if I wished to repeat them all from the Scriptures, it would take too long.

6 Therefore, let us inquire, where is this saving fire? No one can doubt that it is in the holy books, by the reading of which all sins of men are washed away. But as to the second rendering, "the beginning of speech," how it can be applied to the Scriptures, I fear that if I begin to explain I shall seem not so much to be interpreting as bringing force to bear upon the Scriptures.

7 The beginning of speech and of general conversation and all that we say is the Hebrew tongue, in which the Old Testament is written. So universal tradition reports. But after diversity of tongues was imposed because of the offense to God in erecting the tower [of Babel], then a variety of speech was spread abroad over all nations.[44] Therefore, both fire and the beginning of speech may be observed in the two Testaments. And it is not surprising that they stand about God, since it is through them that the Lord Himself may be known.

8 THE ONE HAD SIX WINGS AND THE OTHER HAD SIX WINGS. Our Victorinus[45] interprets these as the twelve apostles. We can accept it also as typifying the twelve stones of the altar[46] *which iron hath not touched,*[47] and the twelve precious

stones[48] of which the priest's emblem was made, which Ezechiel also mentions and concerning which the Apocalypse is not silent.[49]   Which of these interpretations is true, let God judge; which is probable, we shall set forth in what follows.

7.   And: WITH TWO THEY COVERED HIS FACE AND WITH TWO THEY COVERED HIS FEET, AND WITH TWO THEY FLEW. They covered not their own but God's face.   For who can know His beginning, which was in the eternity of things before He founded this [little] world, when He established thrones, dominions, powers, angels, and all the heavenly ministry?

2 AND WITH TWO THEY COVERED HIS FEET: not their own but God's.   For who can know His bounds?   What is to be after the consummation of the age, what after the human race has been judged; what life is to follow: whether there will again be another earth and other elements after the change or if another world and sun must be created.   *Tell me the former things and what shall be at the last,* says Isaias, *and I will say that you are gods;*[50] implying that no one can relate what was before the world and what shall be after the world.

3 AND WITH TWO THEY FLEW: we know only the intermediate events which are revealed to us by the reading of the Scriptures: when the world was made, when man was fashioned, the time of the flood, when the law was given, how the entire expanse of the lands was populated from one man and how, at the end of the age, the Son of God took flesh for our salvation.   But all the other things which we have mentioned these two seraphim have covered in veiling His face and His feet.

4 AND THEY CRIED ONE TO THE OTHER: that is well expressed *one to the other.*   For whatever we read in the Old Testament, that we find also in the Gospel; and what was

gathered together in the Gospel, this is drawn forth from the authority of the Old Testament: nothing is discordant, nothing diverse.

5 And said: Holy, holy, holy the Lord of Sabaoth. In both Testaments the Trinity is made known. But that our Saviour, too, is called Sabaoth, take for example the twenty-third Psalm. The powers that served the Lord cried out to the other celestial forces that they should throw open the door to their returning Lord: *Lift up your gates, O ye princes;* or, as Aquila[51] interprets it: *Lift up your heads, O ye gates, and the King of Glory shall enter in.*[52]

6 And then they, because they see Him clad in flesh, amazed at the new mystery, inquire: *Who is this King of Glory?* and receive the reply: *The Lord of Virtues, He is the King of Glory.*[53] In Hebrew this is written Lord of Sabaoth, and we should realize that wherever the seventy translators[54] have used the expression *dominum virtutum* and *dominum omnipotentem,* there is found in the Hebrew "Lord of Sabaoth." Aquila renders this "the Lord of Hosts." The very word "Lord" here consists of the four letters properly used for God: iod, he, iod, he; that is JA repeated. These letters when doubled form the ineffable and glorious name of God.[55]

7 All the earth is full of His glory. As yet this is said by the seraphim concerning the advent of our Lord the Saviour, how the preaching of Him is spread abroad into all the world, and the sound of the apostles penetrating the limits of the earth.

8. Next: And the lintel of the door was lifted up at the voice of them that cried. We read in the Old Testament that the Lord always spoke to Moses and Aaron at the door of the Tabernacle, as though before the Gospel He did not yet lead them into the Holy of Holies.[56] Just as

the Church was afterwards brought in and said: *The king hath brought me into his room.*[57]

2 So when our Lord descended to the earth, that lintel of the door—that is, an obstacle of some sort—was removed from those desiring to enter, and this whole world was filled with smoke, that is, with the glory of God. But where we read in Latin *elevatum* (i.e., "lifted up"), in the Greek *sublatum*[58] is used. But as the ambiguity of the word makes possible either translation, our [scholars] have interpreted *elevatum* as meaning "removed" (*ablato*).

3 AND THE HOUSE WAS FILLED WITH SMOKE. God, as we have said above, is fire. When He had descended to Moses on Mt. Sinai, at His coming lights were seen flitting about, and the whole mountain was filled with smoke.[59] Whence the saying in the Psalms: *who touchest the mountains, and they will smoke.*[60] From fire, therefore, since we cannot apprehend its entire essence, a certain lighter and, if I may say so, rarer quality, smoke, is spread abroad. Taking this as an example, we may say: *We know in part, and we prophesy in part,*[61] and *we see now through a glass in a dark manner.*[62]

9. AND SERAPHIM STOOD ABOUT HIM: THE ONE HAD SIX WINGS AND THE OTHER HAD SIX WINGS. One of the Greeks, a man particularly learned in the Scriptures,[63] has explained that the seraphim are certain powers in the heavens which, standing before the tribunal of God, praise Him and are sent on various errands and particularly to those who are in need of cleansing and (by reason of former sins) in some measure need punishment. "Moreover," he says, "that the lintel of the door was lifted up, and the house filled with smoke, is a sign of the destruction of the Jewish temple and the burning of all Jerusalem."

2 Some, however, while agreeing with the preceding, dissent from the latter part [of the interpretation]. For they say that the lintel of the door was lifted up at that time when the veil of the temple was rent[64] and the whole house of Israel was confused by a cloud of error when, as Josephus relates,[65] the priests heard the voice of the heavenly powers from the sanctuary of the temple [saying]: "Let us leave this abode."

10.   But there is a man from whom I rejoice to have learned a great deal, and who has so refined the Hebrew speech that among their scribes he is regarded as a Chaldean.[66] He approaches the matter by a far different route.   For he says that none of the prophets except Isaias has seen seraphim standing about God, and that seraphim are not even to be read about elsewhere; furthermore, that this was a premonitory indication of the end and captivity of Jerusalem which took place under Nabuchodonosor.

2 Now from Ozias, under whom he began to prophesy, to Sedecias,[67] who reigned last and who was blinded and taken to Babylon, there were eleven kings.   The twelfth was Godolias,[68] whom the king of Babylon had set up over the land.   Him Ismael, the son of Nathanias, slew in the midst of a banquet—that parricide of the remnant of his countrymen.[69]   These kings [he says] are the twelve wings, with four of which they veil their faces (as is found in some manuscripts), with four they fly, and with four they cover their feet.

3 As a matter of fact, only four of these twelve kings were righteous kings: Ozias, Joatham, Ezechias, and Josias.   These being exalted in various captivities dare to glorify God: *Holy, holy, holy, the Lord of Sabaoth*.   But the rest on account of their sins veil their faces, and others because they were led into captivity hide the tracks of their feet.   But the uplifted lintel of the door and the house filled with smoke (as we have

said before) he explained as the destruction of Jerusalem and the burning of the temple.

11. Since I have once started to refer to his opinion, I shall touch also on those points not yet alluded to by me: he declared that the tongs by which the live coal was taken from the altar and the mouth cleansed refer to the passion of Isaias himself. He was put to death under Manasses.[70] It was then, when his mouth was truly cleansed, that he said to the Lord: *Lo, here am I, send me,* and he said: *Woe is me (because I felt remorse).*

2 So long as Ozias lives, O Isaias, you do not know that you are wretched, you are not conscience-smitten, you are not moved; but when he is dead, you perceive that you have unclean lips, then you know that you are unworthy of the vision of God. But would that I, too, were more conscience-smitten, and that after my remorse I might be made worthy to preach of God. Because, as I am a man and have unclean lips, I live also in the midst of a people that have unclean lips.

3 Isaias, being a righteous man, had sinned in speech only; therefore he had only unclean lips. But I, who use my eyes for lust and am scandalized hand and foot[71] and transgress with all my members, have all things unclean and, because I have defiled my garment after once being baptized by the Spirit, am in need of the cleansing of a second baptism, that is, by fire.[72]

12. The words of Scripture are not simple, as some suppose; much is concealed in them. The letter indicates one thing, the mystical language another.[73] For example, our Lord in the Gospel is girt with a towel, He prepares a basin to wash the disciples' feet, He performs the service of a slave.[74] Granted, it is to teach humility, that we may minister to each other in turn. I do not deny that. I do not reject it.

What is it that He says to Peter upon his refusal? *If I wash not thy feet, thou shalt have no part with me.* And he replied: *Lord, not only my feet, but also my hands and my head.*[75] 2 Because His apostles, as men walking the earth, still had feet stained by the pollution of sin, the Lord, being about to ascend to heaven, desires to free them entirely from their transgressions, that the words of the prophet may be applicable to them: *How beautiful are the feet of those that preach peace!*[76] And that they may have the power to imitate the words of the Church when she says: *I have washed my feet, how shall I defile them?*[77] So that, even if some dust shall cling to them after the resurrection, they may shake it off against the impious city in evidence of their labor,[78] because thus far they have struggled for the salvation of all: for the Jews as Jews,[79] for the Gentiles as Gentiles, so that they have to a certain extent polluted the soles of their own feet.

3 Therefore, to get back to the main point, just as the apostles needed the cleansing of their feet, so because Isaias had sinned only in speech he had unclean lips; and, as I think, he had unclean lips because he had not seized Ozias when he dashed into the temple and, following the example of Elias, in bold words proclaimed him impious.[80]

4 AND I DWELL IN THE MIDST OF A PEOPLE THAT HATH UNCLEAN LIPS. Isaias, because he was conscience-stricken and called men to witness that he was wretched, was made worthy of cleansing. But the people, not only failing to show penitence but not even knowing that they had unclean lips, did not deserve the remedy of cleansing. With this as an example, we must take care not only to be righteous ourselves, but not to tarry with sinners, because the prophet considers this also a part of sin and misery.

13. Next: AND I HAVE SEEN WITH MY EYES THE KING

THE LORD OF SABAOTH. The Jews say[81] that it was for this reason that Isaias was slain by their ancestors, because though Moses saw God's back parts,[82] this man writes that with the eyes of flesh he has seen the Lord of Sabaoth, and concerning this God said: *No man shall see my face and live.*[83]

2 We will inquire of them how God in the law says that He is revealed to other prophets in a vision and in a dream, but speaks to Moses face to face;[84] and what is the meaning of the statement: *No man shall see my face and live,* since He admits that He spoke to Moses face to face. They will reply, of course, that God was seen according to human ability, not as He is, but as He wished to be seen. To this we shall say that He was seen in the same manner also by Isaias. The fact remains that Moses either saw God or did not see Him.

3 He saw Him. Then Isaias was impiously put to death by you for saying that he had see Him, because God can be seen. He did not see Him. Then put Moses to death also with Isaias, because he is guilty of the same falsehood in saying that he saw Him who cannot be seen. Whatsoever opinion they had in their interpretation of this passage about Moses, we too will apply to the vision of Isaias.

14.   Next: AND ONE OF THE SERAPHIM WAS SENT TO ME, AND IN HIS HAND HE HAD A LIVE COAL, WHICH HE HAD RE-CEIVED WITH THE TONGS OFF THE ALTAR. AND HE TOUCHED MY MOUTH AND SAID: BEHOLD, THIS HATH TOUCHED THY LIPS, AND IT SHALL TAKE AWAY THY INIQUITIES AND SHALL CLEANSE THY SINS. Now conceive of the seraphim according to all the explanations which we have indicated above: whether you wish to interpret them as the two Testaments, or as certain virtues that reveal themselves among the heavenly powers, or as a kind of foreshadowing of a future revelation—a sign of the captivity.

2 We, because we are following the first opinion, declare

that which was sent to the prophet was the evangelical Testament,[85] because having within itself the two series of commandments—that is, both its own and those of the Old Testament—it comprehended the glowing speech of God[86] in its double line of precepts. When the lips were touched, whatever ignorance there was (because we interpret the unclean lips in this way) was expelled by the truth of the cleansing he received.

3 As to the tongs, they are what Jacob saw in the ladder.[87] This is the sharp, two-edged sword.[88] These are the two mites which the woman who was a widow cast in as her gift to God.[89] This is the stater, consisting of two denarii, which was found in the fish's mouth and given as tribute for the Lord and Peter.[90] The live coal with this twofold power, comprised by their union, was grasped and sent to the prophet. In the one hundred and nineteenth Psalm, when the prophet besought God, saying: *O Lord, deliver my soul from wicked lips and a deceitful tongue,*[91] after the question of the Holy Spirit: *What shall be given to thee, or what shall be added to thee, to a deceitful tongue?* it was said: *The sharp arrows of the mighty, with coals that lay waste.*[92] 4 We know that this live coal also was granted to the prophet—since, indeed, the coal that layeth waste, which makes the tongue clean from sin, is the divine speech, of which it is said also in Isaias: *You have coals of fire, you shall sit beside them, they will be of service to you.*[93]

15. AND I HEARD THE VOICE OF THE LORD SAYING: WHOM SHALL I SEND? AND WHO WILL GO TO THAT PEOPLE? AND I SAID: LO, HERE AM I, SEND ME. AND HE SAID: GO AND SAY TO THIS PEOPLE: YE SHALL HEAR WITH THE EAR AND NOT UNDERSTAND. These are the words of the Lord asking—not giving commands: whom He should send, and who is to go to the people. To whom the compliant prophet

replies: *Lo, here am I, send me.* And after his promise he received an order to speak: *Go and say to this people: Ye shall hear with the ear and not understand, and perceiving ye shall behold and shall not see,* and the rest, which the language of the prophecy itself provides as context.

2 I have heard no inconsiderable disputation of my Hebrew teacher on this passage. I will set down a few words of it, that you may perceive this man's interpretation. He used to say: "Let us ask concerning Moses and Isaias which did better: whether Moses, who when sent by God to the people says: *I beseech thee, Lord, I am not worthy,* and again: *Look for another to send;*[94] or Isaias, who, though he had not been chosen, voluntarily offered himself, saying: *Lo, here am I, send me.*

3 "I am not unaware," he used to say, "that it is hazardous to argue concerning the merits of the saints, and to wish to claim something either less or more for him whom the Lord has crowned. But since He Himself said: *Seek and you shall find, knock and it shall be opened to you,*[95] we too ought to inquire what the question involves, not in order to detract from anyone, but that knowing the meaning of the Scripture we may apply ourselves to its precepts.

4 "He that upholds Moses," he said, "speaks of his humility and meekness, because he was exalted for judging himself unworthy to serve God. But Isaias, because he voluntarily offered himself, at the outset of his prophetic work started with curses: *Ye shall hear with the ear and not understand, and perceiving ye shall behold and shall not see.*

5 "For this he suffered much and was considered insane by all the people. And when the divine voice said to him a second time: *Cry,* knowing what he had endured for offering himself so readily before, he did not say: *Lo, here am I, send me,* but he asked what it was he should cry. *And I said, says he, what shall I cry?*[96]

6 "This is like that saying of Jeremias: *Take the cup of this pure wine at my hand and thou shalt make all the nations to drink thereof, unto which I shall send thee. And they shall drink and vomit and be mad and shall fall before the face of the sword which I send in their midst.*⁹⁶ᵃ When the prophet had heard this, he did not refuse. He did not say, after the example of Moses: *I beseech thee, Lord, I am not worthy,* and: *Look for another to send.* But being a lover of the people and thinking that hostile nations would be slain and would fall by drinking of the cup, he gladly accepted the cup of wine, not knowing that Jerusalem too was included among all the nations.

7 "Finally, among the rest of the nations: *And I took,* he says, *the cup at the hand of the Lord, and I presented it to all the nations to drink of it, to which the Lord sent me: to wit, Jerusalem, and the cities of Juda, and the kings thereof, and the princes thereof: to make them a desolation, and a trackless waste, and a hissing.*⁹⁷ Regarding this prophecy— although in many manuscripts the order is changed—hear what he says also in another passage: *Thou hast deceived me, O Lord, and I am deceived; thou hast held me and thou hast prevailed. I am become a laughingstock, all the day I am held up to derision.*⁹⁸

8 "On the other hand," [my teacher] used to say, "one who defends Isaias might advance this argument: the prophet trusted not so much his own merit as the mercy of God, after he had heard the seraphim say: *Behold, this hath touched thy lips, and it shall take away thy iniquities and shall cleanse thy sins.* He was unwilling to remain idle in inactivity, but voluntarily offered himself for the service of God with the zeal of faith, as a man freed from his sins.

9 "But Moses excused himself because he had been trained in secular studies and, after killing the Egyptian,⁹⁹ his conscience had grown a little tarnished (whence also the voice

came to him out of the bush, saying: *Come not nigh hither. Put off the shoes from thy feet: for the place whereon thou standest is holy ground*[100]), and because he knew that his struggle would be against the magicians, against Pharaoh, that most wicked king. He said: *I beseech thee, Lord, I am not worthy.*[101] For this we read in the Hebrew: *I have not circumcised lips.* The seventy translators have expressed the sense rather than given a literal rendering.

10 "From this it may clearly be understood that Isaias also, after his lips were circumcised, offered himself for God's service, and Moses, whose lips were as yet uncircumcised, refused so great a service."

16. YE SHALL HEAR WITH THE EAR AND NOT UNDERSTAND, AND PERCEIVING YE SHALL BEHOLD AND SHALL NOT SEE. This entire passage, as the Saviour indicates in the Gospel, applies to that time at which He himself deigned to descend to earth and performed signs which the Jews did not understand.[102]

2 And inasmuch as a manifold explanation continues even to the end of the chapter, and we have now filled the wax tablets that receive our words, let it be sufficient to have dictated this much.[103] Because a discourse which is not revised by a stylus in one's hand is not merely crude in itself: it becomes much more annoying if it doubles its tediousness by its verbosity. Tormented by the pain in our eyes, we attend only with our ears and tongue.

LETTER 18B

To Damasus[1]

1(17). The Seventy have: AND ONE (*unum*) OF THE SERAPHIM WAS SENT TO ME; Aquila and Theodotion: AND ONE (*unum*) OF THE SERAPHIM FLEW TO ME; Symmachus: AND ONE (*unus*) OF THE SERAPHIM FLEW TO ME.[2] Daily a seraph (*seraphim*) is sent to us, daily the lips of those who groan and say: *Woe is me (because I have felt remorse)*, are cleansed, and when they have been released from their sins, they prepare themselves for the service of God.

2 But regarding the use of "flew" instead of "was sent" by the other interpreters, understand it [as referring] to the swift coming of the divine utterance to us who are adjudged worthy of association with Him. There is a difference of gender also. The Seventy, Aquila, and Theodotion have translated *seraphim* in the neuter gender, Symmachus in the masculine. It is inconceivable that sex exists among God's agencies, since even the Holy Spirit, in accordance with the usages of the Hebrew tongue, is expressed in the feminine gender, *ruach*, in Greek in the neuter, *to pneuma*, in Latin in the masculine, *spiritus*.

3 Hence we must understand that when there is discussion concerning the above [-mentioned words: i.e., *seraphim*] and something is set down in the masculine or feminine, it is not so much an indication of sex as an expression of the idiom of the language; because God Himself, the invisible and incorruptible, is represented in almost all languages in the masculine gender, and since sex does not apply to Him.

4 The mistake—although a pious one—of those also is to be reprehended who in their prayers and oblations venture

to say: "Thou that sittest above the cherubim and the sera-phim." For it is written that God sits above the cherubim, as in the passage: "Thou that sittest above the cherubim, show thyself,"[3] but no Scripture states that God sits above the seraphim, and we do not even find in all the Scriptures the seraphim themselves standing around God, except in the present passage.

2(18). The Seventy [have]: AND IN HIS HAND HE HAD A LIVE COAL, WHICH HE HAD TAKEN WITH THE TONGS OFF THE ALTAR. AND HE TOUCHED MY MOUTH. Aquila [reads]: AND IN HIS HANDS A PEBBLE IN THE TONGS (*forcipe*) WHICH HE HAD TAKEN OFF THE ALTAR, AND HE TOUCHED MY MOUTH. Theodotion: AND IN HIS HAND A PEBBLE IN THE TONGS (*forcipe*) WHICH HE HAD TAKEN OFF THE ALTAR, AND HE TOUCHED MY MOUTH. Symmachus: AND IN HIS HAND A PEBBLE IN THE TONGS (*forcipibus*) WHICH HE HAD TAKEN OFF THE ALTAR, AND HE CARRIED IT TO MY MOUTH.

2 As concerns the narrative, God appears to be seated in the Temple at Jerusalem, and before Him (according to the Seventy) a live coal is carried from the altar to Isaias, that is, from the altar of incense or of whole burnt offerings. But as concerns the mystical interpretations, that fire is sent them which Jeremias could not bear.[4] When it has penetrated the secret places of our soul, it so dissolves us, so purifies us changing from the old man into the new, that we are able to give utterance to that cry: *And I live, now not I, but the grace of God, which is in me.*[5]

3 According to the other interpreters, we should under-stand the tongs also (although they were always included in the apparatus of the priests) as diverse graces, whereby at sundry times and in divers manners God in times past spoke to the fathers by the prophets.[6] Because in the Hebrew we read *a pebble* instead of *a live coal*, and the others are in

agreement about this, it seems to me that by the word *pebble* divine speech is indicated. For as a pebble is a kind of stone very hard and round and very smooth because absolutely pure, so God's speech, which can yield to no contradictions of heretics or of any adversaries, is called a pebble.

4 With this stone Sephora circumcises her son,[7] and Jesus cleanses the people from their sins.[8] And in the Apocalypse the Lord promises to those that overcome that they shall receive a stone and that a new name shall be written upon it.[9] Moreover, it seems to me that the Seventy in translating it *anthraka* intended the same meaning as the rest. Because *anthrax*, which we translate as "carbuncle,"[10] is a kind of flashing and shining stone, which we find also among the twelve stones.

5 Therefore, whether we accept the stone as a pebble or a carbuncle, in the pebble of divine speech there is truth and inflexibility, in the carbuncle a clear and shining doctrine is shown: *The words of the Lord are pure words: as silver of the earth tried by the fire, refined seven times.*[11] And elsewhere: *The commandment of the Lord is lightsome, enlightening the eyes.*[12]

6 But as to his saying: IN HIS HAND HE HAD A LIVE COAL, by *hand* let us understand operation, as in the passage: *Death and life are in the power (manu) of the tongue;*[13] and in the Psalm: *They shall fall by the power (in manu) of the sword.*[14] Or, of course, the hand was actually visible, so that by reason of the likeness to the human form the prophet might not be afraid when he saw hands stretched out; just as we have seen God and the angels changed into the appearance of men to take away fear from the beholders.

3(19). The Seventy [have]: AND HE SAID: BEHOLD, THIS HATH TOUCHED THY LIPS, AND IT SHALL TAKE AWAY THY INIQUITIES AND SHALL CLEANSE THY SINS. Aquila: BEHOLD,

THIS HATH TOUCHED THY LIPS, AND THY INIQUITY SHALL DEPART, AND THY SIN SHALL BE FORGIVEN. All the other translators agree with Aquila's version.

2 It is first necessary that our lips be touched. Then, when they have been touched, the iniquity will be driven away, and when the iniquity has been put to rout, the Lord will be appeased, because with Him is the propitiation[15] and according to the Apostle *He is the propitiation for our sins.*[16] Now after our sins have been cleansed, we shall hear the voice of the Lord say: *Whom shall I send?* And we shall reply: *Lo, here am I, send me.*

4(20). The Seventy [have]: AND I HEARD THE VOICE OF THE LORD SAYING: WHOM SHALL I SEND AND WHO WILL GO TO THAT PEOPLE? Aquila, Theodotion, and Symmachus: AND I HEARD THE VOICE OF THE LORD SAYING: WHOM SHALL I SEND AND WHO WILL GO FOR US? We have discussed elsewhere[17] the comparison of Isaias with Moses, how the one refused the commission, the other, offering himself voluntarily, suffered hardships.

2 But lest we seem to have passed over any of those expressions which the Jews call δευτερώσεις[17a] and on which they expend all their learning, let us now touch briefly upon the question, why in the Hebrew there stands: AND WHO WILL GO FOR US? For even as in Genesis the saying is: *Let us make man to our image and likeness,*[18] so here also I think it was said: WHO WILL GO FOR US? Now by *us* what others are to be understood save the Father and the Son and the Holy Spirit, for whom he goes, whosoever obeys their will?

3 And as for the fact that the person of one speaker is presented, God is one. But as for the saying *for us,* a diversity of persons is indicated. We read in the Canticle of Canticles the voice of the bridegroom saying to his spouse:

Arise, come, my nearest, my spouse, my dove, for lo, winter is past, the rain is over and gone.[19] For when the soul is established in the tranquility of thought, when its faith is founded upon a rock[20] and fixed with a deep root, all the billows of temptations pass over each other and do not pass over him who is tempted.

4 Be it observed how in response to what the Lord had said: WHOM SHALL I SEND AND WHO WILL GO FOR US? the prophet made answer in part: LO, HERE AM I, SEND ME, and was silent as to the rest, knowing that no man was worthy to go for God and to make all his journey that of Him who sent him. The Lord, observing this humility, that he considered himself unworthy of the second part of the commission, gave the command that follows, saying: Go.

5(21). The Seventy [have]: AND I SAID: LO, HERE AM I, SEND ME. Aquila and Theodotion: LO, I AM PRESENT, SEND ME. Symmachus: LO, SEND ME. God, who called those things that are not as though they were,[21] and who said *I am who am,* and elsewhere *He who is hath sent me,*[22] makes all whom He calls stand firm, because all things that are apart from Him do not exist.

2 Hence the prophet, cleansed from his sins, dared to say: LO, HERE AM I (*Ecce ego sum*)—although in the Latin manuscripts the *sum* is not added because of the variety of the opinions of the translators. Some think we should observe to which prophets the expression "sending" or "sent" (which in Greek is *apostolus*) is applied. They claim that there is this difference, that those who are sent are both prophets and apostles, but those to whom the speech of Him who sends is not addressed are merely prophets. This I consider superfluous.

3 And as we have once come to consider this word, be it

known that the name of Paul's colleague "Silas" means in Hebrew "apostle." He writes several letters in conjunction with Paul; and "Silvanus"[23] is an incorrect reading for "Silas"; for we do not read of a Silvanus in the Acts of the Apostles.

LETTER 19

A letter of Damasus to Jerome[1]

To his most beloved son Jerome, Damasus, bishop, sends greeting in the Lord.

As I was reading in Greek and in Latin what has been written both heretofore and recently by men of our persuasion, that is, the orthodox, on the interpretation of the Gospels, I found that they put forth not only differing but mutually conflicting explanations of the saying *Hosanna to the son of David.*[2]

I wish you would write, with the ardent impulse of your affectionate zeal—doing away with mere opinions and exploding ambiguities—stating what the meaning is in the Hebrew, in actual terms, so that our solicitude may render you thanks in Christ Jesus concerning this, as in many other instances.

LETTER 20

To Damasus[1]

1. Many persons have devised varying explanations of this word. Of their number our[2] Hilary,[3] in his commentaries on Matthew, has made the statement: *"Osanna* in the Hebrew means 'the redemption of the house of David.'" Now in the first place, "redemption" in the Hebrew tongue is expressed by *pheduth;* then "house" is *beth;* moreover, it is apparent to all that the name "David" is not inserted in this passage. Others have supposed that *osanna* means "glory." Now "glory" is called *chabod.* Some translate it "grace," although "grace" is named *thoda* or *anna.*

2. It remains, therefore, to forsake the rivulets of opinion and hasten back to the source whence it was taken by the Evangelists.[4] For even as we can find neither in Greek nor in Latin manuscripts [the words] *that it might be fulfilled which was said by the prophets: that he shall be called a Nazarene,*[5] and the following: *out of Egypt have I called my son,*[6] so now it is from Hebrew codices that the truth must be extracted: how it came to pass that the crowd, and particularly a throng composed of children, burst forth in this utterance. As Matthew says: *And the multitudes that went before and that followed cried, saying: Hosanna to the son of David; blessed is he that cometh in the name of the Lord; hosanna in the highest.*[7]

2 But Mark has expressed it thus: *They cried, saying: Hosanna, blessed is he that cometh in the name of the Lord. Blessed be the kingdom of our father David that cometh in the name of the Lord: hosanna in the highest.*[8] John also

agrees, with like language: *and cried: Hosanna, blessed is he that cometh in the name of the Lord, the King of Israel.*

3 Only Luke has not set down the word "hosanna," though agreeing in the rest of his interpretation: *Blessed be the king who cometh in the name of the Lord, peace in heaven and glory on high.*[10] Therefore, as I have said, the Hebrew words themselves must be set down and the opinions of all interpreters be digested, that the reader by considering them all may the more readily discover for himself what he is to think about it.

3. In Psalm 117,[11] where we read: *O Lord, save me; O Lord, give good success. Blessed be he that cometh in the name of the Lord,* the reading in the Hebrew is *anna adonai, osianna, anna adonai, aslianna; baruch abba basem adonai.* This Aquila, Symmachus, Theodotion, and the fifth version[12] (lest we seem to change anything in the Latin) translate as follows: ὦ δὴ κύριε, σῶσον δή, ὦ δὴ κύριε, εὐόδωσον δή· εὐλογητὸς ὁ ἐρχόμενος ἐν ὀνόματι κυρίου.

2 Only the sixth version is so far in agreement with the Seventy that, where the rest have set down ὦ δή, it has written ὦ. And that *osianna,* which we through ignorance incorrectly call *osanna,* means "save" or "make safe," has been recognized by the interpretation of all. Now the question is, what the word *anna* alone signifies—without the addition of the word "saving." 3 It must be realized that in this passage *anna* is used three times; and, indeed, the first and second time it is written in the same letters: aleph, nun, he. But the third time it is written heth, nun, he. Therefore, Symmachus, who had agreed with the interpretation of all in Psalm 117, that he might afford us a clearer understanding, in Psalm 115,[13] where we read: *O Lord, deliver my soul,* has rendered it: *I beseech thee, O Lord, deliver my soul.*

4 Besides, where the Seventy have translated by ὦ and

he by "I beseech thee" (obsecro)—whereas Aquila and the other editions interpret by ὦ δή—in Hebrew the reading is *anna*, but so written that it has aleph at the beginning, not heth. Hence we observe that if *anna* is written with an aleph, it means "I beseech thee" (obsecro), but if it is written with a heth, it is a conjunction or an interjection which among the Greeks is expressed by δή and is found in the phrase σῶσον δή, whose meaning the Latin language cannot reproduce.

4. But because these fine points and the inner meaning of this sort of disputation offend the reader on account of the barbarity both of our language and our literature,[14] I have recourse to a brief explanation. I shall speak of Psalm 117, which clearly is a prophecy of Christ and is often read in synagogues of the Jews. Hence it was very well known to the people that these verses had been chosen because He that was promised of the line of David was to come to save Israel. As David says: *The stone which the builders rejected, the same is become the head of the corner. This is the Lord's doing: and it is wonderful in our eyes. This is the day which the Lord hath made: let us be glad and rejoice therein. O Lord, save me; O Lord, give good success. Blessed be he that cometh in the name of the Lord. The Lord is God, and He hath shone upon us.*[15]

2 Whence also the account of the Evangelists records that the Pharisees and scribes were moved with indignation at these things, because they saw the people understanding that the entire prophecy of the Psalm has been fulfilled in Christ, and because the children were crying: *Hosanna to the son of David.*[16] And they said to Him: *Hearest thou what these say?* And Jesus replied: *Have you never read, "Out of the mouth of infants and of sucklings thou hast perfected praise"?*[17] Thus He confirmed Psalm 117 by the declaration of Psalm 8.

3 Moreover, concerning that which could easily be expressed: *Blessed is he that cometh in the name of the Lord,* the writing of all the Evangelists is in accord. But as regards the word *osianna,* because they could not translate the term— as we have seen has also been the case with *alleluia* and *amen* and many others—they set down the actual Hebrew and said *osianna.*

4 But Luke, who was the most learned in the Greek language of all the Evangelists—being both a physician and the author of a Gospel in Greek—because he saw that he could not translate the idiomatic meaning of the word, thought it better to omit it than to set down something that would raise a question in the reader's mind.

5. In short, just as we have in the Latin tongue also certain interjections, so that we say in exultation *va* and in admiration *papae* and in grief *heu,* and when we wish to command silence we bare our teeth and restrict our breath and constrain it to make the sound *st,* so the Hebrews too have among other peculiarities of their language an interjection. So, when they wish to importune the Lord, they set down a word that indicates petition and say *anna* Lord, which the Seventy have rendered "O Lord."[18]

2 Accordingly, *osi* is translated "save," and *anna* is an interjection of entreaty. If you wish to make a compound word of these two, you will say *osianna,* or, as we pronounce it, *osanna,* eliding the medial vowel; just as we are accustomed to do in poetry, when we scan *mene incepto desistere victam* as *men incepto*[19]—because *aleph,* the first letter in the following word, encountering the final letter of the preceding word, has squeezed it out.

3 Accordingly—to return to the original question—when we read in Latin: *o domine, salvum fac, o domine, bene conplace; benedictus, qui venit in nomine domini,*[20] we

might, in accordance with the meaning of the Hebrew, say: *obsecro domine, salvum fac; obsecro domine, prospera, obsecro; benedictus, qui venit in nomine domini.* However, *salvum fac* is written that we may read between the lines "thy people Israel," or, more generally, "the world."

4 Finally, Matthew, who wrote his Gospel in the Hebrew tongue, has expressed it thus: *osianna barrama,* that is, *hosanna in the highest.*[21] Because, when the Saviour was born, salvation came all the way to heaven—that is, to the highest—peace being made not only on earth, but also in heaven, so that now at last it might cease to be said: *My sword is inebriated in heaven.*[22]

Here you have an interim explanation that I have dictated, briefly and concisely, to the best of my ability. But let Your Beatitude know that in dissertations of this kind, boredom on the part of the reader should not arise. For we too might have told some lying tale to solve the question by a single word—just as we have shown others have done. But it is more seemly to exert oneself a little on behalf of truth and to adapt our ear to a foreign tongue, rather than to bring over from the language of others an invented meaning.[23]

LETTER 21

To Damasus[1]

1.   The question of Your Beatitude was a theme for argument, and to have posed questions thus is to have opened a way for a reply.   Indeed *wisdom will be ascribed to one who questions wisely.*[2]   You say: "Who is that father in the Gospel who divided unto his two sons his substance?   Who are the two sons?   Who is the elder or who is the younger?   In what sense does the younger waste the substance he has received with harlots?   How is he put in charge of swine by the prince of that country when famine comes?   How does he eat the husks, return to his father, receive a ring, a robe, and the fatted calf killed for him?   Who is that elder brother and how, as he returns from the field, is he envious of the reception of his brother?   And the rest, which is set forth more fully in the Gospel."

2 You add besides: "I know that many have said various things about this passage and have assumed that the elder brother is the Jew, the younger the Gentile.   But I ask how the story can be adapted to the Jewish people: *Behold, for so many years do I serve thee, and I have never transgressed thy commandment, and yet thou hast never given me a kid to make merry with my friends,*[3] and the following: *Son, thou art always with me, and all I have is thine.*[4]   But," you say, "if we wish to have the parable refer to the righteous and the sinner, it cannot apply to the righteous that he should be annoyed at the salvation of another, and especially of his brother.   For if death came into the world because of the devil's envy,[5] and they who are of his party imitate him, never can such inordinate envy be in keeping with the

character of the just, that he would stand outside and ob-
stinately resist and, being tormented by envy, be the only
one unwilling to participate in the rejoicing of the house."

2.   Therefore, as we are accustomed in the other parables
which were not explained by the Saviour to inquire why
they were spoken, so we should do also in the case of this.
Why did the Lord give utterance to such words? Because
of what question was this kind of reply given?

The scribes and the Pharisees murmured, saying: *Why
doth this man receive sinners and eat with them?*[6] Now the
preceding verse had said by way of preface: *Now the publicans and sinners drew near unto Him to hear Him.*[7] 2
Therefore, all their envy has this source: the question why
the Lord did not avoid speech and intercourse with those
whom the precepts of the law condemned. This is what
Luke reports. But Matthew speaks as follows: *And it came
to pass as He was sitting at meat in the house, behold many
publicans and sinners came and sat down with Jesus and His
disciples. And the Pharisees seeing it, said to His disciples:
Why doth your master eat with publicans and sinners? But
Jesus hearing it, said: They that are in health need not a
physician, but they that are ill. Go then and learn what this
meaneth: I will have mercy and not sacrifice. For I am not
come to call the just, but sinners.*[8]

3 Mark also agrees, using the same language.[9] Therefore,
as we have said, every question arose out of the law. Now
the law, being firmly devoted to justice,[10] was without mercy.
So every adulterer, murderer, perjurer, and—to put it briefly
—whoever was guilty of a crime worthy of death, gained
no absolution because of favor shown to repentance. He was
ordered to pay a tooth for a tooth, a life for a life.[11] Accordingly *all have turned out of the way, they are become unprofitable together; there was none that did good, there was*

not so much as one.[12] *But where sin abounded, grace did more abound,*[13] and *God sent His Son, made of a woman,*[14] who breaking down the middle wall [of partition][15] made both one and tempered the severity of the law by the grace of the gospel.

4 Whence also Paul, writing to the churches, says: *Grace to you and peace from God the Father and from the Lord Jesus Christ*[16]: grace, which is not a payment due to merit,[17] but has been granted as a gift; and peace, whereby we have been reconciled to God, having as propitiator[18] the Lord Jesus, who forgave us our sins and expunged what was the handwriting of death against us, nailing it to the cross; and He made principalities and powers a show, triumphing over them on the tree.[19]

5 But what clemency can be greater than that the Son of God should be born a son of man, that He should endure the tedium of ten months of gestation,[20] await the arrival of birth, be wrapped in swaddling clothes, become subject to His parents,[21] grow through successive ages, and after the insulting words, blows, and scourging become for us accursed on the cross, in order to free us from the curse of the law,[22] being made obedient unto the Father, even unto death?[23] And He fulfilled in deed that which He had previously prayed for in the character of mediator, saying: *Father, I will that as thou and I are one, they also may be one in us.*[24]

6 Accordingly, as it had come to this, that what the law could not do,[25] because no one was justified by it,[26] should by His ineffable mercy be brought to pass, He called the publicans and sinners to repentance, even seeking their company, so that they might be taught also in the midst of their banquets, so that it might be clear to one who had read the Gospel with care how His food and drink and His going about and all that He did procured the salvation of men.

The scribes and Pharisees, seeing this, said that He was acting in opposition to the law: *Behold a man [that is] a glutton
and a wine drinker, a friend of publicans and sinners.*[27]   For
they had rebuked Him even before, asking why the Lord
healed on the Sabbath day.[28]

7 Therefore, that He might refute this accusation of theirs
by means of clemency, He set before them three parables.
One of them is that of the ninety-and-nine sheep left in the
hills and of the one that was lost—which was carried back
on the shepherd's shoulders.[29]   Another is that of the groat
which the woman sought diligently, lighting a candle.   And
when she had found it, she called her neighbors to celebrate
with her, saying: *Rejoice with me, because I have found the
groat which I had lost.*[30]   And the third is of the two sons—
concerning which you bade me give a brief explanation.[31]

3.   And indeed of the sheep and the groat, although they
refer to a single idea, this is not the time to discuss them.
Let it suffice to say only this much, that these parables were
set forth for this purpose: as in the finding of the sheep and
of the groat there is joy of the angels and of the neighbors
round about, so at the repentance of publicans and sinners
there should be joy on the part of all who have no need to
repent.   2 Hence I am greatly surprised that Tertullian in
the book he wrote concerning chastity[32] opposed repentance
and replaced an old conviction by a new point of view.   He
wished to believe this, that the publicans and sinners who ate
with the Lord were the pagans; as the Scripture says: *There
shall be no tax weigher of Israel.*[33]   As though, indeed, Matthew the publican were not of the circumcision,[34] and he who
dared not lift his eyes to heaven as he prayed with the
Pharisee in the Temple[35] were not a publican of Israel, and
as though Luke did not say: *And all the people hearing, and
the publicans, justified God, being baptized with John's*

baptism.[36]   Or as if it could appear credible to anyone that a pagan had entered the Temple, or that the Lord had eaten with pagans.   For He was particularly on His guard lest He should appear to be breaking the law,[37] and came first to the lost sheep of the house of Israel,[38] and replied also to the woman of Canaan who besought Him on behalf of her daughter's health: *One should not take away the bread of the children and give it to the dogs.*[39]   And elsewhere He commanded His disciples: *Go ye not into the way of the Gentiles, and into the cities of the Samaritans enter ye not.*[40]

3 By all this we are taught that among "the publicans" we may include not so much the Gentiles as all sinners generally, that is, both those that were Gentiles and those who were Jews.   But because he was defending this dogma before his mad women,[41] Tertullian argued vainly (being unwilling that penitent Christians should be taken back) that "publicans" might be understood to refer to Gentiles only.   Therefore, not to make a long story of it, I shall set forth the very words of the Gospel and like a commentator subjoin my interpretation to each passage.[42]

4.   A CERTAIN MAN HAD TWO SONS.   That God is called a man is made evident by many instances.   Take the following example: *The testimony of two men is true.   I give testimony of myself; also the Father that sent me.*[43]

2 In one parable He is called a shepherd,[44] in another a householder,[45] in one He plants a vineyard,[46] in another He invites to a wedding,[47] and under various comparisons indicates the same thing, that He disapproves of the pride of the Jews and approves of the repentance of all sinners alike, whether of Gentiles or of Israel.   But as to His saying *two sons*, almost all the Scriptures are full of the calling of two peoples to the sacraments.

5.   AND THE YOUNGER SAID TO HIM: FATHER, GIVE ME

THE PORTION OF SUBSTANCE THAT FALLETH TO ME. Everything is the substance of God: life, reason, thought, speech. This is the gift God has bestowed upon all alike, and in equal measure. As the Evangelist says: *That was the true light, which enlighteneth every man that cometh into the world.*[48]

2 This is the right eye which is to be preserved from scandals;[49] this is the light of the body;[50] this is the talent which is not to be laid up in a napkin,[51] that is, by a life of ease and luxury, nor to be buried in the earth, that is, to be dulled by earthly thoughts.

6. AND HE DIVIDED UNTO THEM HIS SUBSTANCE. In the Greek the reading is more vivid: διεῖλεν αὐτοῖς τὸν βίον. That is, he gave them free choice, he gave their hearts' desire, that each might live, not in accordance with God's command, but to please himself; that is, not out of necessity, but by free will,[52] in order that virtue might have its place, so that, like God, we have the privilege of doing what we wish, differing in this from all the other animals. Hence the judgment against sinners is just, and a reward shall be bestowed upon the saints or the virtuous.

7. AND NOT MANY DAYS AFTER, THE YOUNGER SON, GATHERING ALL TOGETHER, WENT ABROAD INTO A FAR COUNTRY. If God holds heaven in the hollow of His hand, and the earth between His fingers,[53] and Jeremias says: *a God at hand and not a God afar off,*[54] and it is said also by David that no place is without Him,[55] how does His son journey afar and depart from his Father?

2 We must understand, therefore, that it is not by spatial distances but through affection that we either are with God or depart from Him. For just as He says to His disciples: *Behold I am with you all days, even to the consummation of the world,*[56] even so He says to those who have preferred their

own pretensions and do not deserve to be with the Lord: *Depart from me, I know you not, you that work iniquity.*[57]

8.   Accordingly, the younger son left his father, with his substance, and set out for foreign parts. So Cain, too, went out from the face of the Lord[58] and dwelt in the land of Naid,[59] which may be translated "wandering." Whosoever departs from God is straightway shaken by the waves of the world and swept off his feet.[60]

2 For after men left the East and departed from the true light, they then built against God the tower of their iniquity. It was then they contrived proud dogmas, desiring in their curiosity to penetrate the forbidden altars of heaven itself. And that place was called Babel, that is, "confusion."[61]

9.   AND THERE HE WASTED HIS SUBSTANCE, LIVING RIOTOUSLY. Riotous living is hostility to God. Being hostile to the virtues, it destroys the substance of the Father, and charming with pleasure for the moment does not permit future poverty to be thought of.

10.   AND AFTER HE HAD SPENT ALL, THERE CAME A MIGHTY FAMINE IN THAT COUNTRY. He had received his faculties from his Father, so that he knew His invisible attributes from those that were visible,[62] and consequently understood the Creator from the beauty of His creatures. He who detains the truth in injustice[63] and worships idols instead of God, consumes the universal goods of nature. Having consumed all, he began to be in want of the virtues —having forsaken the source of the virtues.

2 THERE CAME A MIGHTY FAMINE IN THAT COUNTRY. Every place in which we dwell without the Father is a place of famine, penury, and want. Moreover, this is the country of mighty famine μετὰ ἐκτάσεως[64] of which it is said by the prophet: *Ye who dwell in the region of the shadow*

of death, light will shine upon you.[65] But on the other hand, there is another country which we are to possess through purity of heart even in our lifetime, which the holy man desires, saying: *I believe to see the good things of the Lord in the land of the living.*[66]

11. AND HE BEGAN TO BE IN WANT, AND HE WENT AND CLEAVED TO ONE OF THE PRINCES OF THAT COUNTRY. Having forsaken his preserver, who at his first cry had bestowed all good things upon him, he cleaved to the prince of this world,[67] that is, the devil, the ruler of that darkness,[68] whom the Scripture calls now the enemy,[69] now the unjust judge,[70] now the dragon,[71] now Satan,[72] now the hammer,[73] now a partridge,[74] now Belial,[75] now a roaring lion,[76] now Leviathan,[77] now "the heads of the dragons,"[78] and by many other names.

2 But that he says *to one of the princes,* it is to be understood that there are many who flit through the air and by the trickery of various forms of vice enslave the race of men.

12. AND HE SENT HIM INTO HIS FARM TO FEED SWINE. The pig is an unclean animal, because it delights in swill and filth. Such is the horde of demons, which, through the instrumentality of idols made by hand, feed on the blood of beasts and finally are satiated by a certain richer offering—the death of man himself. Accordingly, he sent him into his property, that is, he made him his servant, that he might feed his swine, sacrificing to them his own soul.

13. AND HE WOULD FAIN HAVE FILLED HIS BELLY WITH THE HUSKS THE SWINE DID EAT, AND NO MAN GAVE UNTO HIM. And that which in Ezechiel is spoken chidingly to Jerusalem: *And it hath happened in thee contrary to the custom of women in thy fornication, and after thee there are no fornicating women, for thou gavest rewards, and rewards*

were not given to thee,[79] we see fulfilled in the case of the younger son.

2 He lost his substance in the country of the prince, and after losing his wealth, being sent to the swine, he was consumed by want. The food of demons is drunkenness, luxury, fornication, and all the sins. These are persuasive and lascivious; they soothe the senses with pleasure; and immediately upon their appearance they provoke a man to use them. And this is why the young man, given to excess, could not be satisfied: because pleasure always creates a hunger for itself and when indulged does not satisfy.

3 When Satan has deceived someone by his craft and placed his own yoke upon him, he does not give further attention to the multiplication of vices, knowing that the man is dead already; even as we see many idolaters in rags, exhausted by misery and want. These are they in whom the word of the prophet is fulfilled: *Gifts are given to all harlots; but thou hast given hire to all thy lovers and didst not take rewards.*[80]

4 We may also interpret the husks in another fashion. The food of the demons is the songs of poets, secular wisdom, the display of rhetorical language. These delight all with their sweetness; but while they captivate the ears with fluent verses of charming rhythm, they penetrate the soul as well and bind the inmost affections. But when they have been read with the greatest enthusiasm and effort, they afford their readers nothing more than empty sound and the hubbub of words. No satisfaction of truth, no refreshment of justice is found. They who are zealous for these things continue to hunger for truth, to lack virtue.[81]

5 A type of this sort of wisdom is described in Deuteronomy under the figure of a captive woman. The divine voice com-

mands that if an Israelite desires to have her as a wife, he shall make her bald, pare her nails, and shave her hair. When she has been made clean, then she shall pass into the victor's embrace.[82]   If we understand that literally, isn't it ridiculous?[83]   6 And yet we ourselves are accustomed to do this when we read the philosophers, when the books of secular wisdom come into our hands.   If we find anything useful in them, we apply it to our own doctrine; but if we find anything —with regard to idols, love, the care of secular things—that is inapplicable, these we shave off, for these we decree baldness, these we cut away like our nails with a very sharp blade. 7 Hence the Apostle forbids anyone to sit at meat with an idol, saying: *But take heed lest perhaps this your liberty become a stumbling block to the weak.   For if a man see him that hath knowledge sit at meat in the idol's temple, shall not his conscience—being weak—be emboldened to eat those things which are sacrificed to idols?   And through thy knowledge shall the weak brother perish, for whom Christ died?*[84] 8 Doesn't he seem to say, in other words, don't read the philosophers, the orators, the poets, lest you find your peace in reading them?   Let us not flatter ourselves if we do not believe these things that are written; for the conscience of others may be wounded, and we may be thought to approve of the things which we do not condemn as we read them. Otherwise, what opinion can we entertain of the Apostle when he approved of the knowledge of one who ate in an idol's temple and called him perfect whom he knew to be eating those things that are sacrificed to idols?   Never let a Christian mouth utter "Almighty Jove" and "By Hercules" and "By Castor," or swear by the rest of those monstrosities rather than gods.

9 But as it is, we see even priests of God slighting the Gospels and the prophets, reading comedies, reciting love

passages from bucolic verse, cherishing Vergil and voluntarily making themselves guilty of that which in the case of children is done under compulsion. It is thus we must be on our guard not to wish to have a captive to wife, not to recline at meat in an idol's temple. If we have been deceived by love of her, let us at least cleanse her and free her from all the horror of uncleanness, lest a brother for whom Christ died be caused to stumble when he hears uttered by a Christian voice songs composed for the praises of idols.

14. AND RETURNING TO HIMSELF HE SAID: HOW MANY HIRED SERVANTS IN MY FATHER'S HOUSE ABOUND WITH BREAD, AND I HERE PERISH WITH HUNGER. By hired servants, according to one interpretation, we refer to those of the Jews who keep the precepts of the law merely for the sake of present advantages; that is, they are just and merciful, not because of justice itself or because of the actual virtue of mercy, but that they may secure the reward of fertility of the soil and of long life.

2 But he who desires those things is compelled by fear to obey the commandments, lest by violation of what was enjoined he may lose what he desires. Further, where there is fear, there is no love. *But perfect love casteth out fear.*[85] For he who loves keeps the commandments, not because he is compelled by fear of punishment or by the desire for reward, but because the very thing that is commanded by God is best. Therefore, the meaning is as follows: "How many of the Jews are obedient to God merely on account of present advantages, and I am perishing of hunger!"

15. I WILL ARISE AND WILL GO TO MY FATHER. *I will arise* is well said. For in the Father's absence he had not stood upright. For it is characteristic of sinners to lie prone, of the just to stand erect.[86] It is said to Moses: *But stand thou here with me;*[87] and in Psalm 133: *Behold now bless ye*

the Lord, all ye servants of the Lord who stand in the house of the Lord.[88] So the prophet urges those in the house of the Lord to stand to bless the Lord.

16. AND I WILL SAY TO HIM: FATHER, I HAVE SINNED AGAINST HEAVEN AND BEFORE THEE; I AM NOT WORTHY TO BE CALLED THY SON. He had sinned against heaven, since he had forsaken the heavenly Jerusalem, his mother;[89] he had sinned before his father, in that deserting his Creator he had worshiped idols of wood; he was not worthy to be called a son of God, since he had preferred to be the servant of idols. For everyone that commits sin is born of his father the devil.[90]

17. MAKE ME AS ONE OF THY HIRED SERVANTS. "Make me," he says, "as one of the Jews, who honor you because of promises of merely present advantages. Receive a repentant son, you who have very often spared your hired servants when they sinned."

18. AND HE CAME TO HIS FATHER. We come to the Father when we leave off feeding swine, according to the saying: *As soon as you return and make lamentation, you shall be saved.*[91]

19. AND WHEN HE WAS YET A GREAT WAY OFF, HIS FATHER SAW HIM AND WAS MOVED WITH COMPASSION. Before he returned to his ancient father by worthy works and true repentance, God, with whom all future events are already past[92] and who knows beforehand all that is to be, runs forward to his coming and by His Word, which took flesh by a virgin, anticipates the return of His younger son.

20. AND RUNNING TO HIM FELL UPON HIS NECK. He came to earth before the sinner entered the house of confession, He fell upon his neck—that is, He assumed a human body—and just as John leaned on the bosom,[93] he who was made the confidant of His secrets, so He placed upon the younger son (by grace rather than because of merit) His

light yoke, that is, the easy precepts of His commandments.[94]

21. AND KISSED HIM. Accordingly, in the Canticle of Canticles the Church prays concerning the coming of her Spouse: *Let Him kiss me with the kisses of His mouth,*[95] saying: "I do not wish Him to speak to me through Moses nor through the prophets; let Him take my body, let Him kiss me in the flesh." So that we may adapt to this thought also what is written in Isaias: *If you seek, seek and dwell by me in the forest.*[96]

2 And there, indeed, the Church, weeping, is bidden to exclaim by reason of Seir[97]—because Seir means "hairy" and "bristly"—to indicate likewise their ancient horror of the Gentiles, by a corresponding simile: *I am black and beautiful, O daughter of Jerusalem.*[98]

22. AND THE SON SAID TO HIM: FATHER, I HAVE SINNED AGAINST HEAVEN AND BEFORE THEE: I AM NOT NOW WORTHY TO BE CALLED THY SON. He says he is not worthy to be given the name of son, and nevertheless, by reason of the voice of nature, by reason of that substance which his father had once bestowed upon him, in his agitation he breaks out into the very name, saying: *Father, I have sinned against heaven.* 2 In vain, therefore, do certain persons argue that the name "father" is suitable only for the saints, since even he who confesses that he is unworthy of the name of son calls God "Father"; unless, perchance, it is for this reason that he dares call Him "Father," because he has been fully converted.

23. AND THE FATHER SAID TO HIS SERVANTS: BRING FORTH QUICKLY THE FIRST ROBE: that robe which Adam had forfeited by sinning, the robe which in another parable is called a wedding garment,[99] that is, the covering of the Holy Spirit, without which no one can attend the banquet of the King.

24. AND PUT A RING ON HIS HAND: a sign of likeness to

Christ, according to the saying: *Believing, ye were signed with the Holy Spirit of promise.*[100] And to the prince of Tyre, who had lost his likeness to the Creator: *Thou art the seal of resemblance and the crown of beauty, thou wast born in the delights of the paradise of God.*[101]

2 Isaias also speaks of this sign: *Then shall they be made manifest who are sealed.*[102] This sign is given by the hand, when the Scripture indicates works of justice, as in the text: *The word of the Lord came by the hand of Aggeus the prophet;*[103] and to Jerusalem: *I decked thee also with ornaments,* he says, *and put bracelets on thy hands.*[104] 3 Another place for the sign is revealed to that man who was clothed in a long garment: *Go through the midst of Jerusalem and mark a sign upon the foreheads of the men that sigh and mourn for all the abominations that are committed in the midst thereof.*[105] Why? That they may afterwards say: *The light of thy countenance, O Lord, is signed upon us.*[106]

25. AND SHOES ON HIS FEET. For he has lost the dignity of a bridegroom. He could not celebrate the Passover with bare feet. These are the shoes of which the Lord says: *And I shod thee with violet-colored shoes.*[107] *And shoes on his feet,* lest anywhere a lurking snake might attack the sole of his foot as he walked,[108] and that he might tread upon serpents and scorpions,[109] that he might be prepared for the gospel of peace,[110] no longer walking according to the flesh but according to the spirit,[111] and that the prophetic saying might be applicable to him: *How beautiful are the feet of those that preach peace and that bring good tidings!*[112]

26. AND BRING HITHER THE FATTED CALF AND KILL IT, AND LET US EAT AND MAKE MERRY, BECAUSE THIS MY SON WAS DEAD AND IS COME TO LIFE AGAIN, WAS LOST AND IS FOUND. The fatted calf, which is sacrificed for the safety of

penitents, is the Saviour Himself, on whose flesh we feed, whose blood we drink daily.

2 My believing reader,[113] you understand with me with what fatness we have been filled that we burst forth to the utterance of His praises, saying: *My heart hath uttered a good word, I speak my works to the king;*[114] although some—superstitiously rather than truly, and not considering the text of the Psalm—think this is to be understood of the Person of the Father.

3 Moreover, as to the saying: *Let us eat, because this my son was dead and is come to life again, was lost and is found,* it refers to the same interpretation of the former parable, wherein it is said: *So I say to you, there shall be joy before the angels of God upon one sinner doing penance.*[115]

27. AND THEY BEGAN TO BE MERRY. This banquet is celebrated daily, daily the Father receives a Son. Christ always sacrifices Himself for believers.

28. NOW HIS ELDER SON WAS IN THE FIELD. Thus far we have discussed the character of the younger son. According to the present parable, we must accept him as among the publicans and sinners who were called by the Lord to repentance. But according to the mystical interpretation, it is also a prophecy concerning the future calling of the Gentiles.

2 Now the story goes on to the older son, whom many interpret simply as the person of all the saints, but many—quite correctly—refer to the Jews. As to the saints, the identification is not difficult, since it is said: *I have never transgressed thy commandment,* although the fact that he is jealous of the brother's return may seem at variance with this. But while envy at his brother's salvation may fit in with the Jews, this is not in agreement, that he says he has never trans-

gressed His commandment.[116]   We shall attempt at the proper time to make clear what we think about these points.

3 Now HIS ELDER SON WAS IN THE FIELD, sweating at the labor of earthly tasks, far from the grace of the Holy Spirit, banished from his father's counsel.   This is he who says: *I have bought a farm, and I must needs go out and see it: I pray thee, hold me excused.*[117]   This is he who buys five yoke of oxen[118] and weighted down by the burden of the law enjoys the pleasure of earthly sensations.   This is he who married a wife[119] and cannot go to the wedding feast: being made flesh, he can by no means be one with the spirit;[120] in his person the laborers of that parable also find a parallel, wherein they are sent to the vineyard at the first, third, sixth, and ninth hour —that is, at the various times of their being called—and are angry that the laborers chosen at the eleventh hour are made equal with them.[121]

29.   AND WHEN HE CAME, HE DREW NIGH TO THE HOUSE AND HEARD MUSIC AND DANCING.   The superscription of a certain Psalm, "for Maheleth," is in accord with this meaning, because *meleth* is said of a harmonious chorus.[122]   It is a mistake when some Latin interpreters suppose a symphony to be a kind of organ; because the concordant harmony in God's praise is expressed by this word: *symphonia* is represented in Latin by *consonantia*.[123]

30.   AND HE CALLED ONE OF THE SERVANTS AND ASKED WHAT THESE THINGS MEANT.   And now Israel asks why God rejoices at the adoption of the Gentiles.   In their zeal to torture, they cannot understand the Father's will.

31.   AND HE SAID TO HIM: THY BROTHER IS COME, AND THY FATHER HATH KILLED THE FATTED CALF, BECAUSE HE HATH RECEIVED HIM SAFE.   The cause of rejoicing, which is sung in praise of God with equal fervor all over the world, is

the salvation of sinners. The angels rejoice, every creature unites in happiness, and of Israel alone is it said:

32. AND HE WAS ANGRY AND WOULD NOT GO IN. He is angry because his brother was received in his absence; he is angry that he is alive whom he thought dead. And now Israel stands outside, and now, while the disciples hear the good news in church, his mother and his brethren stand seeking him.[124]

33. HIS FATHER THEREFORE COMING OUT BEGAN TO ENTREAT HIM. How kind and merciful a father! He entreats His son to become a participant in the joy of the house; He asks him through the apostles, preachers of the gospel. Of these Paul says: *For Christ, we beseech you, be reconciled to God;*[125] and elsewhere: *To you it behoved us first to speak the word of God; but because you have judged yourselves unworthy, behold we turn to the Gentiles.*[126]

34. AND HE ANSWERING SAID TO HIS FATHER: BEHOLD, FOR SO MANY YEARS DO I SERVE THEE. The father as suppliant begs him to make peace. But he, following the justice that is in the law, is not obedient to the justice of God.[127] And besides, what is greater than the justice of God, greater than forgiving the penitent and saving a son who returns? *Behold, for so many years do I serve thee, and I have never transgressed thy commandment.* As if this very thing were not transgression of a commandment: to begrudge another his salvation, to boast before God of his justice, when no one is clean in His sight.[128] 2 For *who will rejoice that he has a pure heart,* though he be but an infant of a single day?[129] David makes confession and says: *For behold I was conceived in iniquities, and in sins did my mother conceive me,*[130] and elsewhere: *If thou, O Lord, wilt mark iniquities, who shall stand it?*[131] And this man says he has never transgressed a

commandment, after having so many times been given into captivity because of idolatry.[132]

3 BEHOLD, FOR SO MANY YEARS DO I SERVE THEE, AND I HAVE NEVER TRANSGRESSED THY COMMANDMENT. This is what the Apostle Paul speaks of: *What then shall we say? That the Gentiles, who followed not after justice, have attained to justice, even the justice that is of faith; but Israel, by following after the law of justice, is not come unto the law of justice. Why so? Because they sought it not by faith, but as it were of works of the law.*[133]

4 This might also be said of the person of one who, in the words of the same apostle, conversed without blame according to the justice that is in the law;[134] although it seems to me that the Jew boasts more than he tells the truth, after the fashion of that Pharisee: *O God, I give thee thanks that I am not as the rest of men, extortioners, unjust, adulterers, as also is this publican.*[135] 5 I ask you, does not this man seem to be saying of his brother what the Pharisee had said about the publican: *he who hath devoured all his substance living with harlots?* Moreover, as to this that he says: *I have never transgressed thy commandment,* the father's speech is not in accord with it; for he did not agree that what his son had said was true, but assuaged his anger by another means: *Son, thou art always with me.* 6 He doesn't say, does he, "You speak well, and you have done everything that I ordered"? But he says: *Thou art always with me.* You are with me under the law by which you are bound; you are with me while you are being trained by me, even in bondage; you are with me, not because you have fulfilled my precepts, but because I have not suffered you to depart into a far country. You are with me to the end, in accordance with my saying unto David: *If his children forsake my law and walk not in my judgments, if they profane my justices and keep not my commandments,*

I will visit their iniquities with a rod, and their sins with stripes. But my mercy will I not take away from him.[136]

7 By this testimony also that of which the elder son boasted is proven to be false, since he did not walk according to the judgments of God and did not do His commands. And we are informed how he was always with his father, though he failed to do these things: while doing iniquity he is visited with the rod, and upon being so visited mercy is not denied him.

8 Nor is it to be wondered at that he dared to lie to his father—this man who could envy his brother. Especially since on the Day of Judgment some impudently lie, saying: "Have we not eaten and drunk in thy name and done many miracles and cast out devils?"[137] But the meaning of *and all I have is thine* will be explained more appropriately in its own place.

35. AND THOU HAST NEVER GIVEN ME A KID TO MAKE MERRY WITH MY FRIENDS. What Israel is saying is: "So much blood has been shed, so many thousands of men have been slain, and none of them has become the redeemer of our salvation. Josias himself, who did that which was right in thy sight,[138] and more recently the Maccabees, who fought for thy inheritance, were slain by the swords of the enemy in violation of the right of sanctuary, and no blood has restored our liberty. Lo, we are still subject to the Roman empire.[139] No prophet, no priest, no just person was sacrificed for us, and it is for that son devoted to riotous living[140]—that is, for the Gentiles—for sinners of all creation that the glorious blood was shed. Whereas thou hast not given less to the deserving, thou hast bestowed more upon the undeserving.[141] *Thou hast never given me a kid to make merry with my friends.*"

2 You are making a mistake, Israel. Say rather: "That I might make merry with thee." Can there be any rejoicing

unless the Father celebrates the banquet with you? At least be taught by the present instance. When the younger son returns, both the father and the servants rejoice. *Let us eat, he says, and let us make merry.* Not "eat and make merry." But you, persisting in the attitude because of which you envy your brother, because of which you withdraw from your father's sight and are always in the field, now also wish to enter upon a banquet without him.

3 THOU HAST NEVER GIVEN ME A KID. The Father never gives trivial gifts. You have a calf that has been killed: go in, eat with your brother. Why do you ask for a kid, you to whom a Lamb has been sent? And lest you pretend not to know that it was sent, John points Him out to you in the wilderness: *Behold the Lamb of God, behold Him who taketh away the sins of the world.*[142] And the Father, indeed, being merciful and granting you repentance, urges you to the calf, not sacrificing the kid, which he knows to be stationed on the left.[143] But it is you who will sacrifice a kid for yourself—even Antichrist. With your friends, the unclean spirits, you must be sated with its flesh, fulfilling the prophecy: *Thou hast broken the heads of the dragon; thou hast given him to be meat for the people of the Ethiopians.*[144]

36.   BUT AS SOON AS THIS THY SON IS COME, WHO HATH DEVOURED HIS SUBSTANCE WITH HARLOTS, THOU HAST KILLED FOR HIM THE FATTED CALF. Israel confesses even now that it was the fatted calf that was slain; they know that Christ has come, but they are tormented by envy and are unwilling to be saved unless their brother perishes.

37.   BUT HE SAID TO HIM: SON, THOU ART ALWAYS WITH ME, AND ALL I HAVE IS THINE. He calls him son, although he is unwilling to enter. But how are all God's possessions the property of the Jews? Angels, thrones, dominions, and the other powers—they are not, are they? Therefore, by

"all" we are to understand the law, the prophets, the divine utterances. 2 These He gave him that he might meditate on His law day and night;[145] according to that canon of the Scriptures which we have often explained, "all" is not to be referred to the sum of things but to the majority, as in the passage: *They are all gone aside, they are become unprofitable together;*[146] and in another place: *All who have come before me were thieves and robbers.*[147] And Paul to the Corinthians: *I became,* he says, *all things to all men, that I might save all.*[148] And to the Philippians: *For all seek the things that are their own, not the things that are Jesus Christ's.*[149] Although it must be believed that He denied him nothing, whom He urged to eat the fatted calf.

38. BUT IT IS FIT THAT WE SHOULD MAKE MERRY AND BE GLAD, FOR THIS THY BROTHER WAS DEAD AND IS COME TO LIFE AGAIN; HE WAS LOST AND IS FOUND. We have faith that we too can live through penance who were dead in sin. And here, indeed, the son himself returns; but in the preceding parables—namely, that of the sheep and that of the coin—that which had strayed is brought in, and that which had been lost is found.[150] 2 And the three parables close with a similar ending: *was lost and is found,* that we may understand that under diverse comparisons there is the same indication of the reception of sinners.

39. And these, indeed, are spoken in the person of Gentile and Jew. But let us see how the parable may be understood concerning the saint and the sinner in general. And in other respects there is no doubt that they are applicable to the just man. The following is the point at which a scruple is felt by the reader: why a just man should begrudge a sinner his salvation and should be so filled with anger that he is moved neither by sympathy for his brother nor by his father's entreaties nor by the rejoicing of the whole house.

2 To this we shall reply briefly that all the justice of the world is not justice in comparison with that of God.[151]   For even as Sodom is justified by the sins of Jerusalem,[152] not because she is just but because lesser failings become justice in comparison with greater failings, so too the universal justice of men is not justice compared with God.

3 Therefore Paul, who had said: *Let us, therefore, as many as are perfect, be thus minded,*[153] in another passage makes confession and exclaims: *O the depth of the riches of the wisdom and of the knowledge of God!   How incomprehensible are His judgments and how unsearchable His ways!*[154] And elsewhere: *We know in part, and we prophesy in part;*[155] and: *We see now through a glass in a dark manner;*[156] and to the Romans: *Unhappy man that I am, who shall deliver me from the body of this death?*[157]

4 By all of these passages we are taught that the justice of God alone is perfect: who makes His sun to rise upon the good and the bad, and sends the evening and the morning rain upon the deserving and the undeserving alike,[158] who calls to the marriage men from the streets, the corners, and the highways,[159] and seeks the sheep which—like the repentant son—could not or would not return of itself, and having found it, carries it upon His shoulders.[160]   He had labored for one that had gone far astray.

40.   Moreover, that we may be taught that envy may befall even the saints, and that absolute mercy is left as an attribute of God alone, let us consider the example of the sons of Zebedee, for whom their mother, moved by her love and affection, had asked too much.[161]   The remaining ten disciples were angry.   *And Jesus called them to Him and said: You know that the princes of the Gentiles lord it over them; and they that are the greater exercise power upon them.   It shall not be so among you: but whosoever will be the greater*

among you, let him be your minister; and he that will be first among you shall be your servant. Even as the Son of Man is not come to be ministered unto, but to minister, and to give His life a redemption for many.[162]

2 Let none think it perilous, let none think it blasphemous, that we have said that the sin of envy could creep even upon the apostles, since we believe this even of the angels. For the stars are not pure in His sight, and in His angels He found wickedness.[163] And in the Psalms it is said: *In His sight no living creature shall be justified.*[164]

3 He does not say "no man shall be justified," but "no living creature,"[165] that is, no Evangelist, no apostle, no prophet—I advance to higher orders: no angel, no thrones, no dominations, no principalities and the other powers. It is God alone upon whom sin falls not.[166] All the rest, since they have free will because of the fact that man too was made in the image and likeness of God,[167] may direct their will in one way or the other.

4 But if you are not in accord with this view, at least be influenced by the authority of that parable in which laborers are sent into the vineyard throughout the entire day.[168] And at the first hour Adam is called, and Abel and Seth; in the third, Noe; in the sixth, Abraham; in the ninth, Moses; in the eleventh, the people of the Gentiles, to whom it is said: *Why stand you here all the day idle?* And they reply: *No man hath hired us.*[169] But that the last hour is the advent of our Saviour, John is witness when he says: *Brothers, it is the last hour. For as you have heard that Antichrist cometh, even now there are become many Antichrists; whereby we know that it is the last hour.*[170]

5 If this interpretation displeases you, I follow wherever you lead, yet with the understanding that you admit that those who were called first are the just. When I obtain this

admission, I shall quote: And as just people, *they mur-mured against the master of the house, saying: These who came last and have worked but one hour, hast thou made them equal to us, that have borne the burden of the day and the heat?*[171] They seem, indeed, to say with justice that the pay of him who has sweated from the first hour even until night, and of him who was engaged in the work for but one hour, ought not to be equal. But that justice herself has a taint upon her: why should she envy another's happiness?

6 Finally, the Master too accuses them of having an envious eye, saying: *Or is thy eye evil, because I am good?*[172] Hence, also, God alone is called just by the Apostle,[173] He alone is called immortal, not because the angels are unjust and mortal, but because He Himself is immortal and just compared with whom all justice is found to be iniquity.

41. Moreover, that you may understand—in this same parable which we have now set forth—the injustice of those that were hired, pay attention for a little. He who was hired at the first hour deserves more than he who was sent to the vineyard at the third hour. Again, the workman of the third hour has precedence over the one of the sixth hour. How, therefore, do they all envy the workman of the last hour, and not demand the same justice of themselves? 2 You who were hired at the ninth hour, why do you envy him who was sent into the vineyard at the eleventh hour? Whatever reply you make, however diverse you claim the labor was—so as to deserve a greater reward for a different sort of work—you will deserve the same criticism in the opinion of the man of the sixth hour. And you who were hired at the sixth hour and are envious of the man of the eleventh hour, asking why he obtains, like you, a penny—that is, equal salvation—although there is a differing glory of salvation for your work: the third-hour man can say the same about you, and the first-hour man

again about the third-hour man.   3 But they respectively
accept gladly equal reward for work that is not equal and for
the differing periods of their calling.   They object only in
the case of the last workmen—that is, in the case of the salvation of the Gentiles—and do their Master a wrong, and in
all the parables are found guilty of envy.

42.   I have no doubt that this discourse of our insignifi-
cance seems crude to you.   But I have often argued that a
topic cannot be perfected without being polished by the
proper hand.   Therefore, pardon my smarting eyes—that is,
forgive me for dictating[174]—especially since in ecclesiastical
matters it is not words that are sought but meanings.   That
is, life must be sustained by bread, not by husks.[175]

LETTER 22

To Eustochium[1]

1. *Hearken, O daughter, and see, and incline thy ear, and forget thy people and thy father's house; and the king shall greatly desire thy beauty.*[2] In Psalm 44, God is speaking to the human soul: that, following the example of Abraham,[3] it should go out from its own country and its kindred and forsake the Chaldeans (that is, by interpretation, the demons) and dwell in the land of the living, which elsewhere the prophet sighs for, saying: *I believe to see the good things of the Lord in the land of the living.*[4]

2 But it is not enough for you to go out from your native country, unless you forget your people and your father's house and, despising the flesh, are united in your bridegroom's embraces. *Look not back,* it says, *neither stay thou in all the country about; save thyself in the mountain, lest perchance thou be taken captive.*[5] It is not profitable, after putting one's hand to the plow, to look back,[6] nor to return home from the field, nor after accepting Christ's tunic to descend from the roof to put on any other garb.[7]

3 A great marvel: a father exhorts his daughter: "Do not remember your father." *You are of your father the devil, and the desires of your father you will do.*[8] This is said to the Jews. And elsewhere: *He that committeth sin is of the devil.*[9] In the first place, being born of such a parent we are black; after repentance (having not yet ascended to the pinnacle of virtue) we say: *I am black and beautiful, a daughter of Jerusalem.*[10]

4 I went out from the home of my infancy, I forgot my father, I am reborn in Christ. What do I receive as a reward

for this? The Bible says: *And the king shall greatly desire thy beauty.*[11] This, accordingly, is the great sacrament:[12] *Wherefore a man shall leave father and mother, and shall cleave to his wife, and they shall be two—in one flesh?*[13] Now not, as in that text, in one flesh, but in one spirit.[14]

5 Your bridegroom is not arrogant. He is not proud. He has married an Ethiopian woman.[15] As soon as you desire to hear the wisdom of the true Solomon[16] and come to Him, He will divulge to you all that He knows. And the King will conduct you into His chamber,[17] and when your color has been changed in marvelous fashion that passage will be applicable to you: *Who is this that cometh up, being made white?*[18]

2. I write this to you, my lady Eustochium[19]—I must call you lady, as the bride of my Lord—for this reason, that from the very beginning of my dissertation you may learn that I am not now about to speak the praises of virginity (which you have so excellently demonstrated by adopting it), nor to enumerate the disadvantages of wives: pregnancy, a wailing infant, the torment of a husband's unfaithfulness, household cares, and how death at last cuts off all fancied blessings. For married women have their place: honorable wedlock and an undefiled bed.[20] But I would have you understand that as you go out from Sodom, you must be warned by the fate of Lot's wife.[21] 2 There is no flattery in this book; for the flatterer is a persuasive enemy. There will be no display of rhetorical speech to set you now among the angels and put the world beneath your feet through the beauty of virginity.

3. I do not wish pride to come upon you by reason of your decision, but fear. If you walk laden with gold, you must beware of a robber. This mortal life is a race. Here we struggle, that elsewhere we may be crowned. No one walks without anxiety amid serpents and scorpions. *My*

sword is inebriated, saith the Lord, *in heaven*,[22] and do you think of peace on earth, which brings forth thorns and thistles which the serpent eats?[23]

2 *Our wrestling is not against flesh and blood, but against the principalities and powers of this world and of this darkness, against the spirits of wickedness in the high places.*[24] We are surrounded by the hosts of our foes. All places are full of enemies. The flesh is weak and in a little while will be ashes. 3 It fights alone with many. But when it has been dissolved, and the prince of that world has come and has found nothing in it, then you shall listen, carefree, to the words spoken in prophecy: *Thou shalt not be afraid of the terror of the night, of the arrow that flieth in the day, of the business that walketh about in the dark, of invasion, or of the noonday devil. A thousand shall fall at thy side, and ten thousand at thy right hand; but it shall not come nigh thee.*[25]

4 But if the multitude of your foes throws you into confusion, and you begin to burn in response to the individual enticements of sin, and your mind says to you: *What shall we do?* Eliseus will reply: *Fear not; for there are more with us than with them.* And he will pray, saying: *Lord, open the eyes of thy handmaid, that she may see.*[26] And when your eyes are opened, you will see a chariot of fire, which will carry you to the stars, like Elias.[27] And you shall sing joyfully: *Our soul hath been delivered as a sparrow out of the snare of the fowlers; the snare is broken, and we are delivered.*[28]

4. As long as we are imprisoned within this frail little body, as long as *we have this treasure in earthen vessels*,[29] and the spirit lusteth against the flesh and the flesh against the spirit,[30] there is no sure victory. Our adversary the devil, as a roaring lion, goes about seeking what he may devour.[31] *Thou hast appointed darkness*, says David, *and it is night.*

In it shall all the beasts of the woods go about, the young lions roaring after their prey and seeking their meat from God.[32]

2 The devil seeks not unbelievers, not those that are without[33] and whose flesh the Assyrian king boils in a pot:[34] he makes haste to drag victims from the Church of Christ. The elect, according to Habacuc,[35] are his food. He seeks to pervert Job,[36] and after he has devoured Judas seeks authority to sift the apostles.[37] The Saviour came not to send peace on the earth but the sword.[38]

3 Lucifer, who arose in the morning,[39] is fallen from heaven; and he who was reared in the paradise of pleasure[40] deserved to hear: *Though thou be exalted as an eagle, thence will I bring thee down, saith the Lord.*[41] For he has said in his heart: *I will exalt my throne above the stars of heaven, I will be like the Most High.*[42] That is why God daily says to those who descend by the ladder while Jacob dreams:[43] *I have said: you are gods and all of you the sons of the Most High. But you, like men, shall die, and shall fall like one of the princes.*[44]

4 For the devil fell first, and when God stands in the assemblage of the gods and publicly passes judgment on gods,[45] the Apostle writes to those that cease to be gods: *For when there are among you contentions and envyings, are you not men, and walk according to man?*[46]

5. If the Apostle Paul, a vessel of election[47] and prepared for the gospel of Christ,[48] because of the stings of the flesh and the enticements of the vices, chastises his body and brings it into subjection,[49] lest while preaching to others he himself should be rejected—but in spite of everything he sees another law in his members,[50] contending against the law of his mind and subjugating him to the law of sin; if after nakedness, fasting, hunger, imprisonment, stripes, punishments, he exclaims to himself: *Unhappy man that I am, who shall deliver*

me from the body of this death?[51] do you think you should consider yourself safe?

2 Take care, I pray, lest sometime God may say of you: *The virgin of Israel has fallen; there is none to raise her up.*[52] I speak audaciously: although God can do all things, He cannot raise up a virgin after she has fallen. He has power, indeed, to free her from the penalty, but He has no power to crown one who has been corrupted.[53]

3 Let us fear that prophecy, lest it be fulfilled in us: *and good virgins shall faint.*[54] Note what he says: *good virgins shall faint*—because there are also bad virgins. *Whosoever shall look on a woman to lust after her,* He says, *hath already committed adultery with her in his heart.*[55] Virginity, therefore, may be lost even by thinking. Those are the bad virgins, virgins in the flesh, not in the spirit: foolish virgins who, having no oil, are shut out by the bridegroom.[56]

6. But if those virgins are also virgins, but because of other faults are not saved by bodily virginity, what will become of those who have prostituted the members of Christ and have turned the temple of the Holy Spirit into a brothel?[57] 2 Straightway they shall hear: *Come down, sit on the ground, O virgin daughter of Babylon, sit on the ground: there is no throne for the daughter of the Chaldeans, for thou shalt no more be called delicate and tender. Take a millstone and grind meal, strip off thy covering, make bare thy legs, pass over the rivers. Thy nakedness shall be discovered and thy shame shall be seen.*[58] And this after the bridechamber of God the Son, after the kisses of her cousin and her bridegroom; this is she of whom once prophetic speech proclaimed: *The queen stood on thy right hand, in gilded clothing, surrounded with variety.*[59]

3 She shall be stripped and her hinder parts shall be bared in her own sight.[60] She shall sit by the waters of solitude[61]

and putting down her pitcher shall open her feet to every one that passes by[62] and shall be polluted from head to foot. It would have been better to have submitted to marriage with a man, to have walked on the level, than to fall into the depths of hell while striving to attain the heights. 4 I beseech you, let not the faithful city of Sion become a harlot,[63] lest after receiving the refuge of the Trinity, demons may dance there and sirens and satyrs make their nests there.[64] Let not the band about the bosom be loosed, but as soon as desire tempts the senses and the persuasive glow of pleasure suffuses us with its sweet warmth, let us burst forth into the cry: *The Lord is my helper: I will not fear what the flesh can do to me.*[65]

5 When the inner man has begun to waver a little between vices and virtues, say: *Why art thou sad, O my soul? And why dost thou trouble me? Hope in God, for I will give praise to Him: the salvation of my countenance, and my God.*[66] I would not have you permit such a thought to arise. Let nothing that is of Babylon, nothing of confusion, grow up within you. While the enemy is small, destroy him. Let wickedness be nipped in the bud.

6 Hear the Psalmist who says: *O daughter of Babylon, miserable: blessed shall he be who shall repay thee thy payment; blessed be he that shall take and dash thy little ones against the rock.*[67] Because, therefore, it is impossible for a man's senses to escape being assailed by the well-known inner passion,[68] that man is praised, he is called blessed, who as soon as he begins to cherish such thoughts, stifles his imaginings and dashes them against the rock. *And the rock is Christ.*[69]

7. How often, when I was established in the desert[70] and in that vast solitude which is scorched by the sun's heat and affords a savage habitation for monks, did I think myself amid

the delights of Rome! I would sit alone because I was filled with bitterness.[71] My limbs were roughly clad in sackcloth— an unlovely sight. My neglected skin had taken on the appearance of an Ethiopian's body. Daily I wept, daily I groaned, and whenever insistent slumber overcame my resistance, I bruised my awkward bones upon the bare earth. 2 Of food and drink I say nothing, since even the sick drink only cold water, and to get any cooked food is a luxury. There was I, therefore, who from fear of hell had condemned myself to such a prison, with only scorpions and wild beasts as companions. Yet I was often surrounded by dancing girls. My face was pale from fasting, and my mind was hot with desire in a body cold as ice. Though my flesh, before its tenant, was already as good as dead, the fires of the passions kept boiling within me.

3 And so, destitute of all help, I used to lie at Jesus' feet. I bathed them with my tears, I wiped them with my hair.[72] When my flesh rebelled, I subdued it by weeks of fasting. I do not blush at my hapless state; nay rather, I lament that I am not now what I was then. I remember that I often joined day to night with my lamentation and did not cease beating my breast until peace of mind returned with the Lord's rebuke. I was afraid even of my little cell—as though it were conscious of my thoughts. Angry at myself and tense, I used to go out alone into the desert. 4 Whenever I saw some deep valley, some rugged mountain, some precipitous crags, it was this I made my place of prayer, my place of punishment for the wretched flesh. And—as my Lord Himself is witness—after many tears, after fixing my eyes on the heavens, I sometimes seemed to myself to be surrounded by companies of angels and rejoiced, singing happily: *We run after thee to the odor of thy ointments.*[73]

8. But if those who with emaciated frame are assailed

by their thoughts alone, endure such trials, what must a girl endure who is thrilled by luxuries? Of course, the Apostle has said it: *She is dead while she is living.*[74] Therefore, if there can be any good counsel in me, if credence may be placed in one who has had experience, in the first place I advise you—I entreat you as the bride of Christ—avoid wine like poison. 2 This is the first weapon used by demons against youth. Less effective are the shattering of greed, the inflation of pride, the delight of ambition. We readily rid ourselves of the other vices. This foe is shut up within. Wherever we go, we carry the enemy with us. Wine and youth doubly inflame the fires of pleasure. Why do we add fuel to a poor body that is ablaze? 3 Paul writes to Timothy: *Do not still drink water, but use a little wine for thy stomach's sake and thy frequent infirmities.*[75] Note for what reasons a drink of wine is condoned: scarcely does this pain in the stomach and a chronic ailment merit it. And lest perhaps we should become indulgent because of sickness, he recommends that only a little should be taken, rather upon prescription by a physician than by an apostle—though an apostle too is a spiritual physician—and to avert the danger of Timothy's being unable to go about and preach the gospel because of being overcome by weakness. Besides, he remembered that he had said: *wine, wherein is luxury,*[76] and: *It is good for a man not to drink wine and not to eat flesh.*[77]

4 Noe drank wine and became drunk when the world was still uncivilized,[78] and then for the first time planted the vine. Perhaps he did not know that wine was intoxicating. And that you may understand the mystery of the Scripture at all points—for the word of God is a pearl and can be pierced from side to side—after his drunkenness followed the uncovering of his thighs: lust is close to wantonness. First the belly and then the rest; *for the people ate and drank, and*

they rose up to play.[79]   Lot, the friend of God,[80] after he was saved upon the mountain as the one man out of so many thousands found to be righteous, was made drunk by his daughters.   And although they thought that the race of men had come to an end and did this rather because of a desire for children than out of lust, nevertheless they knew that a righteous man would not act thus unless he was drunk. Finally, he did not know what he had done.   And—although his wrongdoing was not deliberate—the penalty of the fault followed: there were born of these unions the Moabites and the Ammonites, enemies of Israel, who unto the fourteenth generation—and even forever—shall not enter into the church of God.[81]

9.   Elias, when he was fleeing from Jezabel and lay exhausted under an oak, was aroused by an angel who came and said to him: *Arise and eat.*   And he looked, and behold there was at his head a hearth cake and a vessel of water.[82] Could not God indeed have sent him spiced wine and cakes seasoned with oil and meats made tender by pounding?

2 Eliseus invites the sons of the prophets to dinner.   And as he was feeding them with herbs from the fields, he heard them say with one accord as they ate: *Death is in the pot, O man of God.*[83]   He was not angry with the cooks (for he was not accustomed to an elaborate repast), but by casting in meal he sweetened the bitterness[84] by the same spiritual virtue whereby Moses had changed the waters of Mara.[85] 3 Hear, too, with what food he ordered those men to be refreshed who had come to seize him.   After they had been blinded both in sight and in mind, when he had led them into Samaria unawares, he said: *Set bread and water before them; and let them eat and drink and let them be sent back to their master.*[86]

4 Daniel, too, might have had very luxurious courses,

served from the king's table, but it was a reaper's dinner that Habacuc brought him: rustic fare, I suppose.[87] And therefore he was called "a man of desires," because he did not eat the bread of desire nor drink the wine of lustfulness.[88]

10.   Countless are the passages dispersed through Holy Writ which condemn gluttony and approve of simple food. But because it is not now my purpose to discuss fasting, and to list all the references would require a separate treatise and a whole book, let these few examples out of many suffice.

2 Besides, you may learn for yourself from these examples how the first man was cast out of Paradise[89] into this vale of tears[90] for obeying his belly rather than God.   It was with hunger that Satan tempted the Lord Himself in the desert.[91] The Apostle exclaims: *Meat for the belly, and the belly for meats, but God shall destroy both it and them,*[92] and of the wanton he says: *whose God is their belly.*[93]   Actually, each one worships what he loves.   Wherefore we must take anxious care that abstinence may bring back those whom repletion expelled from Paradise.

11.   But if you wish to make reply that you—a girl born of noble family always reared on delicacies, always surrounded by down pillows—cannot abstain from wine and luxurious foods, and that you cannot live more austerely under these regulations, I shall reply: "Live then by your law, since you cannot live by the law of God."   Not because God, the Creator of the universe and its Lord, takes delight in the rumbling of the intestines, the emptiness of our stomach, or the inflammation of our lungs, but because chastity cannot be preserved otherwise.

2 Job was dear to God and by his own testimony was pure and a man of integrity.[94]   Hear his estimate of the devil: *His strength is in his loins, and his power in his navel.*[95]   For the sake of propriety, the male and female organs of genera-

tion are called by other names. 3 Hence the promise that one from the loins of David is to sit upon his throne;[96] and the seventy-five souls that entered Egypt are said to have issued from Jacob's thigh.[97] And after the breadth of his thigh shrunk as he wrestled with the angel, Jacob ceased to beget children.[98]

One who is about to celebrate the Passover is bidden to do so with loins girt up and mortified.[99] And God says to Job: *Gird up thy loins like a man.*[100] John too wears a leather girdle.[101] The apostles are ordered to gird their loins and hold in their hands the lamps of the gospel.[102] 4 To Jerusalem, moreover, when found in the plain of error all sprinkled with blood, Ezechiel says: *Thy navel was not cut.*[103] Accordingly, all the strength of the devil against men is in the loins, all his force against women is in the navel.

12. Do you wish to be reassured that it is as we say? Samson was stronger than a lion and harder than rock. Alone and without armor he put to flight a thousand men. In the embraces of Delilah he became weak.[104] David was chosen as a man after the Lord's heart,[105] and with his holy lips he had often prophesied the coming of Christ, yet after he was ensnared by the naked beauty of Bethsabee while walking on the roof of his house, he added murder to adultery.[106] 2 Wherein take brief note of this fact also, that even in one's own home it is never safe to look. Wherefore David in penitence says to God: *To thee only have I sinned, and have done evil before thee.*[107] For he was a king and feared no one else but God. Solomon, through whom wisdom herself spoke, *who treated* [about trees] *from the cedar of Libanus, unto the hyssop that cometh out through the wall,*[108] went back from the Lord because he was a lover of women.[109] And lest anyone put confidence in blood rela-

tionship, Amnon, her brother, was inflamed by an unlawful passion for Thamar, his sister.[110]

13. It becomes wearisome to tell how many virgins fall daily; what important personages Mother Church loses from her bosom;[111] over how many stars the proud enemy sets his throne; how many rocks the serpent makes hollow and then enters through their openings. You may see many who were widowed before they were wed, shielding a guilty conscience by a lying garb. Did not a swelling womb or the crying of their infant children betray them, they would go about with head erect and on skipping feet.

2 But others drink potions to ensure sterility and are guilty of murdering a human being not yet conceived. Some, when they learn they are with child through sin, practice abortion by the use of drugs. Frequently they die themselves and are brought before the rulers of the lower world guilty of three crimes: suicide, adultery against Christ, and murder of an unborn child.[111a] 3 These are the women who are accustomed to say: *All things are clean to the clean.*[112] The approval of my conscience is enough for me. A pure heart is what God desires. Why should I abstain from foods which God created to be used? And whenever they wish to appear bright and festive, and have drowned themselves in wine, they say—adding sacrilege to drunkenness: "God forbid that I should abstain from the blood of Christ." And whenever they see a woman pale and sad, they call her a poor wretch, a nun, and a Manichean: and with reason, for according to their belief fasting is heresy.

4 There are women who make themselves conspicuous in public by their walk and draw a throng of young men after them by furtive winks. It is they to whom the words of the prophet inevitably apply: *Thou hadst a harlot's face, thou*

wouldst not blush.[113] Let them have but a little purple in their dress and a head loosely bound, so that the hair may fall, tawdry sandals, and over their shoulders a fluttering little cloak,[113a] tight sleeves clinging to their arms, and a loose-kneed manner of walking: this is all such a person's virginity amounts to. Let women of that sort have their admirers and let them exact more pay for their ruin because of their reputation for virginity. With such I rejoice to be unpopular.[114]

14. I am ashamed to speak of so scandalous a thing; it's sad but true. How has this disgrace of "dearly beloved sisters" come into the Church? Whence this other use of the name "wives" for the unwed? Nay, whence this new kind of concubines? I will go even farther: whence these one-man harlots? They are sheltered by the same house, by a single bedroom, often by one bed—and they call us suspicious if we think anything about it.

2 A brother deserts his unmarried sister, a virgin despises her bachelor brother, and (although they pretend to be devoted to the same aim) they seek spiritual solace among strangers—to have carnal intercourse at home. In the Proverbs of Solomon God makes accusation, saying: *Can a man hide fire in his bosom and his garments not burn? Or can he walk upon hot coals and his feet not be burnt?*[115]

15. Let us, therefore, drive off and banish those who wish not to be but to seem virgins. Now all I have to say is directed to you. Since you are the first woman of high rank in the city of Rome who has undertaken to be a nun,[116] you will have to strive the more earnestly not to lose both present and future advantages. You have, to be sure, learned from an example in your own family the sorrows of wedlock and the uncertainties of marriage. For your sister Blesilla, older in years but weaker in strength of will, after taking a husband

became a widow in the seventh month.[117]   2 O unhappy mortal lot, so ignorant of the future! She has lost both the crown of virginity and the joy of marriage, and although she may keep the second degree of chastity, yet what torment do you suppose she endures every moment, seeing daily in her sister what she herself has lost? While it is harder for her to do without the pleasure she has experienced, she receives less credit for continence. Still she may be at peace, she may rejoice: the hundredfold and the sixtyfold harvest come from the same seed of chastity.[118]

16. I would not have you consort with married women. I would not have you visit houses of the distinguished. I would not have you see frequently what you disdained in your desire to be a virgin. If ordinary women pride themselves because their husbands are judges and dignified by some high rank, if an emperor's wife is thronged by self-seeking flatterers, why do you insult your Husband? Why do you, the bride of God, make haste to call on the wife of a mortal man? Attain a holy pride in this relationship.   2 Know that you are better than they. Nor do I desire only that you avoid association with those women who are puffed up by their husbands' honors, whom crowds of eunuchs surround, and in whose garments are woven metallic threads. Avoid those also whom necessity has made widows. Not that they ought to wish for the death of their husbands, but that they should gladly seize an opportunity for chastity. But as it is, they change merely their dress; their former ruling passion is unchanged. A row of eunuchs precedes their spacious sedan chairs. Their red lips and their sleek, plump skin would make you think not that they had lost a husband but that they were seeking one.   3 Their houses are full of guests—full of flatterers. Even the clergy, who should have afforded guidance and merited respect, kiss the

brows of their patronesses. They extend a hand, so that you might suppose they wished to bestow a blessing upon them— did you not know that they are accepting a fee for their visit! Meanwhile the women, when they see that the priests are in need of their help, are puffed up with pride and, because they prefer the liberty of widowhood after having experienced a husband's domination, are called chaste nuns, and after a luxurious repast[119] they dream about apostles!

17.   Let your companions be those whom you may see to be thin from fasting, of pallid countenance, approved years and manner of life, who daily sing in their hearts: *Where is it thou feedest, where is it thou liest in the midday?*[120] who lovingly say: *I desire to be dissolved and to be with Christ.*[121]   Be subject to your parents:[122] imitate your Spouse. Appear in public infrequently. Let the martyrs be sought by you in your own bedroom. Never will the occasion for going out be lacking if you intend always to go out—when it is necessary and when it is not. Take food in moderation and never to repletion. There are very many women who, although they are sober as regards wine, are intoxicated by overindulgence in food. When you arise at night for prayer, let not indigestion but hunger affect your breathing. Read much and learn as much as possible. Let sleep creep upon you with a book in your hand, and let the sacred page catch your head as you nod. Fast daily, and let refreshment fall short of satiety. There is no advantage in carrying an empty stomach for two or three days, if it is correspondingly overwhelmed with food, if the fast is compensated by gorging. The mind when sated grows sluggish, and watered ground puts forth thorns of lust.

3 Whenever you observe your outer man[123] sighing for the flowering of youth; when the charming procession of desires assails you while you are resting on your couch after you have

eaten—snatch up the shield of faith, whereby the fiery darts of the devil are extinguished.[124] *They are all adulterers, their hearts are like an oven.*[125] But do you accompany Christ's footsteps and be intent on His words. Say: *Was not our heart burning within us in the way whilst Jesus opened to us the Scriptures?*[126] And again: *Thy word is exceedingly refined, and thy servant hath loved it.*[127] 4 It is hard for the human soul not to love, and it is necessary that our mind be drawn into some sort of affection. Love of the flesh is overcome by love of the spirit. Desire is quenched by desire. Whatever diminishes in the one grows in the other. Nay rather, always make lamentation: *In my bed by night I sought Him whom my soul loveth.*[128] The Apostle says: *Mortify your members which are upon the earth.*[129] Whence also he said with assurance: *And I live, now not I, but Christ liveth in me.*[130] 5 He that has mortified his members and walked about in His image does not fear to say: *For I am become like a bottle in the frost;*[131] whatever there was in me of the moisture of lust has been cooked out. And: *My knees are weakened through fasting;*[132] and: *I forgot to eat my bread; through the voice of my groaning, my bone hath cleaved to my flesh.*[133]

18. Be the grasshopper of the night. Wash your bed and water your couch every night with your tears.[134] Keep awake and become like a lonely sparrow.[135] Sing with your spirit, sing also with your understanding,[136] the Psalm: *Bless the Lord, O my soul, and never forget all He hath done for thee, who forgiveth all thy iniquities, who healeth all thy diseases and redeemeth thy life from corruption.*[137]

2 Who of us can say from the heart: *For I did eat ashes like bread and mingled my drink with weeping?*[138] Should I not weep, should I not groan, when the serpent invites me again to the forbidden food,[139] when, in having driven me

from the paradise of virginity, he wishes to clothe me in skins[140] such as Elias cast upon the earth as he was returning to paradise?[141] What have I to do with pleasure which is so soon at an end? What have I to do with this sweet and death-dealing song of the sirens? 3 I would not come under the sentence which was passed upon man upon his condemnation: *In sorrow and anxieties shalt thou bring forth children, O woman* (that law does not apply to me), *and thy turning shall be to thy husband.*[142] She who has not Christ for her husband, let her turning be to her husband, and at the last *thou shalt die the death,*[143] that is, the end of marriage. My undertaking is one independent of sex. Let married women have their own status and title. My virginity is dedicated in the person of Mary and of Christ.

19.   Someone may say: "And do you dare disparage marriage, which was blessed by the Lord?" It is not disparaging marriage when virginity is preferred to it. No one compares evil with good. Let married women glory too, since they come second to virgins. *Increase,* He says, *and multiply, and fill the earth.*[144] Let him who is to fill the earth increase and multiply. Your company is in heaven. 2 This command is fulfilled after Paradise, and nakedness, and the fig leaves that betoken the lasciviousness of marriage.[145] Let him marry and be given in marriage who eats his bread in the sweat of his face, for whom the earth brings forth thorns and thistles, whose crops are choked with brambles.[146] My seed produces fruit a hundredfold.[147] *All men take not God's word, but these to whom it is given.*[148] It is necessity that makes another a eunuch, my own choice makes me so. 3 There is a time to embrace and a time to withhold the hands from embracing, *a time to scatter stones and a time to gather.*[149] After sons of Abraham have been

begotten from the hardness of the heathen, sacred stones began to roll upon the earth.[150] And they pass through the storms of this world and are whirled in God's car with the speed of its wheels. Let them sew themselves coats who have lost the raiment that was without seam, woven from the top throughout,[151] those whom the wailing of infants delights —a cry at the very outset of life, lamenting that they have been born. 4 Eve was a virgin in Paradise. After the garments of skins her married life began. Paradise is where you belong. Continue as you were born and say: *Turn, O my soul, into thy rest.*[152] And that you may know that virginity is natural and that marriage came after the offense: it is virgin flesh that is born of wedlock, restoring in the fruit what it had lost in the root. *There shall come forth a rod out of the root of Jesse, and a flower shall rise up out of the root.*[153] 5 That rod is the mother of the Lord—simple, pure—having no origin of life from without clinging to its untouched body and, like God Himself, fruitful in unity. The flower of the rod is Christ, who says: *I am the flower of the field and the lily of the valleys.*[154] In another passage He is foretold to be a stone cut out of a mountain without hands:[155] a prophecy signifying that He would be born a virgin of a virgin. "Hands" is, of course, to be understood of the marital act, as in the verse: *His left hand is under my head, and his right hand shall embrace me.*[156] That this is the intention of the meaning is shown by the fact that the animals which were led into the ark in pairs are unclean: an unequal number of the clean animals was taken;[157] also from the fact that Moses and Josue, the son of Nave, are bidden to walk with bare feet upon the holy ground,[158] and the disciples are despatched to preach the gospel without the weight of shoes and fastenings of leather;[159] that the soldiers who divided the garments of Jesus had no shoes to carry off.[160] For the Lord could not have what He had forbidden His servants.

20. I praise marriage, I praise wedlock, but I do so because they produce virgins for me. I gather roses from thorns, gold from the earth, the pearl from the shell. And tell me, is the plowman to plow all day long? Shall he not rejoice in the fruit of his labor? Marriage is honored the more when the fruit of the union is more loved. Why, mother, begrudge your daughter her virginity? She was nourished by your milk, taken from your body; she grew in your embrace. You kept her safe by your protecting love. Are you angry because she was unwilling to be a soldier's bride, but would be the bride of the King? She has bestowed a great honor upon you: you have become a mother-in-law of God.[161]

2 *Concerning virgins*, says the Apostle, *I have no commandment of the Lord.*[162] And why? Because he too was a virgin—not by compulsion but of his own free will. Nor should we pay any attention to those who pretend that Paul had a wife. When he discusses continence and recommends perpetual chastity, he says: *For I would that all men were even as myself;*[163] and later: *But I say to the unmarried and to the widows: It is good for them if they so continue, even as I.*[164] And in another passage: *Have we not power to carry about wives as well as the rest of the apostles?*[165] 3 Why, therefore, does he not have a commandment of the Lord concerning virginity?[166] Because that has more value which is not taken by force but is voluntary. Because if virginity had been commanded, marriage would seem to have been forbidden. And it would have been very hard to impose what is against nature and to require of mankind the life of

angels, and in a certain manner to condemn the plan of creation.[167]

21. Under the Old Law there was a different conception of happiness. *Blessed is he who has seed in Sion and a family in Jerusalem, and cursed is the barren who did not bear children.*[168] And: *Thy children shall be as olive plants, round about thy table.*[169] And there is a promise of riches in the statement: *There shall not be one that is feeble in thy tribes.*[170] 2 But now the saying is: *Do not think that you are a dry tree; you have a place for sons and daughters, eternal in the heavens.*[171] Now the poor are blessed, and Lazarus is preferred to the rich in his purple.[172] Now he that is weak is the stronger. The world used to be empty and—to say nothing of those who were types—the only blessing was that of children. 3 That is why Abraham, when already an old man, married Cetura,[173] and Jacob was hired with mandrakes,[174] and why Rachel the beautiful (who is a symbol of the Church) complains of the closing of her womb.[175] But as the crop gradually increased, a reaper was sent in. Elias was a virgin, Eliseus was a virgin, many sons of the prophets were virgins. To Jeremias it is said: *Thou shalt not take a wife.*[176] Having been sanctified in the womb, he was forbidden to take a wife as the time of the captivity drew near.

4 The Apostle says the same thing in other words: *I think, therefore, that this is good for the present necessity, that it is good for a man so to be.*[177] What necessity is this that takes away the joys of marriage? It is the shortening of the time: *It remaineth that they also who have wives be as if they had none.*[178] 5 Nabuchodonosor is near: *The lion is come up out of his den.*[179] What end is to be served by my marrying a wife who will become the slave of a most haughty king? Or children, of whom the prophet says, bewailing them: *The*

tongue of the sucking child hath stuck to the roof of his mouth for thirst; the little ones have asked for bread, and there was none to break it unto them.[180] 6 So then, as we have said, this virtue of continence used to be found solely in men, and Eve continuously bore children in sorrow.[181] 7 But after a virgin conceived in the womb and bore for us a Son upon whose shoulders is the government, God the mighty, the Father of the world to come,[182] the curse has been abrogated. Death came through Eve, life through Mary. And therefore a richer gift of virginity has flowed upon women, because it began with a woman. Immediately after the Son of God set foot on earth, He established a new household for Himself, so that He who was adored by angels in heaven might have angels also on earth.

8 Then chaste Judith severed the head of Holofernes;[183] then Aman, which is, by interpretation, "Iniquity," was burned in his own fire;[184] then James and John, forsaking their father, the net, and the ship, followed the Saviour.[185] They relinquished the ties of blood, the responsibilities of this world, and the care of their home. Then for the first time was heard: *Whosoever will come after me, let him deny himself, and take up his cross, and follow me.*[186]

9 For no soldier goes to battle with a wife. The disciple who desires to go and bury his father is not permitted to do so.[187] *The foxes have holes, and the birds of the air nests, but the Son of Man hath not where to lay his head*[188]—that you might not be sorrowful when in straitened circumstances. *He that is without a wife is solicitous for the things that belong to the Lord, how he may please God. But he that is with a wife is solicitous for the things of this world, how he may please his wife. There is a difference between a married woman and a virgin. The unmarried woman thinketh on the things of the Lord, that she may be holy both*

in body and in spirit. For she that is married thinketh on the things of the world, how she may please her husband.[189]

22. How many annoyances marriage involves, and by how many anxieties it is entangled, I believe I have briefly set forth in the book I wrote against Helvidius on the perpetual virginity of Mary.[190] To repeat the same arguments now would take too long, and anyone who pleases may drink from that little spring.[191] 2 But lest I should appear to have omitted it entirely, I will say now that the Apostle bids us pray without ceasing,[192] and that one who lives up to his obligations in the married state cannot so pray; we either pray continually and are virgins, or we cease to pray in order to be obedient to our marriage vows. *And if a virgin marry, he says, she does not sin; nevertheless, such shall have tribulation of the flesh.*[193]

3 In the beginning of that little book I said by way of preface that I would say little or nothing of the inconveniences of marriage, and now I repeat that announcement. But if you want to know from how many vexations a virgin is free, and by how many a wife is bound, read Tertullian's work *To a Philosopher Friend*[194] and his other treatises on virginity, and the excellent volume of the blessed Cyprian, and the writings of Pope Damasus on this subject[195] in verse and in prose, and the little works of our own Ambrose which he recently wrote for his sister.[196] In these he has expressed himself with such eloquence that he has sought out, arranged, and given expression to all that pertains to the praise of virgins.

23. I'm starting on a new path. I'm not extolling virginity but preserving it.[197] Nor is it enough to know what is good unless what has been chosen is zealously guarded. The former is a matter of judgment, the latter of effort. The former we have in common with many, the latter with few.

He that shall persevere unto the end, He says, *he shall be saved.*[198] And: *Many are called, but few chosen.*[199]

2 Therefore, I adjure you before God and Christ Jesus and His chosen angels not lightly to expose to the public the vessels of the temple, which priests alone are permitted to behold. Let no profane person look within the shrine of God. Ozias, who touched the ark—which was forbidden— was smitten by sudden death.[200] For no gold or silver vessel has ever been so dear to God as the temple of a virgin's body.

3 The semblance preceded, now the reality is at hand.[201] You indeed speak with simplicity and in your kindness do not belittle strangers, but unchaste eyes see differently. They know nothing of beauty of soul but consider only the beauty of bodies. Ezechias showed God's treasure to the Assyrians, but the Assyrians beheld in it merely something to covet.[202] Consequently Judea was torn by frequent wars, and first of all the vessels of the Lord were seized and carried off.[203] Baltasar used them as drinking cups at the feast and amid throngs of concubines,[204] because it is the culmination of vice to pollute what is noble.

24. Incline not your ear to evil sayings.[205] Often men make some lewd remark to a virgin to test the mind's steadfastness. If you show pleasure at what is said, if you are complacent at their jokes, they approve of all you say and deny whatever you deny. They call you "a good sport" as well as a good woman, and one in whom there is no guile. "Look," they say, "a true handmaiden of Christ; she isn't like that rough, countrified fright who probably couldn't find a husband for that reason."

2 We are led astray by a natural tendency to evil.[205a] We are glad to look with favor on our flatterers, and although we say in reply that we are not worthy and a blush suffuses our faces, still the soul within us rejoices to be praised. The bride

of Christ is, like the ark of the covenant, overlaid with gold within and without,[206] a custodian of the law of the Lord. As there was nothing in the ark but the tablets of the covenant, so let there be in you no thought of what is outside. On this place of propitiation the Lord wishes to sit as He does above the cherubim.[207]

3 He sends his disciples to loose you from secular cares as they loosed the ass's colt,[208] that leaving the bricks and straw of Egypt[209] you may follow Moses in the wilderness and enter the land of promise.[210] Let there be none to prevent you— mother, sister, kinswoman, brother. The Lord has need of you. But if they wish to hinder you, let them fear the plagues that befell Pharaoh who, because he was unwilling to let the people of God go to worship Him, suffered as the Scriptures relate.

4 When Jesus entered the Temple, He cast out everything that did not belong to the Temple.[211] For God is jealous[212] and does not wish the Father's house to be made a den of thieves.[213] Besides, where money is counted, where there are cages of doves[214] and simplicity is slain, where anxiety about earthly affairs seethes in a virgin's breast, straightway the veil of the temple is rent;[215] the Bridegroom arises in anger and says: *Your house shall be left to you desolate.*[216] 5 Read the Gospel and see how Mary, seated at the Lord's feet, is preferred to busy Martha—notwithstanding the fact that Martha, with eager devotion to hospitality, was preparing a meal for the Lord and His disciples. *Martha,* He said, *Martha, thou art careful, and art troubled about many things. But few are necessary, or one. Mary hath chosen the good part, which shall not be taken away from her.*[217] Be thou also a Mary. Prefer instruction to food. 6 Let your sisters bustle about and seek means of entertaining Christ. Do you, who have once for all cast away this world's burden, sit at the

Lord's feet and say: "I have found Him whom my soul was seeking; I shall hold Him, and I will not let Him go."[218]   And may He reply: *One is my dove, my perfect one, she is the only one of her mother, the chosen of her that bore her.*[219] The reference is to the heavenly Jerusalem.[220]

25.   Let the secret retreat of your bedchamber ever guard you.   Ever let the Bridegroom hold converse with you within. When you pray, you are speaking with your Spouse.   When you read, He is talking to you, and when sleep comes upon you, He will come behind the wall and He "will put His hand through the opening and will touch your body."[221]   You will arise, trembling, and will say: *I languish with love.*[222]   And again you will hear His reply: *My sister, my spouse, is a garden enclosed; a garden enclosed, a fountain sealed up.*[223] 2 Go not out from home, nor wish to behold the daughters of a strange country, although you have the patriarchs as brothers and rejoice in Israel as your father.   Dina went out and was ravished.[224]   I would not have you seek a bridegroom in the highways, I would not have you go about the corners of the city.   You may say: *I will rise and go about the city; in the streets and the broad ways I will seek Him whom my soul loveth.*[225]   And you may ask: *Have you seen Him whom my soul loveth?*[226]   No one will deign to answer you.   3 Your Spouse cannot be found in the broad ways.   *Narrow and strait is the way that leadeth to life.*[227]   And then follows: *I sought Him and found Him not; I called, and He did not answer me.*[228]   Would that failure to find Him were all!   You will be wounded, you will be stripped, and you will say, lamenting: *The keepers that go about the city found me, struck me, wounded me; they took away my veil from me.*[229] 4 But if this is what she suffers for going out, she who said: *I sleep, and my heart watcheth,*[230] and: *A bundle of myrrh is my cousin to me, he shall abide between my breasts,*[231] what shall

become of us who are as yet young girls, if we remain outside when the bride goes in with her Spouse?²³² 5 Jesus is jealous. He does not wish your face to be seen by others. You may make excuses and plead: "I have drawn my veil, I have covered my face, I have sought thee, I have said: *Tell me, O thou whom my soul loveth, where thou feedest, where thou liest in the midday, lest I become as one that is veiled beside the flocks of thy companions.*"²³³ He will be angry, He will burst forth: *If thou knowest not thyself, O fair one among women, go forth and follow after the footsteps of the flocks, and feed thy kids among the tents of the shepherds.*²³⁴ 6 "You may be fair," He says, "and among all women yours may be the face beloved by the Bridegroom: unless you know yourself and keep your heart with all watchfulness,²³⁵ unless you avoid the eyes of young men, you shall depart from my bridal chamber and shall feed the goats which shall be placed on the left hand."²³⁶

26. Therefore, my Eustochium, daughter, lady, fellow servant, sister—for one name suits your age, another your rank, another our religion, another my affection—hear Isaias, who says: *My people, enter into thy chambers, shut thy door upon thee, hide thyself for a moment, until the wrath of the Lord pass away.*²³⁷ Let the foolish virgins wander abroad.²³⁸ Remain thou within with the Bridegroom. For, if you shut the door and, in compliance with the precept of the Gospel, pray to your Father in secret,²³⁹ He will come and knock and will say: *Behold I stand at the gate and knock. If any man open to me, I will come in and will sup with him, and he with me.*²⁴⁰ And at once you will eagerly reply: *It is the voice of my beloved knocking: Open to me, my sister, my nearest, my dove, my undefiled.*²⁴¹ There is no reason why you should say: *I have put off my garment, how shall I put it on? I have washed my feet, how shall I defile them?*²⁴² 3

Arise straightway and open, lest while you linger He may pass by, and afterwards you lament, saying: *I opened to my cousin, but my cousin was gone.*[243]   For why is it needful that the door of your heart be closed to the Bridegroom?   Let it be open to Christ and closed to the devil, according to the saying: *If the spirit of him that hath power ascend upon thee, leave not thy place.*[244]   Daniel in his upper chamber kept his windows open towards Jerusalem, for he could not remain below.[245]   Do thou also keep thy windows open, but whence thou mayest see the city of God.   Do not open those windows of which it is said: *Death came in through your windows.*[246]

27.   This also you must avoid with great care, not to be captivated by an eager longing for vain glory.   Jesus said: *How can you believe, who receive glory from men?*[247]   See how great an evil that is which prevents its victim from believing.   2 But let us say: *Thou art my glory;*[248] and: *He that glorieth, let him glory in the Lord;*[249] and: *If I yet pleased men, I should not be the servant of Christ;*[250] and: *God forbid that I should glory, save in the cross of my Lord Jesus Christ, by whom the world is crucified to me, and I to the world;*[251] and the following: *In thee we glory all the day long;*[252] and: *In the Lord shall my soul be praised.*[253]   3 When you are giving alms, let God alone see.[254]   When you fast, let your countenance be joyful.[255]   Let your attire be neither rather elegant nor unbecoming, nor conspicuous because of any peculiarity, lest the crowd of those that pass by stand still when they meet you and point their fingers at you.[256]   Your brother is dead;[257] your sister's dear body must be accorded due burial rites: take care that you do not die yourself while attending such funerals too often.   4 Do not try to seem too religious, or more humble than is necessary.   Don't seek the fame of avoiding fame.   Many who avoid having witnesses of their poverty, their tenderness of heart, their fasting, desire

to win approval for the fact that they despise approval. Oddly enough, praise is attracted by being avoided. From all other disturbances by which a person's mind rejoices, grows sick, hopes, or fears, I find many free; but there are few who are without this fault [i.e., of desiring praise]. That man is the best who is disfigured by but few faults—like slight blemishes on a beautiful body.[258] 5 Of course, I do not warn you not to glory in your wealth, or boast of the nobility of your family, or exalt yourself above other people.[259] I know your humility. I know that you can say with sincerity: *Lord, my heart is not exalted, nor are my eyes lofty.*[260] I know that with you and with your mother that pride whereby the devil fell has absolutely no place.[261] Therefore I have refrained from writing about this. For it is very foolish to teach that which your pupil already knows. 6 But let not this very fact —that you have despised the boastfulness of the world— beget boastfulness in you. Let not the thought silently invade your mind that because you have ceased to please in garments of golden threads, you may attempt to win approval in rags. When you come into a gathering of brothers or sisters, don't sit down on a lowly footstool and pretend that you are unworthy. Don't speak in a deliberately whining voice, as though exhausted by fasting, or lean on someone's shoulders, imitating the walk of a person failing in health. 7 Of course, there are women who disfigure their faces that they may appear unto men to fast.[262] As soon as they catch sight of anyone, they start groaning, let their eyelids droop, and cover up their faces—though they manage to leave an eye free to watch the effect. They wear a black dress and a girdle of sackcloth; their hands and feet are soiled. The stomach alone—because it cannot be seen—is busily digesting food.[263] Of them the Psalm is sung daily: *God hath scattered the bones of them that please themselves.*[264] 8 Other women change their garb to male attire, cut their hair short, and blush to be seen as they were born—women; they impudently lift up faces that appear those of eunuchs. Still others dress in garments of Cilician goats' hair and fashion baby bonnets, that they may return to their infancy and imitate owls and nighthawks.

28.   But lest I appear to be speaking only of women, avoid men, too, whom you see with braids: their hair, contrary to the Apostle's admonition, is worn long like a woman's,[265] with beards like goats, a black cloak, and bare feet to show contempt for the cold. All these are the devil's tricks. Antimus some time ago, and more recently Sophronius, were men like that.[266] Rome groaned over them. 2 After they have made their way into the homes of the nobility and have deceived *silly women laden with sins, ever learning and never attaining to the knowledge of the truth,*[267] they pretend to be plunged in sorrow and protract long periods of fasting by means of furtive snacks by night. I'm ashamed to tell you the rest of the story, lest I seem to be writing an invective rather than giving admonition. 3 There are others (I am speaking of men of my own order[268]) who are ambitious of obtaining the priesthood and the diaconate, that they may be able to visit women more freely. All they care about is dress: if they are well perfumed, if their shoes are not baggy because of a loose fold of leather. Their locks show traces of the curling iron, their fingers gleam with rings, and they take little mincing steps so that the wet streets may not bespatter their feet. When you see such men, look upon them as bridegrooms rather than clergymen. 4 Some have devoted a lifetime of effort to the task of learning the names, the households, and the characters of married women. I shall describe briefly and concisely one of them, who is the leader in this art, that knowing the master you may the more

easily recognize the pupils. He arises in haste with the sun.
The order of his calls is arranged for him. He seeks short
cuts. The old gentleman arrives unseasonably and practically forces his way into the bedchambers of his sleeping
parishioners. 5 If he catches sight of a cushion, an attractive
piece of cloth, or some piece of household bric-a-brac, he
praises it, marvels at it, strokes it, and laments that he is
without things like that. He doesn't so much succeed in
having it presented to him: he extorts it from the owner. All
the ladies fear to offend the town gossip. Chastity doesn't
appeal to him, nor does fasting. What he likes is a meal hot
from the kitchen—a fattened bird, the kind usually called a
chirper.[269] 6 His speech is barbarous and impudent, as he is
always provided with abusive epithets. Wherever you turn,
he is the first person you meet. Whatever news is noised
abroad, he is either the author or the exaggerator of the tale.
He changes horses every hour; and they are so sleek and so
spirited that you would suppose him to be a brother of the
King of Thrace.

29. Our crafty foe fights us with various wiles. *The
serpent was more subtle than any of the beasts which the
Lord God made on the earth.*[270] Whence also the Apostle
says: *We are not ignorant of his devices.*[271] Neither the
affectation of shabbiness nor exquisite neatness of attire is
suitable for Christians. 2 If you are ignorant about something, or in doubt about a point of Scripture, inquire of a
man whose manner of living is commendable, whose years
give him the right to speak, and whose reputation is no
reproach to him; a man who can say: *For I have espoused you
to one husband, that I may present you as a chaste virgin to
Christ.*[272] If there is no one who can explain it, it is better to
be serenely ignorant than to learn with some attendant risks.
3 Remember that *thou art going in the midst of snares;*[273] and

many tried virgins have lost their grip on the undoubted crown of chastity at the very threshold of death. If any of your maidservants have joined you in your resolve, do not exalt yourself against them, do not be puffed up as their mistress.[274] You have begun to have one Bridegroom. You sing psalms to Christ together. You receive His body together. Why sit at a separate table? Let other women be challenged by your conduct. Let the honor you pay to virgins be an invitation to others.

4 But if you perceive that some girl is weak in faith, sustain her, console her, caress her, and make her chastity your gain. But if a girl is merely pretending in order to avoid servitude, read aloud to her the saying of the Apostle: *It is better to marry than to be burnt.*[275] Cast from you like the plague those idle and inquisitive virgins and widows who go about to married women's houses, who outdo the parasites in plays by their unblushing impudence. *Evil communications corrupt good manners.*[276] 5 They care for nothing but their bellies and the adjacent members. Such persons are accustomed to exhort you, saying: "Dear little creature, make use of your charms, and live while you're alive," and: "You're not saving anything for your children, are you?" Those that are addicted to wine and wantonness suggest all manner of evil and weaken even resolute souls to pleasurable practices. And *when they have grown wanton in Christ, they will marry, having damnation, because they have made void their first faith.*[277]

6 Do not be too eager to seem to yourself eloquent, or improvise humorous themes in lyric verse. Do not fastidiously imitate the taste of those married women who, now with lips together, now with loose lips, employ a lisping tongue to mutilate their speech, thinking everything natural countrified. Such delight do they take in adultery, even with the

tongue. For *what fellowship hath light with darkness?
And what concord hath Christ with Belial?*[278] 7 What has
Horace to do with the Psalter, Vergil with the Gospels, Cicero
with Paul? Is not a brother caused to stumble if he sees you
sitting at table in the temple of an idol?[279] And although *all
things are clean to the clean,*[280] and *nothing is to be rejected
that is received with thanksgiving,*[281] nevertheless we ought
not at the same time drink Christ's chalice and the chalice of
demons.[282] I'll tell you the story of my own unhappy experience.[283]

30. It was many years ago when, for the sake of the
kingdom of heaven, I had cut myself off from my home, my
parents, my sister, my kinsmen, and—what was even more
difficult—from an accustomed habit of good living.[284] I was
going to Jerusalem to be a soldier of Christ. But I could not
do without the library which I had collected for myself at
Rome by great care and effort. And so, poor wretch that I
was, I used to fast and then read Cicero. 2 After frequent
night vigils, after shedding tears which the remembrance of
past sins brought forth from my inmost heart, I would take in
my hands a volume of Plautus. When I came to myself and
began to read a prophet again, I rebelled at the uncouth style
and—because with my blinded eyes I could not look upon the
light—I thought this the fault not of my eyes but of the sun.

3 While the old serpent was thus having sport with me, in
about Mid-Lent a fever attacked my enfeebled body and
spread to my very vitals, what I say is almost beyond belief,
but without cessation it so wrought havoc upon my wretched
limbs that my flesh could scarcely cling to my bones. Meanwhile preparations for my funeral were being made. My
entire body was already cold. The vital warmth of life still
throbbed feebly only in my poor breast. Suddenly I was
caught up in the spirit and dragged before the tribunal of the

Judge. Here there was so much light and such a glare from the brightness of those standing around that I cast myself on the ground and dared not look up. 4 Upon being asked my status, I replied that I was a Christian. And He who sat upon the judgment seat said: "Thou liest. Thou art a Ciceronian, not a Christian. *Where thy treasure is, there is thy heart also.*"[285] I was struck dumb on the spot. Amid the blows—for He had ordered me to be beaten—I was tormented the more by the flame of conscience. I repeated to myself the verse: *And who shall confess thee in hell?*[286] However, I began to cry aloud and to say with lamentation: "Have mercy on me, Lord, have mercy upon me."[287] The petition re-echoed amid the lashes. 5 Finally, casting themselves before the knees of Him who presided, the bystanders besought Him to have mercy on the young man, granting me opportunity to repent of my error and then to exact the penalty if I ever again read books of pagan literature. Being caught in such an extremity, I would have been willing to make even greater promises. I began to take an oath, swearing by His name, saying: "O Lord, if ever I possess or read secular writings, I have denied thee." After I had uttered the words of this oath, I was discharged and returned to the world above. To the surprise of all, I opened my eyes, which were suffused with such showers of tears that my grief produced belief in the incredulous. That had not been mere sleep or meaningless dreams, by which we are often deceived.[288] As witness I have the tribunal before which I lay, as witness the judgment of which I was afraid. May it never be my fate to undergo such questioning! My shoulders were black and blue, and I felt the blows after I awoke from sleep. After that I read God's word with greater zeal than I had previously read the writings of mortals.

31. You must also avoid the vice of avarice. I don't refer

to the appropriation of the goods of others, for the laws of the state punish that. But you must not keep your own property, which is now alien to you. *If you have not been faithful,* He says, *in that which is another's, who will give you that which is your own?*[289] Alien to us are weights of gold and silver. Our own is a spiritual possession, whereof it is said elsewhere: *The ransom of a man's life are his riches.*[290] 2 *No man can serve two masters. For either he will hate the one and love the other, or he will sustain the one and despise the other. You cannot serve God and mammon,*[291] that is, riches. For in the heathen tongue of the Syrians "mammon" means riches.[292] The thorns that choke our faith are the taking of thought for our life. The root of greed is care for the things of this world.

3 But (you will say) I am a delicately nurtured girl, one who cannot work with my hands. If I live to old age, if I begin to be sick, who will take pity on me? Hear Jesus, speaking to the apostles: *Be not solicitous for your life, what you shall eat, nor for your body, what you shall put on. Is not the life more than the meat, and the body more than the raiment? Behold the birds of the air, for they neither sow nor do they reap, nor gather into barns: and your heavenly Father feedeth them.*[293] 4 If clothing is lacking, consider the lilies.[294] If you are hungry, hear the blessedness of the poor and the hungry.[295] If some pain afflicts you, read: *For which cause I please myself in my infirmities,*[296] and: *There was given me a sting of my flesh, an angel of Satan, to buffet me,*[297] lest I should be exalted.

5 Rejoice in all the judgments of God. For *the daughters of Juda rejoiced because of thy judgments, O Lord.*[298] Let these words be ever upon your lips: *Naked came I out of my mother's womb, and naked shall I return,*[299] and: *We brought nothing into this world, and we can carry nothing out.*[300]

32. But as it is, you may see many women cramming chests with garments, changing their clothing daily, and yet unable to get ahead of the moths.[301] A more religious woman wears out a single dress and trails rags behind her, but has boxes full of clothes. Parchment is stained with purple dye, gold is melted to form letters, books are studded with gems, and Christ dies in nakedness before their doors.[302] When they extend alms they sound a trumpet.[303] When they invite to a love feast, they hire a crier.

2 Recently I saw the most prominent lady in Rome[304] (I do not mention her name, lest you think I am writing satire) in St. Peter's Basilica, attended by her eunuchs. She was dispensing charity to the beggars, giving them a penny apiece. Meanwhile—as might easily have been expected—a certain old woman conspicuous for her years and her rags ran to the head of the line to get another penny. When she had reached the lady in due course, she received instead of the coin a blow with the fist. She was guilty of so great an offense that her blood was shed. 3 *The desire of money is the root of all evils,*[305] and therefore it is called by the Apostle *a serving of idols.*[306] *Seek first the kingdom of God, and all these things shall be added unto you.*[307] The Lord will not destroy a righteous soul with hunger. *I have been young and am now old; and I have not seen the just forsaken nor his seed begging bread.*[308] Elias was fed by ministering ravens;[309] the widow of Sarephta herself and her sons, expecting to die that night, went hungry to feed the prophet, and her canister being miraculously filled, she fed him who had come to be fed.[310]

4 The Apostle Peter said: *Silver and gold I have none; but that which I have I give thee: In the name of the Lord Jesus Christ, arise and walk.*[311] But in our day many are saying by their actions, though without uttering a word: "Faith and

sympathy I have none; and what I do have—gold and silver—
I do not give you. Accordingly, having food and clothing we
are satisfied."[312]   5 Hear what Jacob asks for in his prayer:
*If God shall be with me, and shall keep me in the way by
which I walk, and shall give me bread to eat and raiment to
put on.*[313]   He asked only for the necessities of life, and
twenty years later he returned to the land of Chanaan a rich
lord and a richer father.   Countless instances are available
from Scripture to teach that love of money is to be avoided.

33.   But I am now referring incidentally to a subject
which, with Christ's permission, is being reserved for a separate
treatise.   I shall tell what happened at Nitria not many
years ago.[314]   A certain one of the brethren, who was stingy
rather than avaricious, not remembering that the Lord was
sold for thirty pieces of silver,[315] left behind him at his death
one hundred gold coins, which he had earned by weaving
linen.   The monks (for about five thousand of them dwell in
that neighborhood in separate cells) took counsel together
what was to be done with it.   2 Some said that they should be
distributed to the poor; others that they should be given to the
Church; some advised that it be sent back to his parents.   But
Macarius and Pambos and Isidore,[316] and the rest of those
whom they call fathers—the Holy Spirit speaking with them
—decided that the money should be buried with its owner,
saying: *Thy money perish with thee.*[317]   And let no one suppose
that this was a cruel act.   So great fear has come upon
all throughout Egypt that to leave one gold piece behind is
an offense.

34.   And because I have mentioned the monks and know
you would like to hear about holy things, give ear a little.   In
Egypt there are three classes of monks.   There are the cenobites,
whom they call in their foreign tongue *sauhes;* we
may describe them as those who live in a community.[318]   The

anchorites, who live alone in the desert, are called by this name because they have withdrawn from society. The third class is that which they call *remnuoth*, a very inferior and despised type, the only ones or the principal kind found in our province.[319] These dwell together by twos or threes, not many more, and live according to their own will and independently. They contribute to a common fund part of their earnings, that they may have a general store of food. But they live for the most part in cities and fortified towns, and whatever they sell is very expensive: presumably their craftsmanship, not their life, is sacred. There are often quarrels among them, because, being self-sustaining, they do not submit to being dependent upon anyone. 3 Actually they are accustomed to compete with each other in fasting. They turn what should be done in secret into triumphant rivalry. Among them everything is done for effect. They wear loose sleeves, flapping boots, clumsy clothing. They sigh a great deal, pay visits to virgins, belittle the clergy, and, whenever a feast day comes round, eat themselves sick.

35. So, ridding ourselves of these like the plague, let us come to those that live in common; that is, those whom we have said are called cenobites. The first rule of their association is to obey their superiors and do whatever they command. They are subdivided into tens and hundreds, so that the tenth man is in charge of nine men, and in turn the one hundredth man has ten officers under him. They live separately, but in adjacent cells. 2 Until the ninth hour there is a kind of cessation of intercourse: no one goes to visit anyone else except those whom we have mentioned—the deans. This is in order that anyone who is troubled in mind may be consoled by their conversation. After the ninth hour they meet together, psalms are sung, and the Scriptures are customarily read. When prayers are finished and all are seated, one

whom they call father stands up in their midst and begins to
expound. While he speaks, there is so great silence that no
one dares look at another, no one dares cough. Approval of
the speaker is expressed by the weeping of his hearers. 3
Tears roll silently down their cheeks, and their sorrow is
manifested without even a sob. But when he begins to proclaim Christ's kingdom, their future blessedness, and the
glory to come, you may see all sighing gently, lifting their
eyes to heaven, and saying to themselves: *Who will give me
wings like a dove, and I will fly and be at rest?*[320]

4 After this the congregation is dispersed and every group
of ten goes with its father to the tables, which they serve in
turn for a week at a time. There is no confusion while they
dine; no one speaks while eating. They live on bread, beans,
and vegetables seasoned with salt and oil. Only the old men
receive wine. They often have their meal in company with
the children, so that the age of the one group may be cheered
and the youth of the other not weakened. Thereafter they
arise together and, after singing a hymn, return to their
quarters. There each converses with his companions until
evening, saying: "Have you observed such and such persons?
How full of grace! What powers of silence! How modest
in bearing!" 5 If they see a man who is unwell, they comfort
him. If fervent in love for God, they commend his zeal.
And because each man keeps vigil in his own bedroom, after
the prayers they go around to the individual cells and, placing
an ear to the door, they carefully investigate what each is
doing. If they catch one who is slothful, they do not scold
him but, keeping their knowledge of it secret, visit him
oftener: by first beginning to pray themselves, they challenge
rather than compel him to do so.

6 The work of the day is mapped out. Whatever is presented to a dean is brought to the overseer, and he, with great

trepidation, renders a monthly account to the father of them all. Even the food is tasted by him when it has been prepared, and because no one is allowed to say: "I have no tunic, no cloak, no mattress woven of rushes," he so directs everything that no one need ask for anything and no one need want. 7 But if anyone falls ill, he is moved to a larger room and is nursed by the old men with such care that he misses neither city luxuries nor a mother's affection. On Sunday they devote themselves solely to prayer and readings—though they do so every day when their tasks are finished. 8 Daily they memorize some part of the Bible. Fasting is regular throughout the entire year except for Lent. Then only are they permitted to live more strictly. At Pentecost, midday meals replace dinners at night. Thus ecclesiastical tradition is satisfied and they do not overload the stomach by two heavy meals. That the Essenes lived thus we learn from Philo,[321] who imitated Plato's dialogues, and from Josephus, the Greek Livy, in his second book dealing with the captivity of the Jews.[322]

36. But as I am now writing about virgins, what I have said about monks is almost superfluous. I will go on to speak of the third class, whom they call anchorites. They go out from the common dwellings and take nothing to the desert except bread and salt. The founder of this manner of life was Paul. The man who made it illustrious was Antony.[322a] But to revert to earlier times, John the Baptist was the first. 2 Jeremias the prophet also has described such a man, saying: *It is good for a man when he hath borne the yoke from his youth. He shall sit solitary and hold his peace, because he hath taken it up upon himself. He shall give his cheek to him that smiteth him, he shall be filled with reproaches. For the Lord will not cast him off forever.*[323] The labor of these

anchorites and their life, in the flesh but not of the flesh, I
shall describe to you at another time, if you wish.

3 Now let me return to my subject. For in speaking of the
love of money, I had come to the monks.[324] With their example before you, you will despise, I shall not say gold and
silver and other riches, but even the earth itself and the sky.
United with Christ, you will sing: *The Lord is my portion.*[325]

37. After this, although the Apostle may bid us pray at
all times,[326] and for the saints even sleep may be a prayer,
nevertheless we ought to have appointed hours for praying, so
that if by some chance we shall be detained by work, the time
itself may remind us of our duty. No one is ignorant that
they are the third, the sixth, and the ninth hour, at dawn also,
and in the evening. Take no food until after prayer, and do
not leave the table without giving thanks to the Creator. 2
You must arise two or three times at night and review those
passages of Scripture which we know by heart. Let prayer
fortify us when we leave our lodgings. As we return from
the streets, prayer should be offered before we sit down. Nor
should our wretched body have rest before the soul is fed. At
every act, at every step, the hand should make the sign of the
cross. Belittle no one, and lay not a scandal against thy
mother's son.[327] 3 *Who art thou that judgest another man's
servant? To his own Lord he standeth or falleth. And he
shall stand, for God is able to make him stand.*[328] If you
have been fasting for a couple of days, don't think yourself
better than one who is not fasting. You fast and become
angry; he eats and is perhaps in good humor. You rid yourself of vexation of spirit and desire for food by quarreling; he
eats in moderation and thanks God. 4 Therefore Isaias
proclaims to us daily: *I have not chosen such a fast;*[329] and
again: *For in the days of your fasts your own will is found,*

*and you torment all who are under your authority. You fast
for debates and strife, and strike the lowly with the fist, so
how fast ye unto me?*[330] What sort of a fast can that be
whose wrath, I will not say the sun goes down upon,[331] but
even the full moon finds unchanged? Take thought for
yourself and do not rejoice in another's fall but in your
achievement.

38. And do not take as your models those women who
make provision for the flesh[332] and keep reckoning up the
income from their property and the daily household expenses.
For the eleven apostles were not broken by the betrayal of
Judas; and though Phigellus and Alexander made shipwreck,[333] the rest did not cease in the race of faith. Nor
should you say: "This young man and that are enjoying their
possessions; she is honored by all; her brothers and sisters
flock to her. Has she ceased to be a virgin on that account?"
2 In the first place, it is doubtful whether such a person is a
virgin. *For God shall not see as man seeth. For man looketh
on the countenance, God beholdeth the heart.*[334] Then, even
if she is a virgin, I know not whether she is a virgin in spirit.
Now the Apostle defines a virgin thus: *that she may be holy
both in body and in spirit.*[335] Finally, let her keep her own
glory. Let her surpass Paul's opinion: let her enjoy her
delights and live. 3 Let us follow better examples. Hold up
before you the blessed Mary, who was of so great purity that
she was counted worthy to be the mother of the Lord. When
the Angel Gabriel had descended to her in the form of a man,
saying: *Hail, full of grace, the Lord is with thee,*[336] she was
troubled and could not answer. For she had never been
greeted by a man. Then she recognized the messenger and
spoke to him. She who had been terrified by a man conversed fearlessly with an angel. You too may be the mother
of the Lord.[337]   4 *Take thee a great book, a new book, and*

*write in it with the pen of a man taking away the spoils with
great speed.* And when you have gone unto the prophetess[338]
and have conceived and borne a son, say: *Lord, we have
conceived by thy fear, and have both been in labor and have
delivered; we have wrought the spirit of thy salvation upon
the earth.*[339] Then shall your son also reply to you and shall
say: *Behold my mother and my brethren.*[340] 5 And miraculously He whom a little while before you had inscribed within
the largeness of your heart,[341] whom you had written with a
flying pen upon the newness of your heart, after He has
taken spoils from the enemy, after He has despoiled the
principalities and powers and affixed them to His cross,[342]
having been conceived He grows to manhood and when older
begins to regard you no longer as mother but as His bride. 6
Great is the task, but great the reward: to be as the martyrs,
as the apostles, as Christ. All this is of avail only when done
within the Church;[342a] when we celebrate the Pasch in one
house; only if we enter the ark with Noe;[343] if while Jericho
falls Rahab, who was justified, shelters us.[344]

7 But such virgins as there are said to be among the various
heretical sects and with the most foul Manichean are to be
considered harlots, not virgins.[345] For if the author of their
body is the devil, how can they honor what has been framed
by his foes? But because they know that the very word
"virgin" is glorious, they shelter wolves in sheep's clothing.[346]
Antichrist pretends to be Christ, and they falsely clothe
shamefulness of life by the honor of that name. Rejoice,
sister; rejoice, daughter; rejoice, my virgin: you have begun
to be in truth what other women pretend to be.

39. All these things that I have set forth will seem hard
to him who does not love Christ. But one who counts all the
pomp of the world as but dung[347] and considers all things
under the sun as vanity, if only one may win Christ; who has

died with his Lord and risen with Him,[348] and crucified the flesh and its faults and its lusts,[349] that one will boldly proclaim: *Who shall separate us from the love of Christ? Shall tribulation, or distress, or persecution, or famine, or nakedness, or danger, or the sword?*[350] 2 And again: *But I am sure that neither death, nor life, nor an angel, nor principalities, nor things present, nor things to come, nor might, nor height, nor depth, nor any other creature, shall be able to separate us from the love of God, which is in Christ Jesus our Lord.*[351] The Son of God for our salvation became the son of man. For ten months in the womb He waits to be born, He endures distress, He comes forth covered with blood, He is wrapped in swaddling clothes, He is mocked by caresses. He within whose closed fist the whole world is held,[352] is contained by the narrow confines of a manger. 3 I say nothing of the fact that He was in obscurity up to his thirtieth year, content with the poverty of His parents; He is scourged and is silent; He is crucified and prays for them that crucify Him. *What, then, shall I render to the Lord for all the things that He hath rendered to me? I will take the chalice of salvation, and I will call upon the name of the Lord.*[353] *Precious in the sight of the Lord is the death of His saints.*[354] This is the only worthy return: when blood is paid for with blood, and having been redeemed by the blood of Christ we gladly die for our Redeemer. Who of the saints was crowned without a struggle? The good man Abel is killed,[355] Abraham is in danger of losing his wife,[356] and—not to prolong my book beyond measure—seek and you shall find that every one of the saints suffered various hardships. Solomon alone lived in luxury, and perhaps for that very reason fell. *For whom the Lord loveth he chastiseth; and He scourgeth every son whom He receiveth.*[357] Is it not better to fight for a short time, to carry a camp stake,[358] arms, provisions, to grow faint

under a coat of mail, and afterwards to rejoice as victor, than
to be slaves forever because of failure to endure a single hour?

40.   Nothing is hard for lovers.   No effort is difficult for
one who is passionately eager.   See how much Jacob endured
for Rachel, his affianced wife.   *And Jacob served seven years
for Rachel,* says the Scripture, *and they were in his sight but
as a few days, because he loved her.*[359]   Whence also he himself said later: *Day and night was I parched with heat and
with frost.*[360]   Let us also love Christ, let us ever seek His
embraces.   And we shall find that every difficult thing is
easy.   2 We shall consider short all things long.   Wounded
by His spear, we shall say every moment of each hour: *Woe
is me, that my sojourning is prolonged.*[361]   *For the sufferings
of this world are not worthy to be compared with the glory to
come, that shall be revealed in us.*[362]   *Because tribulation
worketh patience, and patience trial, and trial hope, and hope
confoundeth not.*[363]   3 When it seems to you that your
burden is heavy, read Paul's second letter to the Corinthians:
*in many more labors, in prisons more frequently, in stripes
above measure, in deaths often.   Of the Jews five times did I
receive forty stripes save one.   Thrice was I beaten with rods,
once was I stoned, thrice I suffered shipwreck, a day and a
night was I in the depth of the sea.   In journeying often, in
perils of waters, in perils of robbers, in perils from my own
nation, in perils from the Gentiles, in perils in the city, in
perils in the wilderness, in perils in the sea, in perils from
false brethren.   In labor and painfulness, in much watchings,
in hunger and thirst, in fastings often, in cold and nakedness.*[364]   4 Who of us can claim for himself even the smallest
portion of the catalog of these virtues?   Certainly it was with
confidence that he afterwards said: *I have finished my course,
I have kept the faith.   As to the rest, there is laid up for me
a crown of justice, which the Lord will render to me.*[365]   If

food has been rather insipid, we feel hurt, and we think we are doing God a favor when we drink wine that is too watery. Water that is too warm is paid for with blood: the glass is broken, the table is overturned, there is the sound of lashes.[366] *The kingdom of God suffereth violence, and the violent bear it away.*[367] Unless you use violence, you will not take the kingdom of heaven. Unless you knock importunately, you shall not receive the bread of the sacrament.[368] Does it not seem to you violence when the flesh desires to be what God is, and to ascend to the place whence the angels fell, in order to judge the angels?

41. Come out for a little while, I pray you, from the body, and picture before your eyes the reward for your present labor, *that eye hath not seen, nor ear heard, neither hath it entered into the heart of man.*[369] What shall that day be like when Mary, the mother of the Lord, shall come to meet you, accompanied by bands of virgins? When, the Red Sea passed and Pharaoh drowned with his army, holding a timbrel she shall sing to those who will reply: *Let us sing to the Lord, for He is gloriously magnified. The horse and the rider He hath thrown into the sea.*[370] 2 Then shall Thecla fly rejoicing into your arms.[371] Then, too, shall your Spouse Himself come to meet you and shall say: *Arise, come, my love, my beautiful one, my dove, for winter is now past, the rain is over and gone.*[372] Then the angels shall marvel and shall say: *Who is she that looketh forth as the morning rising, fair as the moon, excellent as the sun?*[373] The daughters shall see you and shall praise you; the queens and concubines shall proclaim you.[374] 3 Then also another chaste company shall come to meet you: Sara shall come with the wedded, Anna the daughter of Phanuel with the widows.[375] Your mother in the flesh[376] and your spiritual mother[377] shall be there, in different companies. The former will rejoice that she bore

you, the latter will exult that she taught you. Then in truth the Lord shall mount His ass[378] and enter the heavenly Jerusalem.[379]   Then the little children, of whom the Saviour says in Isaias: *Behold I and my children whom the Lord hath given me,*[380] waving palms of victory shall sing with one accord: *Hosanna in the highest; blessed is he that cometh in the name of the Lord: hosanna in the highest.*[381]   4 Then the hundred and forty-four thousand shall hold their harps before the throne and in sight of the ancients and shall sing a new song; and no man will be able to say the canticle except the appointed number:[382] *These are they who were not defiled with women,* for they have remained virgins. These are they who follow the Lamb whithersoever He goeth.[383]   5 As often as the world's vain ambition delights you, as often as you see in mundane affairs something that vaunts itself, transport yourself in your thoughts to paradise: begin to be what you shall be. And you shall hear from your Bridegroom: *Put me as a seal upon thy heart, as a seal upon thy arm.*[384]   And fortified both in fact and in mind, you shall exclaim: *Many waters cannot quench charity, neither can the floods drown it.*[385]

NOTES

NOTES

LIST OF ABBREVIATIONS

ACW	Ancient Christian Writers
Bardenhewer	O. Bardenhewer, *Geschichte der altkirchlichen Literatur.* 5 vols. (Freiburg 1902–32)
Cavallera	F. Cavallera, *Saint Jérôme: Sa vie et son oeuvre.* 2 vols. (Louvain–Paris 1922)
CCHS	*A Catholic Commentary on Holy Scripture,* ed. B. Orchard *et al.* (London 1953)
CSEL	Corpus scriptorum ecclesiasticorum latinorum (Vienna 1866–)
DACL	Dictionnaire d'archéologie chrétienne et de liturgie (Paris 1907–53)
DTC	Dictionnaire de théologie catholique (Paris 1903–50)
Fremantle	W. H. Fremantle, with assistance of G. Lewis and W. G. Martley, *The Principal Works of St. Jerome* (A Select Library of Nicene and Post-Nicene Fathers of the Christian Church, Second Series, Vol. 6; Grand Rapids 1954)
Hilberg	*Sancti Eusebii Hieronymi epistulae,* ed. I. Hilberg. 3 vols. CSEL 54–56 (Vienna–Leipzig, 1910, 1912, 1918)
Labourt	J. Labourt, *Saint Jérôme: Lettres.* 8 vols. (Paris 1949 ff.; Vol. 8 expected late 1963 or early 1964)
LTK	Lexikon für Theologie und Kirche. 2nd ed. (Freiburg 1957–)
MG	Patrologia graeca, ed. J. P. Migne (Paris 1844–55)
ML	Patrologia latina, ed. J. P. Migne (Paris 1857–66)
Monceaux	P. Monceaux, *St. Jerome: The Early Years,* tr. F. J. Sheed (London–New York 1933)
MSJ	*A Monument to St. Jerome,* ed. F. X. Murphy (New York 1952)
PSt	Patristic Studies (Washington, D.C. 1922–)

184 THE LETTERS OF ST. JEROME

Quasten *Patr.*	J. Quasten, *Patrology*. 3 vols. thus far (Westminster, Md.–Utrecht–Antwerp): 1 (1950) *The Beginnings of Patristic Literature*; 2 (1953) *The Ante-Nicene Literature after Irenaeus*; 3 (1960) *The Golden Age of Greek Patristic Literature from the Council of Nicaea to the Council of Chalcedon*
SCA	Studies in Christian Antiquity (Washington, D.C. 1941–)
Vallarsi	D. Vallarsi's edition of the letters of St. Jerome as reprinted in ML 22
Wright	*Select Letters of St. Jerome*, tr. F. A. Wright (Loeb Classical Library, London–New York 1933)

INTRODUCTION

[1] *De vir. ill.* 135: . . . *Epistularum autem ad Paulam et Eustochium, quia cotidie scribuntur, incertus est numerus.* The *cotidie* need not, of course, be taken as meaning literally "every day."

[2] Hilberg gives No. 18 as Nos. 18A and 18B; cf. below, n. 1 to Letter 18A.

[3] That Jerome drafted Letter 46 is a conjecture of long standing among editors of the letters. It may be noted here that some manuscripts of the *De vir. ill.* have an addition referring to a letter to Marcella *ex nomine Paulae de scs. locis,* which could be our Letter 46; but the addition to *De vir. ill.* is itself of doubtful authenticity and cannot be taken as confirmation of the conjecture. Cf. Cavallera 2.136; Labourt 1.xlvii f.

[4] The four epistles referred to as recent additions to the corpus are Nos. 151–54 in the Hilberg edition. D. de Bruyne, following his find in the Escorial library, published these in the *Revue bénédictine* 27 (1910) 3–6.—At least a few of the "spurious" letters have advocates for their authenticity; cf., e.g., the comment and additional references cited by C. Favez, *Sancti Eusebii Hieronymi epistulae selectae* (Collection Latomus 4, Brussels 1950) v; also, Labourt 1.165.

[5] On the date and place of Jerome's birth, cf. esp. Cavallera 2.1–12 and 67–71; and by the same author, "La patrie de S. Jérôme," *Bull. de litt. eccles.* (1946) 60–64. For a recent summary of Jerome's life, works, and significance, cf. W. J. Burghardt, "Jerome, Saint," *Encyclopaedia Britannica* 13 (1962 edition) 2–3.

[6] Letter 3.5.2.

[7] *Chron.* 329.

[8] Cf. below, n. 1 to Letter 1. (A number of matters regarding individual letters are mentioned briefly in the Introduction and discussed more fully in the notes; it is not considered necessary hereafter to refer to these notes in each instance.)

[9] Cf. Letter 3.3.1; also n. 8 to Letter 3.

[10] Cf. the discussion in Cavallera 2.56–63. Cavallera argues well for the year 419.

[11] *De vir. ill.* 135.

[12] The over-all stylistic quality is even more impressive when it is recalled that a number of Jerome's letters were evidently written under press of time, and also that a number of them at least were dictated (cf. below, n. 103 to Letter 18A).

[13] J. Leclercq, *The Love of Learning and the Desire for God* (tr. C. Misrahi, New York 1961) 123. Cf. also M. L. W. Laistner, "The Study of St. Jerome in the Early Middle Ages," MSJ 235–56.

[14] Labourt provides (1.lxi–lxvii) a convenient list of the manuscripts used by Hilberg for establishment of the text and notes with each manuscript the letters it was used for. Labourt does not give so detailed a critical apparatus as Hilberg, nor does he give so many biblical references as Hilberg for Jerome's allusions to Scripture; cf. Labourt's explanatory note on this in 1.lix f. Labourt comments on the Hilberg text in 1.xliii–xlvi and lii (". . . sauf exception, c'est au texte établi par ses soins que nous nous sommes attaché"). In any case, the text we have for the letters is good; Hilberg commented in his introductory note to CSEL 54: "In verbis Hieronymi constituendis coniecturis raro opus erat. . . ."

[15] The following editions may be noted: H. Hurter, *S. Eusebii Hieronymi epistolae selectae* (Innsbruck 1870); J.-P. Charpentier, *Lettres choises de s. Jérôme* (with French translation; Paris 1900); L. Laurand, *Saint Jérôme. Lettres choises* (Paris 1916); J. Schmid, SS. *Eusebii Hieronymi et Aurelii Augustini epistulae mutuae* (Florilegium patristicum 22, Bonn 1930); D. Gorce, *Lettres spirituelles de s. Jérôme* (2 vols., Paris 1932–34); F. A. Wright, *Select Letters of St. Jerome* (with English translation; Loeb Classical Library, London 1933); L. Schade, *Hieronymus. Ausgewählte Briefe* (Munich 1936–37); J. Duff, *The Letters of Saint Jerome. A Selection to Illustrate Roman Christian Life in the Fourth Century* (Dublin 1942); C. Favez, *Sancti Eusebii Hieronymi epistulae selectae* (Collection Latomus 4, Brussels 1950).

[16] The letters involved in the Jerome-Augustine exchange have been published, with introduction and notes, by J. Schmid, whose work is mentioned in the preceding note.—To facilitate the locating of these letters among the letters of Augustine, the epistles mentioned are here listed again, this time with the number of each as it occurs in the Jerome collection followed in parentheses by the number it has in the Augustine collection. The eight letters addressed to Jerome by Augustine are 56(28), 67(40), 101(67), 104(71), 110(73), 116(82), 131(166), 132(167). The nine addressed by Jerome to Augustine are 102(68), 103(39), 105(72), 112(75), 115(81), 134(172), 141(195), 142(123), 143(202). The other two letters of Augustine mentioned are 111(74) and 144(202A).

[17] Cf., e.g., Augustine's *De doct. christ.* 2.15, and esp. his *De civ. Dei* 18.42–44. Jerome also had earlier shared the view of various other Christian writers of his time that the translators of the Old Testament into the Greek of the Septuagint were divinely inspired, but he later abandoned the view; cf. below, n. 54 to Letter 18A.

[18] *Dialogus adv. Pelag.* 3.19.

[19] Cf. *Dialogus adv. Pelag.* 1.22.

LETTER 1

[1] This letter, which may well be the oldest of Jerome's extant writings, recounts the story of a recent "miraculous event" (§ 1: *de eius miraculo rei, quae in nostram aetatem inciderat*) and was evidently written at the bidding (§ 1: *saepe a me . . . postulasti*) of the addressee, Innocent, a priest friend of Jerome's. It tells of a woman accused of adultery, her denials of the charge, the tortures to which she was subjected, the amazingly unsuccessful efforts of two different executioners to dispatch her, her apparent death and later recovery, and, following an appeal to the emperor by Jerome's and Innocent's friend Evagrius, her eventual restoration to freedom. While an effort might be made to interpret the story allegorically (cf. the remark in G. Grützmacher, *Hieronymus: Eine biographische Studie zur alten Kirchengeschichte* 1 [Leipzig 1901] 145: "Das Martyrium der des Ehebruchs beschuldigten Christin ist das Martyrium des Christentums unter dem heidnischen Recht"), the tone of the letter and the details cited of place and personalities are certainly testimony that Jerome is giving it as an account of a true incident. Cavallera (1.27) says the story is presented as "un vrai conte," and states: "Le recit est alert, brilliant, précieux même. . . ." On the other hand, Monceaux (90) terms the account "a curious little story, edifying, if macabre," and refers to Jerome's debut as a writer as "a very modest début"; his judgment is sound in stating (92) of this letter: "The thing is not a masterpiece. The style is brilliant, but the narration is artificial," although there are "hints of talent to come, and even of talent achieved."

The actual date of the letter is not known, but belongs in the period 369–75. While it may have been written while Jerome was still at Aquileia, the time of composition seems more likely to have been after his arrival, on his first trip to the East, at Antioch in 374. (It should be noted here—and considered in the following notes—that many dates in the Hieronymian chronology are not firmly established. E.g., Cavallera [2.153] puts Jerome's departure from Aquileia for the East in about 374; F. X. Murphy, in "St. Jerome: The Irascible Hermit," MSJ 6, puts it in 372; etc.) A *terminus post quem* for dating the present epistle is possibly set by the historical references in § 15. Auxentius, the Arian or Arian-tinged predecessor of St. Ambrose in the episcopal see of Milan, was condemned by a Roman synod about 369/370. Or do Jerome's words imply a time of composition after the death of Auxentius in 374? Cavallera (2.12 ff.) discusses the import of Jerome's phrase, *Auxentium Mediolanii incubantem huius excubiis sepultum paene ante quam mortuum*, and the question of how literally the words should be taken; he (2.153) dates the letter in the fall of 374, and in fact in his chronology lists it after Letter 2, which he also dates in the fall of 374. Labourt, who at first (1.4 f.) considered Antioch as the probable place of composition, later (3.255 f.) questioned the traditional identification of the Auxentius mentioned with the predecessor of St. Ambrose at Milan, and suggested the possibility of an earlier initial writing at Aquileia, this then followed by a definitive edition of the letter at a later date. Grützmacher (*op. cit.* 1.53) says the letter was written between 369 and 373. Fremantle (xxxiv, 1) puts it in or about 370. The rhetorical style certainly argues for an early date.—A *terminus ante quem* for dating the letter is provided by the fact that Jerome's addressee, Innocent, died not many months after their arrival in Antioch, possibly in the summer of 375 (cf. the reference to Innocent's death in Letter 3.3.1).

[2] Possibly a reference to his student days at Rome.

[3] . . . *neque eum posse verba deficere, qui credidisset in verbo.* The Latin tongue favors wordplay, but the rhetorical effect is frequently lost in translation. Note here, however, the play on "words" and the divine "Word" of John 1.1.

[4] Regarding Jerome's nautical figures of speech in this section, see similar such usages of nautical allusions in the present volume in Letters 2.4; 3.2 ff.; 7.5; 10.3.3; 14.6.2 f.; etc. Regarding figures of imagery in general in Jerome's letters, cf. J. N. Hritzu, *The Style of the Letters of St. Jerome* (PSt 60, Washington, D.C. 1939) 99–112. Hritzu states that the device of metaphor is "without doubt the most important stylistic feature of the *Letters* of St. Jerome"; he gives a figure of 1768 as the number of examples of metaphor and metaphorical expressions, and 370 as the number of examples of comparison.—Metaphors of life as a voyage, of the Christian in the ship of the Church, etc., were popular with early Christian writers; cf. the discussion and collection of material by H. Rahner, *Griechische Mythen in christlicher Deutung* (Zurich 1945) 430 ff.: "Die Seefahrt des Lebens."

[5] "Euxine Sea" = Black Sea.

[6] Vergil, *Aen.* 3.193. Numerous citations of and allusions to pagan authors are found in Jerome, and Vergil is one of those who seem to be quoted or alluded to most frequently. On the many reminiscences of this poet in Jerome, cf. D. Comparetti, *Vergil in the Middle Ages* (tr. E. F. M. Benecke, New York 1895) 82 f. Cf. also the remarks of Sr. M. Jamesetta Kelly, *Life and Times as Revealed in the Writings of St. Jerome Exclusive of His Letters* (PSt 70, Washington, D.C. 1944) 60–65: "St. Jerome and Pagan Authors," where about ninety non-Christian Greek and Latin authors cited by Jerome are listed. On the general question of Jerome and secular literature, see Letter 22.30 in the present volume for Jerome's own account of the famous "dream" in which he was

accused of being a *Ciceronianus* and not a *Christianus;* cf. n. 283 to Letter 22.

⁷ Cf. Vergil, *Aen.* 3.195; 5.11.

⁸ Vercelli in the *compartimento* of Piedmont.

⁹ Cf. Ps. 7.10.

¹⁰ The prayer here apparently is that of the writer; but the words could be put in the mouth of the woman.

¹¹ Reading here, with Hilberg, *iam igitur et tertius ictus: sacramentum frustraverat trinitatis.* The insertion of the colon after *ictus* makes the present translation possible without adopting—as Labourt (1.161) sees necessary for such a translation—the variant *tertium ictum* found in the Codex Casinensis 91 s. X–XI. Labourt (1.6) gives the text without the colon after *ictus* and translates: "Voici encore le troisième coup également décevant, de par le mystère de la Trinité!"—For an exposition on the meaning *sacramentum = mysterium,* and other meanings and shades of meanings, see J. de Ghellinck, E. de Backer, J. Poukens, F. Labackz, *Pour l'histoire du mot "sacramentum"* 1: *Les Anténicéens* (Louvain 1924); cf. also F. J. Dölger, "Sacramentum militiae," *Antike und Christentum* 2 (1930) 268–80; J. Quasten, *Monumenta eucharistica et liturgica vetustissima* (Florilegium patristicum 7, Bonn 1935–37) index *s. v.;* G. Bornkamm's article *"μυστήριον"* in Kittel's *Theologisches Wörterbuch zum Neuen Testament* 4 (Stuttgart 1942) 809–34; O. Casel, *Das christliche Kultmysterium* (3rd ed. Freiburg 1948); C. Mohrmann, "Sacramentum dans les plus anciens textes chrétiens," *Harvard Theological Review* 47 (1954) 141–52.

¹² Cf. Dan. 3.23–94.

¹³ Cf. Dan. 6.16–23; 14.30–40.

¹⁴ Cf. Dan. 13.

¹⁵ *haec a iudice damnata absoluta per gladium est.*

¹⁶ Vergil, *Aen.* 12.611.

¹⁷ That is, of the second executioner. This is actually the seventh attempt against her with a sword.

¹⁸ Ps. 117.6. Jerome here has *Dominus auxiliator meus* where Vulgate has *Dominus mihi adjutor.* Hereafter in these notes such minor variations will not be pointed out, although a number of more significant differences in reading will be.

¹⁹ *zabulus* for *diabolus;* cf. Lactantius, *De morte pers.* 16; Augustine, *In Ioann. ev. tract.* 5.15; etc.

²⁰ *domi,* possibly meaning the presbytery next to the church.

²¹ *ius summum summa malitia.* Cf. Terence, *Heaut.* 796. Compare the proverbial *summum ius summa iniuria.*

²² Evagrius of Antioch, who was later (388/389) to become bishop of

that see. He is mentioned often by Jerome; cf. Letters 3.2; 4.2.2.; 5.3; 7.1.2; 15.5.1; also *De vir. ill.* 125, where he is mentioned by Jerome as the writer of several treatises and as the translator into Latin of St. Athanasius' *Life of St. Antony.* The version of the *Life of St. Antony* as translated or paraphrased into Latin by Evagrius enjoyed a fame quite apart from Athanasius' Greek original; cf. R. T. Meyer, ACW 10 (1950) 14. It is quite likely the Evagrius version which is referred to in St. Augustine's *Confessions* 8.6.14 f., wherein is told how "a certain Ponticianus" introduced Augustine and Alypius to the story of Antony.

[23] Cf. n. 1 above.

[24] The reference is evidently to the victory in 368 of Pope Damasus over the antipope Ursinus.

[25] Vergil, *Georg.* 4.147 f.; tr. T. F. Royds.

[26] *imperatorem industria adit.* The *imperator* referred to may be Valentinian I, emperor of the West from 364 to his death in 375.

LETTER 2

[1] In this brief epistle Jerome asks for the prayers of Theodosius and the other anchorites, whom Jerome had evidently visited earlier (cf. § 2), that he may have both the will and the power to withdraw from the world. The letter would seem to have been written from Antioch at least some short time before Jerome actually went to stay in the desert. Cavallera (2.153) dates it in the fall of 374. The Theodosius addressed here has sometimes been identified with the founder of the monastery at Rhossus in Cilicia, mentioned by Theodoret, *Hist. rel.* 10 (MG 82.1388 ff.), but this is conjecture and by no means certain.

In the superscription, "living in residence with him" = *intrinsecus commorantes,* a puzzling term which does not appear in all the manuscripts. It may refer to the fact that the monks addressed are not scattered solitaries but rather living in the same monastery (cf. Cavallera 1.26). Labourt, who translates "demeurant a l'intérieur," suggests that possibly the phrase is an inept Latin transcription of the Greek ἀναχωρητάς, "anchorites."

[2] Jerome makes many allusions to his sins; cf. in this present volume Letters 3.1.2; 4.2.2.; 6.2.1; 7.3 f.; 14.6.2; 15.2.2; 18A.11.3; also Letter 22 *passim* for references to forms of temptations one was exposed to in Rome and for a description (§§ 7 f.) of temptations suffered by Jerome even while in the desert. In Letter 49.20 (= 48.20 of the Vallarsi edition printed in ML 22) he wrote: *Virginitatem autem in caelum fero, non quia habeo, sed quia miror, quod non habeo.* Whatever and however many sins Jerome may have committed in his youth—and assuredly

he knew the events of his past better than we—his self-accusations appear
to involve some, perhaps considerable, hyperbole. On this question and
the possible extent of rhetoric and exaggeration involved, cf. Cavallera
1.16 and 2.72–75, Note B, "Les désordres de jeunesse"; and Monceaux
47–52.

³ Cf. Luke 15.3–6.
⁴ Cf. Luke 15.11–32.
⁵ Cf. Vergil, *Aen.* 5.9 and 3.193.
⁶ *in medio . . . elemento.*

LETTER 3

¹ Jerome here writes to Rufinus telling him how he has received news
of Rufinus in Egypt and stating how much he would like to see again
this friend of his days at Rome and at Aquileia; he tells Rufinus of his
own journey to Syria, and of the deaths of Innocent and Hylas; he reports enthusiastically on their mutual friend Bonosus, who has left home
and is living as a hermit on an island; and he closes with a plea that their
friendship will continue. This letter appears to have been written from
Antioch in the year 375; cf. Cavallera 2.14 f. and 154.

The addressee is Rufinus of Aquileia, and the language of this letter
(and of Letter 4) is clear testimony to the sincere friendship that existed
between Jerome and Rufinus in their youth, and in sharp contrast to
the words of both in later years when they were estranged.—Rufinus was
born about 345 in Concordia, a town not far from Aquileia and Jerome's
home town of Stridon. He was one of Jerome's fellow students in Rome
and subsequently attached himself to the group of ascetics in Aquileia.
Apparently it was not long after Jerome left Aquileia for the East that
Rufinus embarked on a journey to Alexandria and Egypt, his fortunes
at about that time becoming linked with those of Melania the Elder
(whom Jerome refers to in § 3.2 of the present letter). It is not certain
whether Rufinus and the wealthy Roman widow met in Italy and traveled together to the East, or whether their companionship began only
after they had both reached Egypt. Melania later established a community for virgins on the Mount of Olives in Jerusalem. Rufinus eventually rejoined her in Jerusalem and founded a community for men.
Some years later, in 397, Rufinus left the East and returned to Italy. He
died in 410.—Rufinus' reputation as an author rests principally on his
translations, often paraphrases, of the works of others. It was in his
Latin translation that the great *Church History* of Eusebius of Caesarea
spread over the West. Of his original works, perhaps the most important
is his *Commentarius in symbolum apostolorum* (= ACW 20). Cf.

J. N. D. Kelly's Introduction and Notes in ACW 20 (1955); F. X. Murphy, *Rufinus of Aquileia, His Life and Works* (Washington, D.C. 1945); Labourt 4.180–83; also Quasten *Patr.* 3 *passim.*

[2] 1 Cor. 2.9.

[3] Cf. Acts 8.26–40 and Dan. 14.33–39. Jerome has *Ambacum* for Habacuc.

[4] Heliodorus of Altinum, a town not far from Stridon and Aquileia, was another of Jerome's friends of his youth, of the school days in Rome, of the period before Jerome set out for the East. He embarked on a pilgrimage to the Holy Places, apparently at about the time or not very long after Jerome departed Aquileia. Heliodorus, who was in military service before he became a monk, subsequently became bishop of Altinum. Jerome's Letters 14 and 60 are addressed to him.

[5] The reference quite possibly is to Catholics exiled in 373 by the Arian emperor Valens (and freed in 378 by an edict of the Catholic emperor Gratian), and perhaps specifically to exiles interned at Heliopolis (Baalbek); cf. Labourt 1.11 f. and 163. Note also the reference to *Aegyptios confessores* in Letter 15.2.2. In the present letter Jerome has *ad Aegyptios confessores et voluntate iam martyres*. Labourt's remark here that the word *confessor* "est, dans la langue chrétienne de cette époque, à peu près synonyme de martyr" is too sweeping a statement; cf. the remarks and references cited by L. A. Arand, ACW 3 (1947) 141 ("But in Augustine's time death for the faith was always implied in the word *martyr* . . .") and by M. Bévenot, ACW 25 (1957) 79.

[6] Rufinus (*Hist. monach.* 28) and Palladius (*Hist. Laus.* 17) testify to the important position of Macarius the Egyptian (also surnamed the Elder, or the Great) in the history of Egyptian monachism. This Macarius had retired to the desert of Scetis around the year 330, is said about ten years later to have received the grace of healing and predicting the future, and became famous for his sermons and instructions; his eloquence won him repeated invitations to address the anchorites in the Nitrian mountains. A contemporary of Macarius the Egyptian was Macarius the Alexandrian, who seems to have possessed the gifts of healing and prediction in a still higher degree. Macarius the Alexandrian had established himself in the desert of Cellia about the year 325, but apparently was for a time in charge of a monastic colony in the Nitrian desert. For both men, cf. Quasten *Patr.* 3.161–69.

[7] Cf. Horace, *Odes* 4.5.9–14.

[8] We do not know what friction with his relatives or with others, or what other causes, had led to Jerome's evidently abrupt departure from Aquileia and his setting out on his first trip to the East. Jerome's words at the beginning of this section are: *Postquam me a tuo latere subitus*

turbo convolvit, postquam glutino caritatis haerentem inpia distraxit avulsio. . . . Had Jerome been guilty of some imprudence, exposed himself to calumny? Is there a connection here with his failure to hear from the virgins of Haemona and the monk Antonius (see Letters 11 and 12) and with the quarrel with his Aunt Castorina (see Letter 13)? Cf. the discussion by Monceaux 75–84; also Cavallera 2.75 ff., Note C, "Le premier départ pour l'Orient et sa cause."

[9] Vergil, *Aen.* 3.194; 5.9.

[10] *. . . e duobus oculis unum perdidi.* Jerome has referred in this letter (§§ 1.2 and 2.3) to his illnesses; in the present instance, however, he is not to be taken literally, but rather as referring to the loss through death of his friend Innocent (addressee of Letter 1 above). The Latin *oculus,* "eye," was at times used as a term of endearment.

[11] *partem animae meae.* Cf. Horace, *Odes* 1.3.8.

[12] Cf. above, n. 22 to Letter 1.

[13] *sanctae Melaniae.* The reference is to Melania the Elder, patroness of Rufinus (cf. n. 1 above). The *sanctae* here, while carrying the implication of Christian moral goodness, is certainly not to be translated as "saint" with its present-day meaning. What we have here is a survival of the earlier usage of "saints" for the members of the living Church on earth. Compare St. Augustine's use (e.g., in *Serm.* 51.11) of *sanctitas vestra,* in the general sense of "my good Christians," in addressing the hearers of his sermons. On the various uses and meanings of *sanctus* (*sanctitas*) in early Christianity, cf. H. Delehaye, *Sanctus. Essai sur le culte des saints dans l'antiquité* (Brussels 1927) esp. ch. 1.

[14] This so-called "stain"—*maculam servitutis*—was of course a social, not a moral, one. Cf. the remarks of St. Augustine, *De civ. Dei* 19.15 f., on the existence of the state of servitude, a result of sin. For a history of slavery during the first Christian centuries, cf. P. Allard, *Les esclaves chrétiens depuis les premiers temps de l'église jusqu'à la fin de la domination romaine en occident* (6th ed. Paris 1914).—The "wound" reopened by Hylas' passing (see the following) is obviously an allusion to the death of Innocent.

[15] Cf. 1 Thess. 4.12. For death regarded as a sleep, cf. Jerome's Letter 75.1; *Vita Pauli* 11; *C. Vigil.* 6. See A. Rush, *Death and Burial in Christian Antiquity* (SCA 1, Washington, D.C. 1941) 12–22.

[16] Very close friend and companion of Jerome's going all the way back to their childhood; see n. 1 above, and also the remarks that follow in this letter and in Letter 7.3 below. Cf. Cavallera 1.5 and *passim.*

[17] Cf. Gen. 28.12 ff.

[18] Cf. Matt. 16.24; Luke 9.23; etc.

[19] Cf. Matt. 6.34: "Be not therefore solicitous for tomorrow. . . ."

[20] Possibly a reference to Lot's wife, who looked back and was turned into a pillar of salt; cf. Gen. 19.26. Cf. also Luke 9.62: "No man putting his hand to the plow, and looking back, is fit for the kingdom of God."

[21] Cf. Ps. 125.5.

[22] Cf. Num. 21.9.

[23] Apparently an island in the Gulf of Quarnero, south of modern Fiume; cf. Cavallera 1.34. As Adam was originally alone with God in Paradise, so Bonosus *quasi quidam novus paradisi colonus* settled on this island.

[24] Cf. Matt. 17.1 f.; Mark 9.1; Luke 9.28 f.

[25] Cf. 1 Thess. 4.16.

[26] Cf. John 4.14; Apoc. 21.6 and John 19.34.

[27] Cf. Vergil, *Georg.* 3.261 f.

[28] Cf. Eph. 6.11–17.

[29] Cf. Apoc. 1.9 ff.

[30] Deut. 8.3; cf. Matt. 4.4; Luke 4.4.

[31] 1 Tim. 6.9. Jerome's "into the trap of temptation" here = *in muscipulam* (literally, "mousetrap") *et temptationes.* The Vulgate reads ". . . fall into temptation, and into the snare (*laqueum*) of the devil. . . ." The "mousetrap" variant is also found in Cyprian, *De laps.* 12; *De dom. or.* 19; *De op. et eleem.* 10.

[32] Cf. Rom. 15.17; Gal. 6.14; 2 Cor. 10.17.

[33] 2 Cor. 12.10 and 9.

[34] Phil. 1.23.

[35] Cf. Eph. 6.16.

[36] Cf. Acts 1.24 and Apoc. 2.23.

[37] Cf. Jonas 2.

[38] Cf. Matt. 5.19: "He therefore that shall break one of these least commandments and shall so teach men. . . ."

[39] Cf. Apoc. 7.9.

[40] John 14.2.

[41] 1 Cor. 15.41.

[42] Cf. Tertullian, *De cult. fem.* 2.7.3.

[43] . . . *cum ego voluerim, ille perfecerit; mihi ignoscas, quia inplere non potui.* . . . This would seem to have been written before Jerome actually went to stay in the desert of Chalcis; cf. n. 1 above.

LETTER 4

[1] Jerome here asks Florentinus to give an enclosed letter to Rufinus, who, Jerome has heard, has come with Melania to Jerusalem. (The

report on Rufinus proved to be false; cf. Letter 5.2.1. Regarding Rufinus and Melania, cf. above, n. 1 to Letter 3.) The enclosure here possibly was Letter 3; that letter, however, makes no mention of a reported arrival of Rufinus in Jerusalem, and the present reference may be to another epistle which has not survived.—Florentinus was a Latin, evidently a man of wealth, who had come to Jerusalem to live the life of a monk; he appears to have been quite charitable and became known as "father of the poor"; cf. Jerome, *Chron. an.* 377. Note the references in this present epistle to Florentinus' good works and to the assistance given by him to Heliodorus (regarding whom, cf. above, n. 4 to Letter 3); cf. also Letter 5.2.3.—Letter 4 probably was written in the year 375; cf. Cavallera 2.14 f. and 154; Labourt 1.16.

The "Your Grace's" in the opening sentence of this letter = *beatitudinis tuae.* Regarding such usage, cf. M. B. O'Brien, *Titles of Address in Christian Latin Epistolography to 543 A.D.* (PSt 21, Washington, D.C. 1930).—In the second sentence, "renown of your charity" = *tuae dilectionis fama.* It is not impossible that, as Labourt (1.162) has suggested, the *tuae dilectionis* is also a protocolary expression here; note, however, the balanced contrast of "some men's sins" and "your charity."

[2] 1 Tim. 5.24.
[3] Cf. Matt. 25.35–40.
[4] Cf. Job 30.19.
[5] Cf. Ps. 50.9. Rufinus had been baptized at Aquileia by Chromatius (regarding whom, cf. below, n. 1 to Letter 7); Jerome had been baptized earlier, while in Rome.
[6] Cf. Matt. 5.26. Regarding Jerome's references to his sins, cf. above, n. 2 to Letter 2.
[7] Ps. 145. 7.
[8] Cf. Isa. 66.2. Jerome here has *super humilem et quietum et trementem verba sua requiescit.*
[9] Cf. John 11.43 f., the recall of Lazarus from the dead.
[10] Cf. above, n. 22 to Letter 1.
[11] Martinianus apparently was a fellow monk of Florentinus.

LETTER 5

[1] Jerome writes again to Florentinus (cf. above, n. 1 to Letter 4), this time evidently in response to a letter stating that Rufinus has not yet come to Jerusalem. Jerome urges that their correspondence continue, makes requests regarding some manuscripts, and offers to supply Florentinus some Bible manuscripts.—The opening words of this letter (*In ea mihi parte heremi commoranti . . .*) tell us that Jerome has actually left

Antioch and entered the desert; the time is possibly late in the year 375.
Hence this may be the first of the group of extant letters of Jerome's
correspondence written during his stay in the desert of Chalcis from 375
to 377(?). In this "desert group" we can perhaps put, in addition to
Letter 5, Letters 6–9 and 11–17. (Regarding Letter 10 and the possibility of dating it in the same general period, cf. n. 1 to that letter
below.) Cavallera (2.15 f.) says that Letters 6 (to Julian), 7 (to
Chromatius, Jovinus, and Eusebius), 8 (to Niceas), 9 (to Chrysocomas),
and 11 (to the virgins of Haemona) are surely of the first months of solitude and without doubt were written about the same time; that one can
suppose 12 (to Antonius, monk of Haemona) was written on the same
occasion as was 11; and that 13 (to Jerome's Aunt Castorina) can likely
be placed in the same time. He adds that Letters 14 (to Heliodorus),
15 and 16 (both to Pope Damasus), and 17 (to Mark, a priest of
Chalcis) would appear to date from the year 376, except that 17 may
belong to early 377. However, it should be remembered here that the
actual date of Jerome's departure from the desert is not certain, and
determination of that date could affect estimates on the timing of some
of these letters.

[2] In the desert of Chalcis, between Immae and Beroea (Aleppo); cf.
Jerome's *Vita Malchi* 3.

[3] *tua dilectio.*

[4] Where Florentinus is.

[5] *ut paene nocuerit proposito, quod profuerit caritate.* The vow or
resolution referred to presumably is one to live as a hermit in the desert.

[6] Jerome had earlier heard that Rufinus had come to Jerusalem with
Melania; cf. Letter 4.2.1.

[7] *in quibus Canticum Canticorum sublimi ore disseruit.* Despite the
high praise here for Reticius' *Commentarius in Canticum Canticorum,*
Jerome was later to criticize the work severely; cf. Letter 37, in § 4.1 of
which he wrote to Marcella: *Frustra igitur a me eiusdem viri commentarios postulas, cum mihi in illis multo displiceant plura, quam placeant.*
This work by Reticius—who had a great reputation in Gaul and who
was sent by the emperor Constantine to Rome to attend the synods of
313 and 314, which dealt with the Donatist controversy—has not survived, except for a fragment in the twelfth-century *Liber apologeticus
pro Abaelardo,* written by Peter Berengarius of Poitiers against Bernard
of Clairvaux. Another work by Reticius, *Against Novatian,* mentioned
by Jerome (*De vir. ill.* 82), also has not survived.

[8] Paul of Concordia, the addressee of Letter 10; cf. below, n. 1 to
Letter 10.

[9] Not preserved.

[10] Following his studies at Rome, Jerome had traveled with Bonosus to

Treves and the "semibarbarous banks of the Rhine" (cf. Letter 3.5.2
above). The reference here is to works of Hilary he transcribed at
Treves for Rufinus. The first work mentioned, *Tractatus super psalmos,*
a voluminous commentary, survives in considerable fragments (CSEL
22; ML 9.231–908). The other work, *De synodis, seu de fide orien-
talium,* likewise survives (ML 10.479–546).

¹¹ Cf. Ps. 1.2.

¹² *habeo alumnos, qui antiquariae arti serviant.* The *alumnos* here pos-
sibly were foundlings who had been adopted and reared by Christians.
Cf. Cavallera 1.42, n. 2. On the status of *alumni* in antiquity and early
Christianity, and on laws pertaining to them, cf. the article by H.
Leclercq, "Alumni," DACL 1.1 (Paris 1924) 1287–1306.

¹³ Cf. above, n. 4 to Letter 3.

¹⁴ Cf. above, n. 22 to Letter 1.

¹⁵ *pueri tui,* of whom nothing further is known.

LETTER 6

¹ Jerome here writes in a light vein, asking pardon that Julian has not
heard from him, expressing pleasure at the news Julian has sent of
Jerome's sister, and asking for further reports. The letter includes references to the illnesses Jerome suffered and to the visit and departure of
Heliodorus (cf. above, n. 4 to Letter 3). The addressee here was one of
the group of ascetics at Aquileia with which Jerome was associated. We
learn from this letter (§ 2.1: "my sister, your daughter in Christ") and
the following (Letter 7.4.1: "My sister is the fruit in Christ of the holy
Julian") that Julian was the spiritual father of Jerome's sister. Jerome
was the oldest of three children; we know the name of his brother
(Paulinianus) but not the name of his sister.—On the dating of this
letter, cf. above, n. 1 to Letter 5.

² A proverb of quite ancient origin. Jerome's version here: *Mendaces
faciunt, ut nec vera dicentibus credatur.* Compare Cicero, *De div.*
2.71.146: *Mendaci homini ne verum quidem dicenti credere.*

³ Horace, *Sat.* 1.3.1 ff.

⁴ Presumably a resolution to dedicate herself to the religious life.

⁵ *Hibera excetra.* The allusion here is not clear. Perhaps there is a
reference to the Lupicinus mentioned in Letter 7.5. The rare word
excetra means "snake," "serpent," but also occurs as an epithet for a
spiteful, or bad, intriguing woman. What Jerome is referring to with
sinistro . . . rumore is also not certain. Is the reference here to something
connected with his departure from Aquileia? Cf. above, n. 8 to Letter 3.

⁶ Horace, *Odes* 3.3.7 f.

⁷ Cf. 1 Cor. 3.14.

LETTER 7

[1] In this affectionate letter to three friends of his Aquileia days, Jerome expresses thanks for the letter he has received from them (and suggests they might have written at greater length), again writes in praise of Bonosus (cf. §§ 4-6 of Letter 3 and n. 16 thereto), asks that his sister (cf. n. 1 to Letter 6) be given advice and encouragement, and sends greetings to the mother and sisters of Chromatius and Eusebius.—The home of Chromatius (who had earlier baptized Rufinus and was later to succeed Valerian as bishop of Aquileia) appears to have been a virtual monastery wherein those practicing asceticism included Chromatius, his brother Eusebius, their mother and sisters, and the archdeacon Jovinus. Visitors here included Jerome and others of the Aquileia group of ascetics. —On the dating of this letter, cf. above, n. 1 to Letter 5.

[2] That is, for the brothers Chromatius and Eusebius.

[3] That is, in the desert of Chalcis. Regarding Evagrius, cf. above, n. 22 to Letter 1.

[4] The Battle of Cannae was fought in the year 216 B.C.; Nola, in 215 B.C.

[5] "by many miles" = *longo . . . spatio.*

[6] *hic enim aut barbarus seni sermo discendus est aut tacendum est.* Jerome gives a small sample of this "barbarous language" in his *Vita Pauli* 6.—Note the use here of the word *seni,* "for an old man" ("in your aging days"). If Jerome was born around the middle of the century, say between 345 and 350, and this letter was written in 375 or 376, then Jerome at this time was at the most thirty or thirty-one years old. References by Jerome to his age, evidently at times exaggerated, have complicated determination of a chronology. On the date of Jerome's birth, cf. Cavallera 2.1–12. Cf. also n. 1 to Letter 14 below.

[7] "Parchment" (= German *Pergament*) is derived from the Latin *pergamenus,* "of or pertaining to Pergamum," an ancient city of Asia Minor where, in the second century B.C., the preparation of parchment suitable for use on both sides was achieved.

[8] *facilius enim neglegentia emendari potest, quam amor nasci.*

[9] *quasi filius* ἰχθύος *aquosa petiit.* The fish, ἰχθύς, early became a symbol for Christ, deriving from the acrostic provided by a formula of faith wherein the initial letters of the five Greek words for "Jesus Christ, Son of God, Saviour" (Ἰησοῦς Χριστὸς Θεοῦ Υἱὸς Σωτήρ) spelled the Greek word for fish. Tertullian (cf. *De bapt.* 1) and the Inscription of Abercius are testimony to the popularity of this formula in the second half of the second century. Cf. Quasten *Patr.* 1.24 and 171–75. In F. J. Dölger's monumental five-volume work ΙΧΘΥΣ. *Der heilige Fisch in den antiken*

Religionen und im Christentum, there is consideration of the present passage in Jerome in Vol. 2 (Münster in Westf. 1922) 508 n. 1. Cf. also J. H. Emminghaus, "Fisch," LTK 4 (1960) 153–55; H. Leclercq, "Poisson," DACL 14.1 (1939) 1246–52.—As for the *aquosa petiit,* this may be a reference to Bonosus' baptism, as suggested by Fremantle (who translates "has taken to the water") and by Wright ("makes for watery places"); or, and perhaps more likely, it may refer to Bonosus' retirement to an island (cf. above, Letter 3.4.6). Labourt translates "a gagné un lieu aquatique." It is also possible, of course, that Jerome deliberately chose a phrase which could serve as allusion to both the baptism and the retirement.

[10] Cf. Gen. 3.14 f.

[11] *potest summum graduum psalmum scandere.* Gradual Psalms = the fifteen "songs of ascents," Pss. 119–33. T. E. Bird, CCHS § 336, comments that it is now generally agreed that these were pilgrimage Psalms, sung by pilgrims "going up" to Jerusalem for the great festivals. Other possibilities are that the title or superscription on each of these Psalms indicates that they were appointed to be sung on the fifteen steps by which people ascended to the Temple; or that the voice was to be raised by steps in the singing of them; or that they were to be sung by the people returning from their captivity and ascending to Jerusalem. There is also the mystical consideration of these steps or ascensions as the degrees by which Christians ascend to virtue and perfection, and to the true temple of God in the heavenly Jerusalem. Jerome has an interesting allusion to these Psalms in a sentence—reminiscent of St. Augustine's fascination with numbers—in Letter 53.8.7: *Iohel, filius Bathuel, describit terram duodecim tribuum eruca, brucho, locusta, rubigine vastante consumptam et post eversionem prioris populi effusum iri spiritum sanctum super servos dei et ancillas, id est super centum viginti credentium nomina, et effusum iri in cenaculo Sion, qui centum viginti ab uno usque ad quindecim paulatim et per incrementa surgentes quindecim graduum numerum efficiunt, qui in psalterio mystice continentur.* (15 Psalms; sum of numbers from 1 to 15 = 120, the number mentioned in Acts 1.15.)

[12] Ps. 120.1.

[13] Cf. Apoc. 10.9 f.

[14] Cf. John 11.43 f., the recall of Lazarus from the dead. Note the same usage in Letter 4.2.2 above.

[15] Cf. Job 40.11.

[16] Cf. Jer. 13.4–7.

[17] A conflation of Ps. 138.13 and Ps. 115.16 f.

[18] Cf. Jer. 39.7.

[19] Cf. 4 Kings 19.28 and Ps. 136.3.

[20] Ps. 145.7 f.

[21] Cf. 1 Cor. 3.6. Regarding the references to Julian and Jerome's sister, cf. above, n. 1 to Letter 6.

[22] Vergil, *Aen.* 4.298.

[23] Cf. above, n. 2 to Letter 2, on Jerome's allusions to his sins.

[24] 1 Cor. 13.7.

[25] *a papa Valeriano.* Valerian was the bishop of Aquileia, and it would seem that the Aquileia ascetics with whom Jerome was associated were grouped around him, or at least had his approval and protection.—The term *papa*, here translated "father," was only many years later to become equivalent to "pope," and in Jerome's time was freely applied to any bishop. Cf. in the present series the remarks of J. N. D. Kelly, ACW 20 (1955) 99 and the references there cited: P. de Labriolle, "Papa," *Bulletin du Cange* 4 (1928) 65–75; H. Leclercq, "Papa," DACL 13.1 (1937) 1097 ff.; H. Janssen, *Kultur und Sprache: Zur Geschichte der alten Kirche im Spiegel der Sprachentwicklung von Tertullian bis Cyprian* (Latinitas christianorum primaeva 8, Nijmegen 1938) 93–96.

[26] Phil. 3.19.

[27] The proverb *patellae dignum operculum* is used by Jerome also in Letter 127.9.1.—Lupicinus (cf. above, n. 5 to Letter 6) is here termed a *sacerdos*, a title which could designate either a priest or bishop. It is not established whether he was of episcopal rank, although it is possible that Stridon was the seat of a bishop.

[28] Cf. Cicero, *De fin.* 5.92.

[29] Cf. Matt. 15.14.

[30] Cf. Matt. 25.1–12, the parable of the wise and foolish virgins.

[31] Cf. Luke 2.36 f.; Acts 21.9; 1 Kings 2.18. Jerome, of course, is referring to Chromatius and Eusebius and their family.

[32] Cf. 2 Mac. 7.

[33] Regarding Fortunatian, Valerian's predecessor in the see of Aquileia, cf. below, n. 11 to Letter 10.

LETTER 8

[1] In this brief epistle, Jerome writes to a friend of Aquileia, Niceas, who, it appears from § 2 of the letter, had recently visited Jerome in the Orient while on a pilgrimage to the Holy Land. The present note provides further evidence that Jerome, though he had retired to the desert, was still eager to receive mail from his friends and to get news from home.—On the dating of this letter, cf. above, n. 1 to Letter 5.

[2] Of whom only some few titles and fragments survive; *floruit* 130 B.C.

³ Cf. Ennius, *Annales* 24: "quam prisci casci populi tenuere Latini." *Cascus* = "old," "very old," "primeval."

⁴ Cf. Cicero, *De invent. rhetorica* 1.2.

⁵ Letter carriers were called *tabellarii*, the name deriving from *tabula*, a "plank," "board," "writing tablet." Scribes were called *librarii*, this deriving from *liber*, the "inner bark" or "rind" of a tree, "paper," "parchment," "book."

⁶ See Letter 7 above.

⁷ Cf. Cicero, *De amic.* (= *Laelius*) 21.76.

LETTER 9

¹ Jerome here again chides an addressee for not writing more. The note is short, and is both laudatory and critical—and, all in all, hardly of a tone likely to awaken a desire on the part of the recipient to write at length. Nothing more is known of the addressee, Chrysocomas (or possibly Chrysogonus; one of the older manuscripts, the one followed by Vallarsi on this name, has *ad crisogonum*), but he would seem to have been a friend of Jerome's youth, possibly one of the Aquileia group of ascetics. This letter would appear to have been written after Heliodorus' arrival in the Orient and visit with Jerome. On dating, cf. above, n. 1 to Letter 5.

² Regarding Heliodorus, cf. above, n. 4 to Letter 3.

³ Cf. 2 Cor. 3.2 f.

LETTER 10

¹ Jerome here writes to the aged Paul of Concordia, a town not far from Aquileia. Much of this friendly letter is devoted to the significance of old age and praise of the addressee. Jerome then asks for some works of various authors, says that he is sending Paul an "older Paul," and suggests that more items will be on the way if desired. Paul of Concordia was mentioned above in Jerome's Letter 5.2.2.

The date of this letter and place of composition are uncertain. The "older Paul" sent to Paul of Concordia seems clearly a reference to Jerome's *Vita Pauli*, or possibly to an early version of this legendary life of Paul of Thebes. Cavallera (2.16 f., 154 f.), who dates the *Vita Pauli* about 377/379, admits the impossibility of dating this letter with certainty but would put it in 380/381, that is, during Jerome's stay in Constantinople, after his stay in the desert and at Antioch. Bardenhewer (3.636 f.) says the *Vita Pauli* was written about 376 in the desert of Chalcis—which would, of course, allow for an earlier dating of this present letter even with the assumption that the "older Paul" is indeed the *Vita Pauli*. Fremantle (xxxiv, 11, 299) dates the *Vita Pauli* in 374 or 375 and says the present letter was written in 374. Labourt (1.163) remarks that Letter 10 seems to be Jerome's first to Paul of Concordia, notes Jerome's reference in Letter 5.2.2 to receipt of a letter from Paul, and thinks Letter 10 was written at the same time as, if not before, Letter 5 (written in the desert of Chalcis); the *Vita Pauli*, then, may have been written at about that time, or perhaps Jerome was sending Paul a different version, possibly an early draft which was only later developed into the work as we know it today.

² Cf. Horace, *Ep.* 2.1.94.

³ Cf. Gen. 5.5, 8, 11, 14, 20, 27.

⁴ Cf. Gen. 6.4–7; also Num. 13.34.—By "baptism" in the following sentence Jerome means the Deluge. For further patristic references to the Deluge as a symbol of baptism, cf. J. Quasten, *Monumenta eucharistica et liturgica vetustissima* (Bonn 1935–37) 118 and 145. Cf. also 1 Peter 3.20 f.

⁵ Ps. 89.10, quoted freely.

⁶ Horace, *Ep.* 2.3.147 (*Ars poetica*). Helen of Troy, according to one myth, and Castor and Pollux were born of twin eggs produced by Leda after she had been visited by Zeus in the form of a swan.

⁷ *et caput ad Christi similitudinem candidum.* Cf. Apoc. 1.14.

⁸ *ingenita levitas et erudita vanitas* (Cicero, *Pro Flacco*, frg. 2), quoted again by Jerome in his *Comm. in Gal.* 1.3.1.

⁹ Cf. Matt. 13.46.

¹⁰ Ps. 11.7. Where the Vulgate has *argentum igne examinatum, probatum terrae, purgatum septuplum,* the Douai reads "as silver tried by the fire, purged from the earth, refined seven times." Jerome's text here as given by Hilberg varies from the Vulgate in that it lacks the word *probatum* as well as the comma after *examinatum.* When Jerome quotes the same text in Letter 18A.6.5, Hilberg gives the same reading as in the present letter, referring in his critical apparatus to the reading in this letter, while noting that six of seven MSS. used for 18A have *probatum* in place of *purgatum.* However, in Letter 18B.2.5, the text is given as ". . . argentum igne probatum terrae, purgatum septuplum."

¹¹ Fortunatian, an African by birth, was Valerian's predecessor as bishop of Aquileia and evidently was tinged with Arianism. Although Jerome in this letter tells Paul he is asking for *margaritam de evangelio,* he was later to refer to Fortunatian's work disparagingly: *in evangelio titulis ordinatis brevi et rustico sermone scripsit commentarios* (*De vir. ill.* 97, wherein Jerome also castigates Fortunatian for his influence on Pope Liberius in the Arian controversies). Cf. Bardenhewer 3.486.

[12] Sextus Aurelius Victor, *floruit* 360 A.D., to whom four small historical works have been ascribed: *De caesaribus; Epitome de caesaribus; Origo gentis Romanae; De viris illustribus Romae.*

[13] Novatian, a gifted, vigorous, and evidently ambitious man, had held a leading position among the clergy at Rome, and it would seem had hopes of becoming bishop of Rome, which position went to Cornelius in March, 251. Novatian took a rigorist position on the question of reconciling apostates, as opposed to the more lenient attitude of Pope Cornelius. The Novatian schism, or sect, became widespread and lasted for several centuries; it seemingly started at least, however, from personal rather than doctrinal differences. Novatian was the first theologian of Rome to publish in Latin; his *De trinitate,* probably written well before the year 250, is important especially for the terminology and precise dogmatic formulas therein. Jerome (*De vir. ill.* 70) mentions, in addition to the *De trinitate,* the names of eight other works of Novatian and says that Novatian wrote many others. The *De trinitate* and *De cibis Judaicis* survive among the works of Tertullian. Two other works, *De spectaculis* and *De bono pudicitiae,* neither of which is cited by Jerome by name, are found among the works of St. Cyprian. As for the epistles of Novatian which Jerome is asking for in the present letter, the reference may be to two letters (30 and 36) found in the correspondence of St. Cyprian, addressed to the bishop of Carthage in answer to questions regarding the *lapsi* and written during the vacancy of the Holy See between the end of Fabian's pontificate and the election of Cornelius. Cyprian testifies that the first of these letters (30) was written by Novatian, and the contents and style of the second (36) seem to prove Novatian's authorship of it; both were sent in the name of the "presbyters and deacons abiding at Rome." A third letter among Cyprian's correspondence (28) may also have been written by Novatian; cf. B. Melin, *Studia in corpus Cyprianeum* (Uppsala 1946) 67–122. On Novatian, his writings and theology, and the Novatian schism, cf. Quasten *Patr.* 2.212–33; also E. Amann, "Novatien et novatianisme," DTC 11.1 (1931) 815–49.

[14] The reference, of course, is to the great bishop of Carthage, St. Cyprian, martyred on Sept. 14, 258. The date of Cyprian's birth is not known (even his great admirer and countryman St. Augustine says in his *Serm.* 310.1: *quando natus sit, ignoramus*) but is presumed to have been between 200 and 210. A convert, Cyprian was baptized in 245 or 246, was raised to the priesthood not long thereafter, and became bishop in 248 or 249. His episcopacy was relatively short, but active and widely influential. Although Cyprian is often described as more a man of action than of thought, a number of his works have come down

to us. Two of these, his *De lapsis* and *De catholicae ecclesiae unitate,* both relevant to his opposition to Novatianism and possibly those or among those Jerome had in mind in the present letter, have appeared in the present series: ACW 25 (1957), tr. M. Bévenot. For Cyprian, his works, his opposition to Novatianism, and his theology, cf. Quasten *Patr.* 2.340–82, wherein numerous other bibliographical references may be found. See also the useful work of X. S. Thani Nayagam, *The Carthaginian Clergy during the Episcopate of Saint Cyprian* (Tuticorin 1950).

[15] *misimus interim tibi, id est Paulo seni, Paulum seniorem.* On this "older Paul," cf. n. 1 above. The traditional dates for the life of Paul of Thebes are 228 to 341 A.D.

[16] Cf. Horace, *Ep.* 1.2.69 f.

LETTER 11

[1] In this note *ad virgines Haemonenses* and the following one to the monk Antonius of Haemona, Jerome complains of his failure to hear from them. The tone, especially of Letter 12 with its stress on the sin of pride, may seem hardly the type one would expect to elicit a friend-to-friend response. Jerome's hurt is evident. The reason for the apparent silence of the addressees is not known, but perhaps was connected with the cause of Jerome's departure from Aquileia; cf. above, n. 8 to Letter 3. Haemona has been identified with the modern Ljubljana (Laibach); cf. Cavallera 2.70. On the date and place of composition of Letters 11 and 12, cf. above, n. 1 to Letter 5.

[2] Cf. 2 Cor. 6.14.

[3] Cf. Luke 7.38.

[4] Cf. Matt. 15.27.

[5] Cf. Matt. 9.13; Mark 2.17; Luke 5.32; 1 Tim. 1.15.

[6] Luke 5.31.

[7] Cf. Ezech. 18.23 and 33.11; Luke 15.7.

[8] Cf. Luke 15.5.

[9] Cf. Luke 15.20–24.

[10] 1 Cor. 4.5.

[11] Rom. 14.4.

[12] 1 Cor. 10.12. The Vulgate reads: "Wherefore, he that thinketh himself to stand, let him take heed lest he fall."

[13] Gal. 6.2.

[14] Cf. Ezech. 18.25; Prov. 14.12.

[15] Cf. 2 Cor. 4.7.

[16] Cf. Matt. 26.69–75.

[17] Cf. Luke 7.47.

[18] Cf. Luke 15.4–7.
[19] Cf. Matt. 20.15: "... is thy eye evil, because I am good?"

LETTER 12

[1] Cf. above, n. 1 to Letter 11.
[2] Matt. 18.3. The Vulgate reads: "... unless you be converted and become as little children, you shall not enter into the kingdom of heaven."
[3] Cf. John 13.5.
[4] Cf. Matt. 26.48 ff.
[5] Cf. John 4.7–29.
[6] Cf. Luke 10.39.
[7] Cf. Mark 16.9.
[8] Cf. Isa. 14.12–15.
[9] Cf. Luke 11.43 and 20.46; Matt. 23.6; Mark 12.39.
[10] Cf. Isa. 40.15.
[11] 1 Peter 5.5; cf. James 4.6 and Prov. 3.34.
[12] Cf. Luke 18.10–14.

LETTER 13

[1] In this brief note, Jerome writes his aunt Castorina urging a reconciliation. The reasons for their break and the anger referred to by Jerome are not known, but may be related to the cause of Jerome's departure from Aquileia; cf. above, n. 8 to Letter 3. Cavallera (2.103–15, Note P) has an interesting note on "Les tribulations de saint Jérôme." In the present epistle with its comments on hate, Jerome says he has written to his aunt earlier, and he indicates that so far as he is concerned, if she is not willing to have a reconciliation now, the blame will be hers. On the date and place of composition, cf. above, n. 1 to Letter 5.
[2] 1 John 3.15.
[3] Ps. 4.5.
[4] Eph. 4.26.
[5] Matt. 5.23 f.
[6] Matt. 6.12.
[7] Cf. John 14.27.

LETTER 14

[1] In this letter to his friend Heliodorus (cf. above, n. 4 to Letter 3), Jerome recalls Heliodorus' visit with him in the Orient and Heliodorus' request for an invitation after Jerome has moved to the desert (§ 1.2:

. . . et tu ipse abiens postularas, ut tibi, postquam ad deserta migrassem, invitatoriam a me scriptam transmitterem . . .); he refers to his effort to persuade his friend also to take to a life in the desert, urges Heliodorus not to shrink from severing family ties, and delivers a virtual eulogy on the life of a hermit. "The cornerstone of St. Jerome's spiritual direction is complete renunciation" (thus E. P. Burke, "St. Jerome as a Spiritual Director," *MSJ* 151), and here we have an excellent and early example; and although Jerome himself was to give up the desert life, his espousal of asceticism and preaching of renunciation continued, with many examples offered in his numerous letters. On the time and place of composition of this letter, cf. above, n. 1 to Letter 5; also n. 2 below.

If the present epistle did not succeed in convincing the addressee to follow all the advice therein, it had nonetheless considerable success and won admiration. The celebrated Roman matron and convert Fabiola is said to have committed it to memory (cf. Jerome's Letter 77.9). The letter is written in a highly rhetorical style, and Jerome himself, writing years later in Letter 52.1.1 f., to Heliodorus' nephew Nepotian, was to speak of it somewhat disparagingly: *Dum essem adulescens, immo paene puer, et primos impetus lascivientis aetatis heremi duritia refrenarem, scripsi ad avunculum tuum, sanctum Heliodorum, exhortatoriam epistulam plenam lacrimis querimoniisque et quae deserti sodalis monstraret affectum. Sed in illo opere pro aetate tunc lusimus et calentibus adhuc rhetorum studiis atque doctrinis quaedam scolastico flore depinximus. . . .*
—Note how Jerome says in Letter 52 that he wrote Letter 14 when he was an *adulescens, immo paene puer.* One can hardly take all of Jerome's references to his age at one time or another in his life completely literally; cf. above, n. 6 to Letter 7.

² Possibly it was at Antioch that the two had discussed plans for the future. This section also suggests that this letter may have been written soon after Jerome's settlement in the desert rather than toward the end of his stay there. Cf. n. 1 to Letter 5.

³ Matt. 6.33. The Vulgate reads: "Seek ye therefore the kingdom of God and His justice, and all these things shall be added (*adjicientur;* Jerome: *adponentur*) to you."

⁴ Cf. Matt. 10.10.

⁵ It will be recalled that Heliodorus had been in military service before deciding to be a monk; cf. § 6.4 of this letter. Here and elsewhere in this letter (cf. esp. § 7.1: *. . . cur tam bene paratus ad bella non militas?*), Jerome draws upon this fact and in effect calls upon Heliodorus to be a dedicated soldier of Christ. The usage of military terminology in referring to the Christian's struggles on earth was, of course, common among early Christian writers; cf. A. Harnack, *Militia Christi: Die*

christliche Religion und der Soldatenstand in den ersten drei Jahrhun-
derten (Tübingen 1905); also E. E. Malone, *The Monk and the Martyr*
(SCA 12, Washington, D.C. 1950) 91–111: "Martyrdom and Monastic
Life as a 'militia spiritualis.'"

⁶ Cf. Apoc. 1.16.

⁷ Luke 11.23; cf. Matt. 12.30.

⁸ Cf. Col. 2.12.

⁹ Reference has already been made above (n. 1) to Heliodorus' nephew
Nepotian, to whom Jerome's Letter 52 is addressed. Jerome's Letter 60,
addressed to Heliodorus, is on the death of Nepotian.

¹⁰ Cf. Horace, *Odes* 1.3.18.

¹¹ Cf. Heb. 12.22.

¹² Cf. Vergil, *Aen.* 4.366 f.

¹³ Cf. Vergil, *Aen.* 2.677 f.

¹⁴ Cf. Persius 3.18.

¹⁵ Vergil, *Aen.* 12.59.

¹⁶ Cf. Exod. 20.12.

¹⁷ Cf. Matt. 8.21 f.

¹⁸ Cf. Matt. 16.22 f.

¹⁹ Acts 21.13. The Vulgate reads: ". . . for the name (*propter nomen;*
Jerome: *pro nomine*) of the Lord Jesus."

²⁰ Cf. Matt. 12.50; Luke 8.21.

²¹ Luke 9.60.

²² Cf. 1 Peter 5.8.

²³ Ps. 9(10).8 f.

²⁴ Cf. Vergil, *Georg.* 2.470.

²⁵ Cf. Phil. 3.19.

²⁶ Cf. 2 Tim. 1.14 and 1 Cor. 3.16 f.

²⁷ Vergil, *Aen.* 7.337 f.

²⁸ Eph. 5.5. The Vulgate reads: ". . . of Christ and of God."

²⁹ Col. 3.5 f.

³⁰ Cf. Matt. 26.15. As Labourt (1.38) remarks, this comparison of
avarice with idolatry is frequent with Jerome. Note in this volume
Jerome's remarks on avarice in Letter 22.31 ff.

³¹ Cf. Rom. 12.1.

³² Cf. Acts 5.1–11.

³³ Luke 14.33.

³⁴ Cf. Matt. 4.22.

³⁵ Cf. Matt. 9.9; Mark 2.14; Luke 5.27 f.

³⁶ Matt. 8.20; Luke 9.58.

³⁷ Cf. Horace, *Odes* 2.15.15.

³⁸ Cf. Rom. 8.17.

[39] *interpretare vocabulum monachi, hoc est nomen tuum: quid facis in turba, qui solus es?* "Monk," *monachus,* μοναχός, as Jerome points out, etymologically equates to "one who lives alone," *solus.*

[40] On the nautical allusions here, cf. above, n. 4 to Letter 1.

[41] Matt. 19.21.

[42] The "made yourself a eunuch" should hardly be taken literally; cf. Matt. 19.12.

[43] Wisd. 1.11.

[44] Cf. Matt. 6.24; Luke 16.13.

[45] Matt. 16.24.

[46] 1 John 2.6.

[47] Cf. John 4.44; Luke 4.24.

[48] Cf. John 6.15.

[49] Cf. Matt. 16.19.

[50] Cf. Matt. 3.10.

[51] Cf. Luke 21.1–4.

[52] Cf. 1 Cor. 5.5.

[53] Cf. Deut. 17.12.

[54] 1 Tim. 3.1. In connection with Jerome's remarks here, it may be worth recalling that it was only subsequent to this letter that he was ordained by Paulinus of Antioch—and perhaps also worth noting that some years later he seems to have seen himself, at least in the eyes of others (and possibly only in retrospect), as a possible successor to Pope Damasus in the papacy (cf. Letter 45.3.1: . . . *omnium paene iudicio dignus summo sacerdotio decernebar . . .*).

[55] 1 Tim. 3.2 f., with some variations from the Vulgate, notably for the Vulgate's *doctorem,* "a teacher," the word *docibilem,* "teachable," "that learns easily" (though the word here may well be being used as in John 6.45: *docibiles Dei,* "taught of God," or 2 Tim. 2.24: *docibilem,* "apt to teach"). Also, as Jerome notes in the following sentence, he has not quoted all the characteristics given in St. Paul's Epistle.

[56] *in tertio gradu.* Clergy of the "third degree" were the deacons; those of the second, priests, or presbyters; those of the first, bishops.

[57] 1 Tim. 3.8 ff.

[58] Cf. Matt. 22.12.

[59] Matt. 22.13. The Vulgate reads: *Ligatis manibus et pedibus ejus, mittite eum . . . ,* "Bind his hands and feet, and cast him. . . ."

[60] Luke 19.22 f.

[61] *qui bene ministrat, bonum gradum sibi adquirit.*

[62] Cf. 1 Cor. 11.27.

[63] Cf. Apoc. 2.6.

[64] A Gnostic sect.

[65] Cf. 1 Cor. 11.28.

[66] Cf. Acts 10.

[67] Cf. Dan. 13.45–62.

[68] Cf. Amos 7.14 f., where, however, reference is made to plucking of *sycomoros* (Douai: "wild figs").

[69] Cf. 1 Kings 16.

[70] John 13.23; 19.26; 20.2; 21.7.

[71] Cf. Luke 14.10.

[72] Cf. Isa. 66.2.

[73] Wisd. 6.7.

[74] Cf. Matt. 12.36.

[75] Cf. Matt. 5.21 f.

[76] Cf. Matt. 27.51.

[77] Cf. Apoc. 2.5.

[78] Cf. Luke 14.28.

[79] Cf. Matt. 5.13. Jerome has *a porcis,* "by swine," where the Vulgate has *ab hominibus,* "by men."

[80] Cf. Cicero, *Tusc.* 4.33.

[81] Cf. Apoc. 21.18–21.

[82] Cf. Matt. 5.3.

[83] Cf. 2 Tim. 2.5.

[84] Cf. 1 Cor. 11.3.

[85] *sed qui in Christo semel lotus est, non illi necesse est iterum lavare.* Cf. John 13.10.

[86] Rom. 8.18.

[87] Cf. 1 Cor. 15.53 f.

[88] Cf. Matt. 24.43–46; Luke 12.37; Apoc. 16.15.

[89] *hic est ille operarii et quaestuariae filius.* The use of *quaestuaria* as a reference to the Blessed Mother is unusual. Fremantle translates: "This is He whose parents were a workingman and a workingwoman." Labourt: "voici ce fils de l'artisan et de la salariée."

[90] Cf. Matt. 27.28 f. On the preceding sentence, cf. Matt. 2.13 ff.

[91] This sentence reads strangely here, but may of course be seen as a reference to John 7.20 ("The multitude answered and said: Thou hast a devil"), 8.48 ("The Jews therefore answered and said to Him: Do not we say well that thou art a Samaritan and hast a devil?"), 10.20 ("And many of them said: He hath a devil and is mad . . .").

[92] Cf. John 19.34.

[93] Cf. Matt. 28.13.

LETTER 15

[1] This is the first of Jerome's extant letters to Pope Damasus. Written perhaps in 376 (cf. above, n. 1 to Letter 5), it asks for guidance, a rule

of conduct, in the matter of the doctrinal (and semantic) controversy then dividing the Church in the East. There were at this time three claimants to the bishopric at Antioch, and of them Jerome writes here (§ 2.2): "I do not know Vitalis. I spurn Meletius. I am unacquainted with Paulinus." The first-named of these, Vitalis, apparently represented the smallest faction; he had been consecrated by Apollinaris of Laodicea, the famous Apollinaris who had fought with Athanasius and Basil against the Arians (and even Jerome was among his pupils), but whose own Christological heresy was condemned. More important here are the rival claims of Meletius and Paulinus. Meletius was successor of the Arian installed after the orthodox Catholic bishop Eustathius of Antioch had been deposed by an Arian synod and sent into exile in 326–30. Paulinus—whose consecration by Lucifer of Cagliari may have prolonged the split by hindering efforts to get Meletius recognized—was the "Eustathian" claimant. It was Paulinus who got Rome's support, whereas Meletius, who turned out to be Catholic rather than Arian, had majority support among the bishops in the East. Meletius died at Constantinople during the Second Ecumenical Council (Constantinople I), after presiding over the early sessions there. Paulinus died in 388 and was succeeded by Jerome's friend Evagrius. The split at Antioch continued, however, into the following century. For a brief summary of the period from Eustathius to 415, cf. Bardenhewer 3.237 ff. Cf. also Cavallera, *Le schisme d'Antioche* (Paris 1905). For various of the personalities involved and their works, cf. Quasten *Patr.* 3, *passim*.

Jerome writes here of the controversy over whether there is one *hypostasis* or three *hypostases* in God—a controversy which was complicated by the history of the word *hypostasis* and the lack of agreement on exactly what the word meant; cf. n. 21 below.

Whether Jerome already knew Damasus personally at this time is not known; the tone of much of the present letter might be taken as evidence that he did. In any case, Jerome emphasizes the primacy of the Roman episcopate and his readiness to abide by the Pope's decision.

[2] Cf. John 19.23.

[3] Cf. Cant. 2.15.

[4] Jer. 2.13.

[5] Cf. Cant. 4.12.

[6] *unde olim Christi vestimenta suscepi.* Jerome had been baptized at Rome. Cf. also Letter 16.2.1: *Christi vestem in Romana urbe suscipiens.*

[7] Cf. Matt. 13.46.

[8] Luke 17.37; cf. Matt. 24.28.

[9] On the "Sun of Justice," *sol iustitiae*, cf. Mal. 4.2; regarding Christ as the *Sol iustitiae*, cf. F. J. Dölger, *Die Sonne der Gerechtigkeit und der*

Schwarze (Liturgiegesch. Forsch. 2, Münster in W. 1918) 100–110. On the "Lucifer, who had fallen . . . ," cf. Isa. 14.12–15.

[10] Matt. 5.14.

[11] Matt. 5.13.

[12] Cf. 2 Tim. 2.20.

[13] Cf. Apoc. 2.27; 18.8 f.

[14] *Quamquam igitur tui me terreat magnitudo, tamen invitat humanitas.* In the following, "Your Beatitude" = *beatitudini tuae.*

[15] Cf. Lev. 19.7. On the preceding sentence, cf. Matt. 16.18.

[16] Cf. Gen. 7.23.

[17] *a sanctimonia tua.*

[18] *ideo hic collegas tuos Aegyptios confessores sequor.* Regarding these *Aegyptios confessores,* cf. above, n. 5 to Letter 3.

[19] Cf. n. 1 above.

[20] Cf. Luke 11.23.

[21] *Nunc igitur—pro dolor!—post Nicenam fidem, post Alexandrinum iuncto pariter occidente decretum trium ὑποστάσεων ab Arrianorum prole, Campensibus, novellum a me, homine Romano, nomen exigitur.*—The first condemnation of Arius, who denied the divinity of the Son and of the Holy Spirit, was at the Alexandria Synod of 318. His theology was condemned at the First Ecumenical Council, that at Nicaea in 325. In the credal formula passed at the Council of Nicaea, the term ὁμοούσιος is used (God the Son is termed ὁμοούσιον τῷ πατρί—*unius substantiae cum Patre [quod Graece dicunt homousion]*; text is given in H. Denzinger–C. Rahner, *Enchiridion symbolorum* [30th ed., 1955] § 54), and in the "anathematizing" section at the conclusion of the Creed the terms ὑπόστασις and οὐσία (*subsistentia, essentia*) are used. Perhaps at least some of the difficulties that arose might have been foreseen. The word ὁμοούσιος—used at Nicaea as meaning *unius substantiae, consubstantialis* —had been used in the past in referring to a heresy of identifying the Father and the Logos as one, and in some quarters at least in the East the word itself stank of heresy. (The Antioch Synod of 268 which condemned Paul of Samosata is said to have expressly repudiated the word ὁμοούσιος as being unfit to describe the Father-Son relationship; cf. St. Hilary, *De synodis* 81.86; St. Basil, *Epist.* 52.) Moreover, *hypostasis* came to mean to Greeks what the Latins called "person," with the result that a statement that the Son is not of another *hypostasis* than the Father (which a Latin would understand as meaning that the Father and Son are of the same nature) might be taken by a Greek in a heretical sense, that is, as meaning that the Father and the Son were one person. As Jerome's present letter makes clear, the controversy developed in part at least into a semantic one.

The Alexandria Synod of 362, presided over by Athanasius, admitted that the term *hypostasis* could be used in the meaning of "person," and that one could therefore speak of three *hypostases*. (Hence Jerome's statement in § 4.1 below that *tota saecularium litterarum schola nihil aliud hypostasin nisi usian novit*, evidently should be taken as irrelevant or exaggerated.) Athanasius' *Tomus ad Antiochenos*, written in the name of the Alexandria Synod, urged the two parties not to press the matter of one or three *hypostases*, since arguments merely over words should not be permitted to divide those who think alike. The decision of the Alexandria Synod of 362 gave rise to misunderstandings and controversies. It was Basil the Great who fixed once and for all the meaning of the words *ousia* and *hypostasis*; he maintained that μία οὐσία, τρεῖς ὑποστάσεις was the only acceptable formula. Basil died before the General Council at Constantinople in 381, which explicitly renewed the *homoousion* definition of Nicaea and which named and condemned the various varieties of Arianism. On various aspects of the questions here discussed, cf. Quasten *Patr.* 2.140 ff.; 3.28 f., 55, 206 f., 228 f., and *passim*; the chapters on the First General Council of Nicaea and the First General Council of Constantinople in P. Hughes, *The Church in Crisis: A History of the General Councils 325–1870* (Garden City, N.Y. 1961) 22–45; also n. 1 above.

The origin and full significance of the term *campenses* (here called *Arrianorum proles;* in § 5.2 below, Jerome says they *cum Tarsensibus hereticis copulantur*) are not known. Cf. the remarks in Labourt 1.163; also the article by Jülicher, "Campenses," in Pauly–Wissowa–Kroll, *Realencyclopädie der klassischen Altertumswissenschaft* 3 (Stuttgart 1899) 1443. G. Bardy, in a translation of this paragraph in "St. Jerome, and Greek Thought," MSJ 88 f., renders *campenses* as "peasants."

The present sentence is also interesting in showing that Jerome, despite his abode in the desert, considers himself a Roman: *a me, homine Romano*.

²² *et sub hac confessione vobiscum pariter cauterio unionis inurimur.* Mierow would take the meaning here as: ". . . marked with the brand of union [i.e., as Sabellian heretics, uniting the Father and the Son in one person]." G. Bardy, *art. cit.* 89, gives: "Because of such a confession, we are branded for being in union with you." The latter interpretation would seem preferable.

²³ Exod. 3.14.

²⁴ Ursinus, the antipope; Auxentius, the Arian or Arian-tinged predecessor of Ambrose in the see of Milan.

²⁵ Cf. 2 Cor. 11.14.

²⁶ Regarding Jerome's friend Evagrius, cf. above, n. 22 to Letter 1.

LETTER 16

[1] Cf. Letter 15 above and the notes thereto. Apparently Jerome had not received a reply from Damasus and writes again, this time more briefly, on the same matter. He again makes clear his own union with the chair of Peter; he says that Meletius, Vitalis, and Paulinus all *tibi haerere se dicunt* and *aut duo mentiuntur aut omnes;* and he reiterates his request for a judgment. A moving plea concludes the letter: *noli despicere animam, pro qua Christus est mortuus.*

[2] Cf. Matt. 15.21–28.

[3] Cf. Luke 11.5–8.

[4] Cf. Luke 19.8 f.

[5] Cf. Jonas 3.

[6] Cf. Luke 23.43.

[7] Cf. Luke 15.20.

[8] Cf. Luke 15.4 f.

[9] Cf. Acts 9.1–22.

[10] Cf. Phil. 1.13 f.

[11] Horace, *Ep.* 1.11.27.

[12] *hinc enim praesidiis fulta mundi Arriana rabies fremit.*

[13] Cf. Matt. 19.28.

[14] Cf. John 21.18.

[15] *municipatum caeli.* Cf. Phil. 3.20: "Nostra autem conversatio in caelis est. . . ."

[16] Cf. 1 Cor. 8.11.

LETTER 17

[1] This letter to the priest Mark indicates that the religious controversy about which Jerome wrote to Pope Damasus in Letters 15 and 16 is now pushing in hard on him despite his protestations of orthodoxy. *Non mihi conceditur unus angulus heremi,* Jerome writes, and he states that he will soon be leaving. On the dating of this letter, cf. above, n. 1 to Letter 5.

[2] Ps. 38.2 f. The Vulgate reads: "I have set a guard to my mouth, when the sinner stood against me. I was dumb. . . ."

[3] Ps. 37.14 f.

[4] Cf. 1 Cor. 13.7.

[5] Cf. Cyprian, *Ep.* 59.13.

[6] Vergil, *Aen.* 1.539 ff.

[7] Cf. Col. 3.15.

[8] Cf. Esth. 4.3.

[9] Jerome's reference to himself as being at this point in his life *eloquentissimus homo in Syro sermone vel Graeco* can be taken as ironical exaggeration.

[10] 2 Thess. 3.10.

[11] Cf. Isa. 42.14.

[12] Cf. John 3.5.

[13] Cf. Horace, *Odes* 2.17.5.

[14] Ps. 23.1.

[15] Gal. 6.14.

[16] It is not known who this Cyril is.

[17] Not otherwise known.

LETTER 18A

[1] This letter provides a commentary on Isaias' vision of the seraphim and of the Lord sitting on a throne (Isa. 6.1–9) and appears to be the earliest of Jerome's biblical works, apart from translations, that have come down to us. It, perhaps in combination with Letter 18B, would seem to be the *brevem . . . subitumque tractatum* on this vision of Isaias which Jerome, writing about thirty years later (*In Isaiam* 1), tells us was composed during his stay at Constantinople, and a likely date of composition is the year 381. The work seems more a treatise or essay than an epistle, but Damasus is the manuscript-named person to whom both Letters 18A and 18B were dedicated or addressed.

Letters 18A and 18B, published earlier as a single epistle or tract but given separately by Hilberg, seem clearly to have been composed at different times. The language of § 16.2 of Letter 18A indicates that a break occurred at that point, and the *in alio loco disputavimus* in § 4 of Letter 18B seems a reference back to § 15 of Letter 18A. Both may have been composed at Constantinople. It is also possible that Letter 18B may have been presented to Damasus personally in Rome; in any case, 18B reads as a sort of supplement to 18A, and one may speculate on whether it might have been in reply to a request for further commentary on the verses treated, or possibly in response to criticism that Jerome had skimped in 18A in treating of the last few verses of the passage under consideration.

On Jerome and his approach to exegesis, cf. the article by L. N. Hartmann, "St. Jerome as an Exegete," MSJ 35–81. Regarding Letter 18, Hartmann (39) comments: "This . . . already shows the exegetical method that he [Jerome] was to follow more or less closely in all his subsequent work: a large dependence on previous commentators combined with a certain independent judgment of his own. Here, for instance, he borrowed freely from Origen; yet, at least in one important point (the interpretation of the two Seraphim as signifying God the Son and the Holy Ghost), he rejected the exegesis of the Alexandrian sage. This rejection was to prove very useful to him when, some years later, he was accused of being a blind follower of Origen. . . ."—Regarding Jerome's general attitude toward Scripture and the unity of Holy Writ, cf., e.g., his comment in § 7.4 of Letter 18A: *quidquid enim in veteri legimus testamento, hoc idem et in evangelio repperimus et, quod in evangelio fuerit lectitatum, hoc ex veteris testamenti auctoritate deducitur; nihil dissonum, nihil diversum est.* On meanings to be found in Scripture, cf., e.g., the excerpt in n. 73 below.

The Oration of the Mass for the feast of St. Jerome (Sept. 30) reads in part: "Deus, qui ecclesiae tuae in exponendis sacris scripturis beatum Hieronymum confessorem tuum, doctorem maximum providere dignatus es. . . ." On the terminology here regarding Jerome, and how it can be interpreted, cf. Hartmann, *art. cit.* 68, where note is also taken of views of L. Murillo, "S. Jerónimo, el 'Doctor Máximo,'" *Biblica* 1 (1920) 447 ff.

[2] 740/739 B.C.

[3] Hilberg here says "gloria *scripsi,*" and as justification for changing from *maiestate* refers to the reading *gloria* at the beginning of § 5 below (where he notes in his critical apparatus that two of seven manuscripts have *maiestate*).

[4] Isa. 6.1–9. Since Jerome considers the text in detail, his reading here is given below side by side with the Latin of the Vulgate:

Letter 18A	*Vulgate*
(1) Et factum est in anno, quo mortuus est rex Ozias: vidi Dominum sedentem super thronum excelsum et elevatum, et plena domus a gloria eius.	(1) In anno quo mortuus est rex Ozias, vidi Dominum sedentem super solium excelsum et elevatum; et ea quae sub ipso erant replebant templum.
(2) Et seraphim stabant in circuitu eius: sex alae uni et sex alae alteri. Et duabus quidem velabant faciem et duabus velabant pedes et duabus volabant.	(2) Seraphim stabant super illud: sex alae uni, et sex alae alteri; duabus velabant faciem ejus, et duabus velabant pedes ejus, et duabus volabant.
(3) Et clamabant alter ad alterum et dicebant: sanctus sanctus sanctus Dominus sabaoth, plena est universa terra gloria eius.	(3) Et clamabant alter ad alterum, et dicebant: Sanctus, sanctus, sanctus Dominus, Deus exercituum; plena est omnis terra gloria ejus.
(4) Et elevatum est superliminare	(4) Et commota sunt superlimin-

a voce, qua clamabant, et domus inpleta est fumo.

(5) Et dixi: O miser ego, quoniam conpunctus sum, quia, cum sim homo et inmunda labia habeam, in medio quoque populi inmunda labia habentis habitem, et regem Dominum sabaoth ego vidi oculis meis.

(6) Et missum est ad me unum de seraphim, et in manu sua habebat carbonem, quem forcipe acceperat de altari.

(7) Et tetigit os meum et dixit: Ecce tetigit hoc labia tua et auferet iniquitates tuas et peccata tua circumpurgabit.

(8) Et audivi vocem Domini dicentis: Quem mittam et quis ibit ad populum istum? Et dixi: Ecce ego, mitte me.

(9) Et ait: Vade et dic populo huic: Aure audietis et non intellegetis, et cernentes aspicietis et non videbitis.

aria cardinum a voce clamantis, et domus repleta est fumo.

(5) Et dixi: Vae mihi, quia tacui, quia vir pollutus labiis ego sum, et in medio populi polluta labia habentis ego habito et regem Dominum exercituum vidi oculis meis.

(6) Et volavit ad me unus de Seraphim, et in manu ejus calculus, quem forcipe tulerat de altari,

(7) et tetigit os meum et dixit: Ecce tetigit hoc labia tua, et auferetur iniquitas tua, et peccatum tuum mundabitur.

(8) Et audivi vocem Domini dicentis: Quem mittam? et quis ibit nobis? Et dixi: Ecce ego, mitte me.

(9) Et dixit: Vade, et dices populo huic: Audite audientes, et nolite intelligere; et videte visionem, et nolite cognoscere.

[5] Isa. 6.1.   Hereafter in the notes the individual verses or parts thereof as quoted by Jerome for exegetical comment will not be identified separately.

[6] Cf. 4 Kings 15.1–7 (where Azarias = Ozias).

[7] Cf. 2 Par. (= Chronicles) 26.

[8] 2 Par. 26.4.

[9] 2 Par. 26.5.

[10] Ps. 82.17.   For the preceding, cf. 2 Par. 18 f.

[11] Cf. Exod. 28.38.

[12] Cf. Ezech. 9.4.   Tav (taw) is the last letter of the Hebrew alphabet, and also means "a sign" or "a mark."   In the ancient Hebrew character the form of the tav was the form of a cross.   The text in Ezechiel, however, does not indicate the nature of the mark.

[13] Ps. 4.7.

[14] Goliath; cf. 1 Kings 17.49 ff.

[15] Cf. 4 Kings 15.2 and 2 Par. 26.3.

[16] "Chronicles" here = *Temporum librum.* (In § 1.2 above, the phrase "in the books of Kings and of the Chronicles" = *in Regnorum et Praeteritorum libris.*) The present reference is to the *Chronicle* of Eusebius of Caesarea. The Greek original of this work, written about 303, has not survived except for some fragments and excerpts. There is, however, an Armenian translation of the sixth century, and also extant is the second part in the Latin version prepared by Jerome in or about 380. Both the Armenian and Jerome's versions are based on a revision which continued the chronicle up to the twentieth year of Constantine's reign; Jerome also added entries, bringing it up to the year 378. Cf. Quasten *Patr.* 3.311 ff., where the *Chronicle* is termed "one of the fundamental books upon which all research on the past of mankind has been based."

[17] *nec in mysterio fidei ter sancti nomen auditum est.*

[18] Cf. Exod. 1.14. For the following sentence, cf. Exod. 3.15.

[19] Exod. 2.23.

[20] Ezech. 11.13.

[21] Rom. 6.12.

[22] Cf. Dan. 7.9.

[23] Cf. Joel 3.12.

[24] Cf. Eph. 1.21; Col. 1.16.

[25] Here we see an example of Jerome's independence of judgment; cf. n. 1 above.

[26] . . . *multo si quidem melius est vera rustice quam diserte falsa proferre.* . . .

[27] John 12.39 ff. The Vulgate reads: "Therefore they could not believe, because Isaias said again: 'He hath blinded their eyes, and hardened their heart, that they should not see with their eyes, nor understand with their heart, and be converted, and I should heal them.' These things said Isaias, when he saw His glory, and spoke of Him." Cf. Isa. 6.10.

[28] *In praesenti volumine Esaiae.*

[29] Acts 28.25 ff.

[30] Ps. 23.1.

[31] John 1.16.

[32] Cf. Prov. 14.1.

[33] Isa. 2.2, with some variation from the Vulgate.

[34] Heb. 3.5 f. Significantly different from the Vulgate version are the last two clauses, which read in the Vulgate: "which house are we, if we hold fast the confidence and glory of hope unto the end." The "of which house are we" in the present epistle = *cuius domus sumus nos,* which could also be translated "whose house are we."

[35] 1 Tim. 3.14 f.

[36] These questions are indirect in the original, dependent on the initial "We wish to know. . . ."

[37] *non minimum pulverem.*

[38] *aut 'incendium' aut 'principium oris eorum' interpretantur.* Cf. Jerome's *De nominibus hebraicis* (ML 23.830): *ardentes vel incendentes.* Regarding this work on Hebrew proper names, note Hartmann's remarks (*art. cit.* 43) that it "has now not much more value than a museum curio" and "offers in most cases mere fanciful and popular etymologies devoid of scientific exactness," although Jerome's *Book on the Sites and Names of Hebrew Places* "will always retain a certain scientific value." The latter reference is to Jerome's translation (with his own additions, and some omissions) of the *Onomasticon* of Eusebius of Caesarea. Both the *Onomasticon* and Jerome's Latin version are extant and "present even today the most important source for the topography of the Holy Land" (thus Quasten *Patr.* 3.336).

[39] Luke 12.49, with variation from the Vulgate.

[40] Luke 24.32, slightly abbreviated.

[41] Cf. Deut. 4.24.

[42] Cf. Ezech. 8.2.

[43] Ps. 11.7. On the variation from the Vulgate here, cf. above, n. 10 to Letter 10.

[44] Cf. Gen. 11.1–9.

[45] Victorinus of Pettau, who died as a martyr, most probably in 304, and to whom Jerome elsewhere refers critically though kindly: *Victorino martyri in libris suis, licet desit eruditio, tamen non deest eruditionis voluntas* (Letter 70.5.2); *Victorinus martyrio coronatus, quod intellegit eloqui non potest* (Letter 58.10.1). In his *De vir. ill.* 74, Jerome mentions a number of Victorinus' works, but of these relatively little has survived. The so-called *Decretum Gelasianum de libris recipiendis et non recipiendis* declared the works of Victorinus "apocryphal," probably because of their chiliastic tendencies. Cf. Quasten *Patr.* 2.411 ff.

[46] Cf. 3 Kings 18.31 f.

[47] Deut. 7.5.

[48] Cf. Exod. 28.17–21 and 39.10–14.

[49] Cf. Ezech. 28.13 and Apoc. 21.19 f.

[50] Isa. 41.22 f., where the Vulgate reads: "Let them come, and tell us all things that are to come: tell us the former things what they were: and we will set our heart [upon them], and shall know the latter end of them, and tell us the things that are to come. Shew the things that are to come hereafter, and we shall know that ye are gods. . . ."

[51] Aquila, second-century A.D. Jewish translator of the Hebrew Old

Testament into Greek.   His translation was quite literal.   Cf. also below, n. 2 to Letter 18B.

[52] Ps. 23.9.

[53] Ps. 23.10.   "Lord of Virtues" here = *Dominus virtutum,* which the Vulgate also has and the Douai translates as "Lord of Hosts."   (The New Psalter has *Dominus exercituum.*)   In the following, Jerome gives *Dominus militiarum* for Aquila's version, translated here as "Lord of Hosts."

[54] That is, the translators of the Septuagint version of the Scriptures. The Septuagint version of the Pentateuch may perhaps date from around 250 B.C., but the production of the whole Septuagint evidently was protracted over a considerable period; cf. E. Power, "The Languages, Texts and Versions of the Bible," CCHS § 23g–j.   Regarding Jerome's attitude toward the Septuagint translation, and his comments later discounting the story of seventy (seventy-two) Hebrew scholars working independently in an equal number of cells and turning out their version of the Pentateuch in seventy (seventy-two) days, cf. Hartmann, *art. cit.* 65 f., and P. W. Skehan, "St. Jerome and the Canon of the Holy Scriptures," MSJ 259–87.

[55] That is, the Tetragrammaton, now rendered as "Yahweh," although the old pronunciation is not known.   It is rendered κύριος (*dominus,* "Lord") in the Septuagint.   Hilberg gives Jerome's text as ". . . iod he iod he, id est duobus IA . . . ," but notes one manuscript reading where the third consonant is given as "vau."   (Iod = J or Y; he = H; vau = W or V.)   Yahweh was, among the Jews, the personal name for God, but was in later times rarely pronounced; cf. J. L. McKenzie, "The Jewish World in New Testament Times," CCHS § 591c.   On the name Yahweh and its occurrence in Scripture, cf. also E. F. Sutcliffe, "Introduction to the Pentateuch," CCHS § 133a–d; E. Power, "Exodus," CCHS § 165a–c.

[56] Cf. Exod. 33.9 f.

[57] Cant. 1.3.   The Vulgate has *cellaria sua,* "his storerooms," where Jerome here has *cubiculum suum.*

[58] i.e., ἐπήρθη.   As Jerome observes in the next sentence, there is *ambiguitas* in the word *sublatum* (which can mean either "lifted up" or "removed," "taken away"); *nostri,* he writes, '*elevatum*' *interpretati sunt pro* '*ablato.*'

[59] Cf. Exod. 19.16–19.

[60] Cf. Ps. 103.32.

[61] 1 Cor. 13.9.

[62] 1 Cor. 13.12.

[63] It is not established to whom this reference is; Labourt (1.64) suggests perhaps Gregory of Nazianzus, if not Origen.

[64] Cf. Matt. 27.51.

[65] Cf. Josephus, *Bell. Iud.* 5.3.—This is the first time in Jerome's extant correspondence that we find the name of this famous Jewish historian of the first century A.D., Flavius Josephus. Note the remark of P. Courcelle, *Les lettres grecques en occident de Macrobe à Cassiodore* (Paris 1943) 71: "Le seul historien profane que Jérôme connaisse à fond et chez lequel il puise perpétuellement pour ses commentaires historiques de l'Écriture, est Josèphe."

[66] Possibly the reference here is to the convert from Judaism to Christianity whom Jerome, as he tells us in Letter 125.12, asked to teach him Hebrew.

[67] Cf. 4 Kings 24.17 f. and 25.7; Jer. 39.7.

[68] Cf. 4 Kings 25.22; Jer. 40.7.

[69] Cf. 4 Kings 25.25; Jer. 41.2.

[70] This is not from the Bible, but rather according to Jewish legend or tradition. Note that in § 13.1 of this letter Jerome says: *Aiunt Iudaei Esaiam a maioribus suis idcirco interemptum.* . . .

[71] Cf. Matt. 5.30 and 18.8 f.; Mark 9.42–46.

[72] *secundi baptismatis purgatione, id est ignis, indigeo.* Cf. Matt. 3.11: ". . . He that shall come after me . . . shall baptize you in the Holy Ghost and fire."—Regarding Jerome's allusions to his sins, cf. above, n. 2 to Letter 2.

[73] *Non sunt, ut quidam putant, in scripturis verba simplicia; plurimum in his absconditum est. Aliud littera, aliud mysticus sermo significat.* Cf. n. 1 above.

[74] Cf. John 13.4 f.

[75] John 13.8 f.

[76] Isa. 52.7, abbreviated and with variation from the Vulgate.

[77] Cant. 5.3.

[78] Cf. Matt. 10.14.

[79] Cf. 1 Cor. 9.20.

[80] Cf. 2 Par. 26.16–19; 3 Kings 21.17–26.

[81] Cf. § 11.1 above and n. 70 thereto.

[82] Cf. Exod. 33.20–23.

[83] Exod. 33.20, considerably abbreviated.

[84] Cf. Exod. 33.11.

[85] *evangelicum testamentum.*

[86] Cf. Prov. 30.5.

[87] Cf. Gen. 28.12 f.

[88] Cf. Apoc. 1.16.

[89] Cf. Mark 12.41–44.

[90] Cf. Matt. 17.24 ff.

[91] Ps. 119.2.

[92] Ps. 119.3 f.

[93] Cf. Isa. 47.14 f.: ". . . there are no coals wherewith they may be warmed, nor fire, that they may sit thereat. Such are all the things become to thee, in which thou hast labored. . . ."

[94] Cf. Exod. 4.10 and 13.

[95] Matt. 7.7.

[96] Isa. 40.6.

[96a] Jer. 25.15 f., with several variations from the Vulgate, esp. *vini meri huius* for the Vulgate's *vini furoris huius*, "wine of this fury."

[97] Jer. 25.17 f. The principal variation here from the Vulgate is in the final part of the quoted section, which in the Vulgate reads: ". . . a desolation, and an astonishment, and a hissing, and a curse, as it is at this day." Also, the Vulgate continues with the listing.

[98] Jer. 20.7, with some variations from the Vulgate.

[99] Cf. Exod. 2.11–15.

[100] Exod. 3.5.

[101] Cf. Exod. 4.10.

[102] Cf. Matt. 13.14 f.; Mark 4.12; Luke 8.10; John 12.39 ff.; Acts 28.25–28; Rom. 11.8.

[103] From the language of this paragraph it seems clear that a break occurred at the end of Letter 18A; cf. n. 1 above.—A number of references to dictating will be found in Jerome's letters. Regarding Jerome's use of stenographic help, and the evidence in his works that he could not always bear the expense of such, cf. Sr. M. Jamesetta Kelly, *Life and Times as Revealed in the Writings of St. Jerome Exclusive of His Letters* (PSt 70, Washington, D.C. 1944) 24 ff.: "Stenographers and Copyists."

LETTER 18B

[1] Cf. n. 1 to Letter 18A.

[2] Isa. 6.6. As in the case of Letter 18A, it is not considered necessary to identify in the notes each verse or part thereof of the passage from Isaias as Jerome sets it out for comment.—Reference has already been made to the Septuagint and to Aquila (nn. 51 and 54 to Letter 18A). Theodotion and Symmachus each translated the Hebrew Scriptures into Greek, Theodotion's version dating from about 180 A.D., Symmachus' from about 200 A.D. The Aquila, Symmachus, Septuagint, and Theodotion versions were contained in the third, fourth, fifth, and sixth

columns respectively of the famous *Hexapla* compiled by Origen about 250 A.D.   The first column of the *Hexapla* had the Hebrew text in Hebrew letters, and the second column had the Hebrew text in Greek letters.   Cf. E. Power, *art. cit.*, esp. § 23k–o; also in the present series, R. P. Lawson, ACW 26 (1957) 359 f.

[3] Ps. 79.2.

[4] Cf. Jer. 20.9.

[5] Cf. Gal. 2.20 ("And I live, now not I, but Christ liveth in me . . .") and 1 Cor. 15.10 (". . . His grace in me . . ."). For the preceding, cf. Col. 3.9 f. (". . . stripping yourselves of the old man with his deeds, and putting on the new . . .").

[6] Cf. Heb. 1.1.

[7] Cf. Exod. 4.25.

[8] Cf. John 15.3.

[9] Cf. Apoc. 2.17.

[10] Cf. Exod. 28.18 and 39.11.

[11] Ps. 11.7.   On the variation here from the Vulgate, cf. above, n. 10 to Letter 10.

[12] Ps. 18.9.

[13] Prov. 18.21.

[14] Ps. 62.11.   The Vulgate reads: "They shall be delivered into the hands (*in manus*) of the sword. . . ."

[15] Cf. Ps. 129.4, where the Douai's "merciful forgiveness" = *propitiatio* in the Vulgate.

[16] 1 John 2.2.

[17] *in alio loco disputavimus.*   Cf. Letter 18A.15; also n. 1 to Letter 18A.

[17a] The reference here is clearly to Jewish traditions.   The word δευτέρωσις, the equivalent of the Hebrew *mišnāh*, means literally "repetition."   In Letter 121.10, Jerome tells us that the Jews call their tradition δευτέρωσις.

[18] Gen. 1.26.

[19] Cant. 2.10 f.   The Vulgate reads: "Arise, make haste, my love, my dove, my beautiful one, and come.   For winter is now past, the rain is over and gone."   For "the rain is over and gone," the Vulgate has *imber abiit, et recessit,* whereas Jerome here has *pluvia abiit sibi.*

[20] Cf. Matt. 7.24 f.; Luke 6.48.

[21] Cf. Rom. 4.17.

[22] Exod. 3.14.

[23] Cf. 1 Thess. 1.1; Acts 15–18, *passim.*   Note that where Jerome says "in Hebrew," *lingua Hebraea,* we would today say "in Aramaic."

LETTER 19

[1] In this brief note Pope Damasus asks Jerome to write regarding the meaning *apud Hebraeos* of the phrase *osanna filio David*. See the following letter.—Jerome left Constantinople in 382, and with Bishops Paulinus and Epiphanius went to Rome. What role he may have played in the Roman synod of 382 we do not know. In the phrase *sicut et de multis* in the last sentence of the present letter we may have an indication, though not a particularly strong one, that Jerome had been in Rome for some time before this note was written. A probable date of composition is 383; cf. Cavallera 2.26 and 155.—The "by men of our persuasion, that is, the orthodox" = *a nostris, id est orthodoxis, viris.*

[2] Matt. 21.9. Cf. Mark 11.10; John 12.13.

LETTER 20

[1] This letter from Jerome to Damasus on the meaning of the word *osanna* presumably was written shortly after the Pope's request in Letter 19, i.e., probably also in 383. Cf. n. 1 to Letter 19. The lack of a preamble or introductory paragraph in the present instance may be further indication that Jerome had been in Rome for some time.—Throughout this letter the word "hosanna" is written without the aspirate, i.e., as *osanna.*

[2] *noster*, "our," in Christian Latin literature can mean that the person in question is a Christian and not a pagan; or also that he is a Latin instead of Greek.

[3] The reference is to St. Hilary, author of a number of works, who was bishop of Poitiers, and who died *ca.* 367.

[4] *ad ipsum fontem, unde ab evangelistis sumptum est.*

[5] Matt. 2.23. Matthew, of course, wrote his Gospel in "Hebrew" (i.e., Aramaic).

[6] Matt. 2.15. Cf. Osee 11.1: ". . . and I called my son out of Egypt."

[7] Matt. 21.9.

[8] Mark 11.9 f. The Vulgate lacks the second "in the name of the Lord."

[9] John 12.13.

[10] Luke 19.38.

[11] Ps. 117.25 f.

[12] *quinta editio.* In the prologue addressed to Pope Damasus which Jerome prefixed to his translation (in or about 383) of two homilies of Origen on the Canticle of Canticles, Jerome mentions the Septuagint, Aquila, Symmachus, and Theodotion translations of the Hebrew Scrip-

tures (cf. above, n. 2 to Letter 18B), "and finally a fifth, which he [Origen] tells us he found on the coast near Actium" (= ACW 26.265). In the following sentence of the present letter, Jerome mentions a *sexta editio*, also anonymous. Eusebius (*Hist. eccl.* 6.16.2 f.) reports Origen as saying he found the *quinta* at Nicopolis, near Actium, and as stating in the *Hexapla* of the Psalms that of the *sexta* and *septima* used by him he had found one version in an earthen jar at Jericho. Epiphanius (*De mens. et pond.* 14 f.) says the *quinta* was found in some jars near Jericho and the *sexta* in some jars at Nicopolis. Cf. the remarks and additional references cited by R. P. Lawson, ACW 26.359 f.

[13] Actually Ps. 114.4.

[14] *propter barbariam linguae pariter ac litterarum.*

[15] Ps. 117.22–27.

[16] Matt. 21.15.

[17] Matt. 21.16; cf. Ps. 8.3.

[18] . . . *ponant verbum petentis affectu et dicant 'anna domine,' quod Septuaginta dixerunt 'o domine.'*

[19] The quotation is from Vergil, *Aen.* 1.37.

[20] Ps. 117.25 f. The Vulgate has *bene prosperare* for Jerome's *bene conplace* here. (But in § 4.1 above, Jerome has *bene prospera*.)

[21] Matt. 21.9.

[22] Isa. 34.5.

[23] *sed magis condecet ob veritatem laborare paulisper et peregrino aurem adcommodare sermoni, quam de aliena lingua fictam ferre sententiam.*

LETTER 21

[1] In this rather long letter, again to Pope Damasus, we have a commentary by Jerome on the parable of the prodigal son (Luke 15.11–32; cf. n. 42 below). Jerome is responding to a number of questions by Damasus. A likely time of composition is the year 383 in Rome; cf. Cavallera 2.26 and 155.

[2] Possibly an allusion to Prov. 17.28: "Even a fool, if he will hold his peace, shall be counted wise: and if he close his lips, a man of understanding."

[3] Luke 15.29.

[4] Luke 15.31.

[5] Cf. Rom. 5.12.

[6] Cf. Luke 15.2; Matt. 9.11; Mark 2.16.

[7] Luke 15.1.

[8] Matt. 9.10–13.

[9] Cf. Mark 2.15 ff.

[10] *lex quippe iusti tenax clementiam non habebat.*

[11] Cf. Exod. 21.23 ff.

[12] Ps. 13.3, quoted in Rom. 3.12. The Vulgate reads: " . . . is none that doth good, there is not so much as one."

[13] Rom. 5.20.

[14] Gal. 4.4.

[15] Cf. Eph. 2.14.

[16] Rom. 1.7. The Vulgate reads: ". . . from God, our Father. . . ."

[17] *gratia, quae non ex merito retributa, sed ex donante concessa est.*

[18] Cf. 1 John 2.2.

[19] Cf. Col. 2.13 ff. The "on the tree" = *in ligno.*

[20] Cf. Vergil, *Ecl.* 4.61. Cf. also Wisd. 7.4: "In the time of ten months . . . ," where perhaps lunar months are meant.

[21] Cf. Luke 2.12 and 51.

[22] Cf. Gal. 3.13.

[23] Cf. Phil. 2.8.

[24] Luke 17.21, somewhat paraphrased and condensed.

[25] Cf. Rom. 8.3.

[26] Cf. Gal. 5.4.

[27] Matt. 11.19; cf. Luke 15.2.

[28] Cf. Matt. 12.10 ff.

[29] Cf. Luke 15.4–7.

[30] Luke 15.9.

[31] Cf. § 1 above.

[32] That is, Tertullian's *De pudicitia* (= ACW 28 [1959] 53–125), termed by W. P. Le Saint (ACW 28.41) "one of Tertullian's most violent Montanist treatises—a passionate, bigoted and yet utterly sincere attack on the doctrine and discipline of the orthodox Church." Jerome writes here: *Unde vehementer admiror Tertullianum in eo libro, quem de pudicitia adversum paenitentiam scripsit et sententiam veterem nova opinione dissolvit.* . . . Regarding the *adversum paenitentiam*, it should, of course, be recalled that Tertullian did not oppose all repentance and penance, and that there was a distinction in his theology between "remissible" sins and sins which were considered to be "irremissible" (i.e., by the Church, not by God). Cf. Le Saint's Introduction (ACW 28.41–52) to his translation of the *De pudicitia.* Jerome goes on to say here that Tertullian *hoc voluisse sentire, quod publicani et peccatores, qui cum domino vescebantur, ethnici fuerint dicente scriptura: non erit vectigal pendens ex Israhel.* . . . Cf. *De pudicitia* 9 (ACW 28.75 f.), where, however, Tertullian concedes that some of the sinners may have been Jews.

[33] *non erit vectigal pendens ex Israhel*—possibly an allusion to Deut. 23.19 f., though there the condemnation is of usury, not of taking of tribute. Tertullian (*De pudicitia* 9: ACW 28.76) has: "There shall be no weigher of tribute from among the sons of Israel."

[34] Cf. Matt. 9.9; Mark 2.14; Luke 5.27.

[35] Cf. Luke 18.13.

[36] Luke 7.29.

[37] Cf. Matt. 5.17.

[38] Cf. Matt. 10.6; 15.24.

[39] Matt. 15.26. The Vulgate has: "It is not good to take the bread of the children and to cast it to the dogs."

[40] Matt. 10.5.

[41] *quia iuxta insanas feminas suas id dogmatis defendebat.* The *insanas feminas* would seem to be a reference to Prisca (Priscilla) and Maximilla, the two "prophetesses" of Montanism. After Tertullian went over openly to the Montanists, he became the head of a special sect among them, the so-called Tertullianists.

[42] The *ipsa evangelii verba* Jerome sets forth to comment on comprise the parable of the prodigal son in Luke 15.11–32, and it is not considered necessary to identify in these notes each verse or part thereof of the passage as quoted by him in the following. To facilitate identification of textual variations, mainly minor here, the Vulgate version and Jerome's version as compiled from quotations in the present letter are given side by side below:

Letter 21	*Vulgate*
(11) Homo quidam habebat duos filios.	(11) Ait autem: Homo quidam habuit duos filios.
(12) Et dixit illi adulescentior: Pater, da mihi portionem substantiae, quae me contingit. Qui divisit eis substantiam.	(12) Et dixit adolescentior ex illis patri: Pater, da mihi portionem substantiae quae me contingit. Et divisit illis substantiam.
(13) Et non post multos dies collectis omnibus adulescentior filius peregre profectus est in regionem longinquam. Et ibi dissipavit substantiam suam vivens luxuriose.	(13) Et non post multos dies, congregatis omnibus, adolescentior filius peregre profectus est in regionem longinquam, et ibi dissipavit substantiam suam vivendo luxuriose.
(14) Cumque consumpsisset omnia, facta est fames valida per regionem illam. Et ipse coepit egere	(14) Et postquam omnia consummasset, facta est fames valida in regione illa, et ipse coepit egere.

(15) et abiit et coniunxit se uni de principibus regionis illius. Qui misit illum in agro suo, ut pasceret porcos.

(16) Et cupiebat saturare ventrem suum de siliquis porcorum, et nemo illi dabat.

(17) In se autem conversus dixit: Quanti mercenarii patris mei abundant pane, ego autem hic fame pereo!

(18) Surgens ibo ad patrem meum. Et dicam illi: Pater, peccavi in caelum et coram te;

(19) iam non sum dignus vocari filius tuus. Fac me sicut unum ex mercenariis tuis.

(20) Et venit usque ad patrem suum. Cumque adhuc longe esset, vidit eum pater eius et misericordia motus est. Et procurrens incubuit super collum ipsius. Et osculatus est eum.

(21) Dixit autem illi filius: Pater, peccavi in caelum et coram te; iam non sum dignus vocari filius tuus.

(22) Dixit autem pater ad pueros suos: Celerius proferte stolam priorem. Et date anulum in manu illius. Et calciamenta in pedibus eius.

(23) Et adferte vitulum saginatum et occidite, et manducemus et epulemur,

(24) quoniam hic filius meus mortuus fuerat et revixit, perierat et inventus est. Et coeperunt epulari.

(25) Erat autem filius illius senior in agro. Et cum veniret, adpropinquavit domui et audivit symphoniam et chorum.

(15) Et abiit, et adhaesit uni civium regionis illius. Et misit illum in villam suam, ut pasceret porcos.

(16) Et cupiebat implere ventrem suum de siliquis, quas porci manducabant; et nemo illi dabat.

(17) In se autem reversus, dixit: Quanti mercenarii in domo patris mei abundant panibus, ego autem hic fame pereo!

(18) Surgam, et ibo ad patrem meum, et dicam ei: Pater, peccavi in caelum, et coram te:

(19) Jam non sum dignus vocari filius tuus: fac me sicut unum de mercenariis tuis.

(20) Et surgens venit ad patrem suum. Cum autem adhuc longe esset, vidit illum pater ipsius, et misericordia motus est, et accurrens cecidit super collum ejus, et osculatus est eum.

(21) Dixitque ei filius: Pater, peccavi in caelum, et coram te; jam non sum dignus vocari filius tuus.

(22) Dixit autem pater ad servos suos: Cito proferte stolam primam, et induite illum, et date anulum in manum ejus, et calceamenta in pedes ejus,

(23) et adducite vitulum saginatum, et occidite, et manducemus, et epulemur,

(24) quia hic filius meus mortuus erat, et revixit; perierat, et inventus est. Et coeperunt epulari.

(25) Erat autem filius ejus senior in agro; et cum veniret, et appropinquaret domui, audivit symphoniam, et chorum,

(26) Et vocavit unum de pueris et interrogavit, quidnam essent haec. (27) Qui ait illi, quoniam frater tuus venit et occidit pater tuus vitulum saginatum, quoniam incolumem illum recepit. (28) Iratus autem noluit intrare. Egressus autem pater illius coepit rogare eum. (29) Ipse autem respondens ait patri suo: Ecce tot annis servio tibi et numquam mandatum tuum praeterivi. Et numquam dedisti mihi haedum, ut cum amicis meis epularer. (30) Cum autem filius tuus hic, qui comedit omnem facultatem suam vivens cum meretricibus, venit, et occidisti ei vitulum saginatum. (31) Ipse autem dixit illi: Fili, tu mecum es semper et omnia mea tua sunt. (32) Epulari nos oportet et gaudere, quoniam hic frater tuus mortuus fuerat et revixit, perierat et inventus est.

(26) et vocavit unum de servis, et interrogavit quid haec essent. (27) Isque dixit illi: Frater tuus venit, et occidit pater tuus vitulum saginatum, quia salvum illum recepit. (28) Indignatus est autem, et nolebat introire. Pater ergo illius egressus, coepit rogare illum. (29) At ille respondens, dixit patri suo: Ecce tot annis servio tibi, et nunquam mandatum tuum praeterivi, et nunquam dedisti mihi haedum ut cum amicis meis epularer. (30) Sed postquam filius tuus hic, qui devoravit substantiam suam cum meretricibus, venit, occidisti illi vitulum saginatum. (31) At ipse dixit illi: Fili, tu semper mecum es, et omnia mea tua sunt. (32) Epulari autem et gaudere oportebat, quia frater tuus hic mortuus erat et revixit, perierat et inventus est.

[43] John 8.17 f., much condensed.
[44] Cf. Matt. 18.12 ff. and Luke 15.4 ff.
[45] Cf. Matt. 20.1–16.
[46] Cf. Matt. 21.33; Mark 12.1; Luke 20.9.
[47] Cf. Matt. 22.2–14.
[48] John 1.9.
[49] Cf. Matt. 5.29.
[50] Cf. Matt. 6.22; Luke 11.34.
[51] Cf. Luke 19.20.
[52] Cf. Philem. 14.
[53] Cf. Isa. 40.12.
[54] Jer. 23.23. The Vulgate reads: "Am I, think ye, a God at hand, saith the Lord, and not a God afar off?"
[55] Cf. Ps. 23.1; cf. also Ps. 138.7–12.

[56] Matt. 28.20.

[57] Matt. 7.23, with some variation from the Vulgate.

[58] Cf. Gen. 4.16.

[59] Or Nod.

[60] Cf. Ps. 72.2; 93.18.

[61] Cf. Gen. 11.1–9.

[62] Cf. Rom. 1.20.

[63] Cf. Rom. 1.18.

[64] Presumably meaning "everywhere," or "the length of the land." On this Greek phrase, Hilberg is following the oldest of seven manuscripts used for this letter (Lugdunensis 602 s. VI). Readings for the phrase vary considerably.

[65] Cf. Isa. 9.2: "The people that walked in darkness have seen a great light: to them that dwelt in the region of the shadow of death, light is risen."

[66] Ps. 26.13.

[67] Cf. John 14.30.

[68] Cf. Eph. 6.12.

[69] Cf. Matt. 13.39.

[70] Cf. Luke 18.6.

[71] Cf. Apoc. 12.3.

[72] Passim.

[73] Cf. Jer. 50.23.

[74] Cf. Eccli. 11.32.

[75] Passim.

[76] Cf. 1 Peter 5.8.

[77] Cf. Job 3.8.

[78] Cf. Ps. 73.13 f. Jerome here has the Hebrew *tenninim,* but when quoting Ps. 73.14 in § 35.3 below, he has *capita draconis.*

[79] Ezech. 16.34, with some variation from the Vulgate.

[80] Ezech. 16.33 f., condensed.

[81] Compare the remarks here and in the following on secular training and pleasure in secular literature with Letter 22.30 on the famous "dream" in which Jerome was accused of being a *Ciceronianus,* not a *Christianus;* cf. also n. 283 to Letter 22.

[82] Cf. Deut. 21.10–13.

[83] *haec si secundum litteram intellegimus, nonne ridicula sunt?*

[84] 1 Cor. 8.9 ff.

[85] 1 John 4.18.

[86] *peccatorum iacere, stare iustorum est.*

[87] Deut. 5.31.

[88] Ps. 133.1.

[89] *qui Hierusalem caelestem reliquerat matrem.* Cf. Heb. 12.22 ("But you are come to mount Sion, and to the city of the living God, the heavenly Jerusalem . . ."), Gal. 4.26 ("But that Jerusalem, which is above, is free: which is our mother"), and also the various references cited and comments by J. C. Plumpe, *Mater Ecclesia. An Inquiry into the Concept of the Church as Mother in Early Christianity* (SCA 5, Washington, D.C. 1943) esp. 1–17: "Scriptural Prototypes and Contemporary Pagan-Gnostic Analogies."

[90] Cf. 1 John 3.8.

[91] *statim ut conversus ingemueris, salvus eris.* Cf. Isa. 30.15: ". . . If you return and be quiet, you shall be saved. . . ."

[92] Cf. Eccle. 3.15; Wisd. 8.8.

[93] Cf. John 13.23 and 25.

[94] Cf. Matt. 11.30.

[95] Cant. 1.1.

[96] Cf. Isa. 21.12 f.

[97] Cf. Isa. 21.11.

[98] Cant. 1.4. The Vulgate has: ". . . O ye daughters of Jerusalem." Jerome's text here (the same as in Letter 22.1.3) could be rendered: "I am black and beautiful, a daughter of Jerusalem."

[99] Cf. Matt. 22.11 f.

[100] Eph. 1.13.

[101] Cf. Ezech. 28.12 f.

[102] Cf. Isa. 8.16.

[103] Ag. 1.1 and 2.2.

[104] Ezech. 16.11.

[105] Ezech. 9.4. The principal variation from the Vulgate here is Jerome's *da signum* for *signa thau* (Douai: "mark Thau"). Cf. above, n. 12 to Letter 18A.

[106] Ps. 4.7.

[107] Ezech. 16.10. Jerome here has *calceavi te hyacinthum,* where the Vulgate has *calceavi te ianthino.*

[108] Cf. Gen. 3.15.

[109] Cf. Luke 10.19.

[110] Cf. Eph. 6.15.

[111] Cf. Gal. 5.16.

[112] Isa. 52.7, with variation from the Vulgate.

[113] *Fidelis . . . lector.* Jerome perhaps was aware of the wide circle of readers this commentary would reach.

[114] Ps. 44.2.

[115] Luke 15.10.

[116] Cf. Luke 15.29, and § 34 below.

[117] Luke 14.18.
[118] Cf. Luke 14.19.
[119] Cf. Luke 14.20.
[120] Cf. 1 Cor. 6.16 f.
[121] Cf. Matt. 20.1–16.
[122] Cf. Pss. 52.1 (*pro Maeleth*) and 87.1 (*pro Maheleth*). Hilberg gives Jerome's reading as *pro meleth*. This superscription, according to T. E. Bird, "The Psalms," CCHS § 336, is among those which "await solution."
[123] The basic meaning of the Greek *symphonia* (συμφωνία) and the Latin *consonantia* are the same: "a sounding together." In late Latin *symphonia* was used for a kind of musical instrument.
[124] Cf. Matt. 12.46.
[125] 2 Cor. 5.20.
[126] Acts 13.46, with some variation from the Vulgate.
[127] Cf. Rom. 10.3 ff.
[128] Cf. Job 4.17.
[129] Cf. Prov. 20.9: "Who can say: My heart is clean, I am pure from sin?"
[130] Ps. 50.7.
[131] Ps. 129.3.
[132] That is, identifying the elder son with the Jews; cf. § 28.2 above.
[133] Rom. 9.30 ff. The principal variation from the Vulgate is that the Vulgate lacks the final "of the law."
[134] Cf. Phil. 3.6.
[135] Luke 18.11.
[136] Ps. 88.31–34.
[137] Cf. Matt. 7.22 and Luke 13.26.
[138] Cf. 4 Kings 22.2.
[139] Jerome refers to the successful resistance of the Jewish people to foreign domination, the revolt of the Jews under the Maccabees against the Syrians; cf. 1 and 2 Mac. Judas Maccabaeus was slain in 160 B.C.; Jonathan was treacherously captured in 143/142, and subsequently slain by Tryphon, the general of Antiochus IV; Simon was treacherously slain at a banquet by his ambitious son-in-law, Ptolemy, in 135/134. But the Jews were later to suffer Roman domination—in 63 B.C. Pompey was in Jerusalem—and Jerome here has Israel saying: *ecce adhuc Romano imperio subiacemus.*
[140] Referring, of course, to the prodigal son of the parable.
[141] *cumque merentibus minora non dederis, immeritis maiora tribuisti.*
[142] John 1.29.
[143] Cf. Matt. 25.33.

[144] Ps. 73.14.
[145] Cf. Jos. 1.8 and Ps. 1.2.
[146] Ps. 13.3.
[147] John 10.8.   The Vulgate reads: "All, as many as have come, are thieves and robbers."
[148] 1 Cor. 9.22.
[149] Phil. 2.21.
[150] Cf. Luke 15.4–10.
[151] Cf. Job 4.17.
[152] Cf. Luke 10.12.
[153] Phil. 3.15.
[154] Rom. 11.33.
[155] 1 Cor. 13.9.
[156] 1 Cor. 13.12.
[157] Rom. 7.24.
[158] Cf. Matt. 5.45.
[159] Cf. Matt. 22.9–14.
[160] Cf. Luke 15.4 ff.
[161] Cf. Matt. 20.20–28.
[162] Matt. 20.25–28.
[163] Cf. Job 15.15 and 4.18.
[164] Ps. 142.2.   The Vulgate reads: "For in thy sight. . . ."   The Douai gives "no man living" for *non . . . omnis vivens;* the reason for the rendering here, "no living creature," is immediately evident from the following.
[165] *Non ait 'non iustificabitur omnis homo,' sed 'omnis vivens'.* . . .
[166] Cf. 1 John 3.5; 1 Peter 2.22; Isa. 53.9.
[167] Cf. Gen. 1.26.
[168] Cf. Matt. 20.1–16.
[169] Matt. 20.6 f.
[170] 1 John 2.18.   The Vulgate has *filioli,* "little children," where Jerome here has *fratres,* "brothers."
[171] Matt. 20.11 f., with slight variations from the Vulgate.
[172] Matt. 20.15.
[173] Cf. 1 Tim. 1.17 and 6.16.
[174] Cf. above, n. 103 to Letter 18A.
[175] Cf. Luke 15.16 f.

LETTER 22

[1] This letter, one of the most famous of the entire collection, provides a treatise on motivations and rules of conduct for a life of virginity.

Included in the letter are some graphic observations on Roman society, autobiographical bits (Jerome's account of his celebrated "dream" is in § 30; cf. also n. 283 below), and notes regarding monasticism as practiced in Egypt. Written in Rome, quite likely in the spring of 384 (cf. Cavallera 2.155; Labourt 1.112), it is addressed to the young third daughter of the now widowed Paula, Eustochium, who together with her mother was later to go to the East after Jerome's departure from Rome in 385, and who was subsequently to succeed her mother as head of the convent established in Bethlehem.

The letter is long, more a pamphlet- or booklet-length tract than an ordinary epistle, and Jerome himself was to refer to it as a *libellus* (cf. his Letters 31.2.2 and 52.17.1). The language of the letter and the criticisms expressed in it are strong; and it is not difficult to understand how some of Jerome's remarks would be resented in certain quarters of Rome, or how some critics of Jerome would feel that he was supplying ammunition to the enemies of the Church. Rufinus (*In Hier.* 2.5) was to write of this letter: *Libellum quemdam de conservanda virginitate, Romae positus, scripsit, quem libellum omnes pagani et inimici Dei, apostatae et persecutores et quicumque sunt qui christianum nomen odio habent certatim sibi describebant pro eo quod omnem ibi Christianorum ordinem, omnem gradum, omnem professionem universamque pariter foedissimis exprobationibus infamavit Ecclesiam et ea quae gentiles falso in hos conferre crimina putabantur iste vera esse, immo multo peiora a nostris geri quam illi criminabantur asseruit.*

In this letter and elsewhere in his writings, Jerome puts heavy emphasis on virginity and continence, and the pictures he paints of married life are in sharp contrast. Time and time again he makes it clear that virginity is not commanded, but counseled; that marriage has its place and is not condemned by the Church, nor indeed by him; and that marriage is a good. Some of his comments, however, with the rhetorical attention he gave the seamy side of social marriage and the relatively small amount of space he devoted to the noble side of marriage, were such that it is not altogether surprising that his teaching has at times been misunderstood. Regarding Jerome's doctrine on virginity, continence, and marriage, cf. E. P. Burke, "St. Jerome as a Spiritual Director," MSJ, esp. 155–63.

[2] Ps. 44.11 f.
[3] Cf. Gen. 12.1.
[4] Ps. 26.13.
[5] Gen. 19.17. The principal variation from the Vulgate here is the last clause, which reads in the Vulgate: *ne et tu simul pereas* (Douai: "lest thou also be condemned").

⁶ Cf. Luke 9.62.

⁷ Cf. Matt. 24.17 f.

⁸ John 8.44.

⁹ 1 John 3.8.

¹⁰ Cant. 1.4, with the same variation from the Vulgate as in Letter 21.21; cf. n. 98 to Letter 21.

¹¹ Ps. 44.12.

¹² *hoc ergo illud magnum est sacramentum.* Cf. Eph. 5.32.

¹³ Gen. 2.24; cf. Eph. 5.31; also Matt. 19.5; Mark 10.7.

¹⁴ *iam non, ut ibi, in una carne, sed spiritu.* Cf. 1 Cor. 6.17: "But he who is joined to the Lord, is one spirit."

¹⁵ Cf. Num. 12.1 ff.

¹⁶ Cf. Matt. 12.42.

¹⁷ Cf. Cant. 1.3.

¹⁸ Cf. Cant. 8.5, which, however, in the Vulgate lacks the *dealbata,* "being made white." Cf. Cant. 6.9: "Who is she that cometh forth as the morning rising, fair as the moon, bright as the sun . . . ?"

¹⁹ *mi domina Eustochium*—to which Jerome, as it were explaining his form of address, adds: *dominam quippe debeo vocare sponsam domini mei.* Cf. § 26 below: *Itaque, mi Eustochia, filia, domina, conserva, germana—aliud enim aetatis, aliud meriti, illud religionis, hoc caritatis est nomen. . . .*

²⁰ *habent enim et maritatae ordinem suum, honorabiles nuptias et cubile immaculatum.* Cf. Heb. 13.4: "Marriage honorable in all, and the bed undefiled" (Vulgate: *Honorabile connubium in omnibus, et thorus immaculatus*).—The quotation from Heb. 13.4 is "in the class of favored quotations," and although Jerome was later for a while to reflect contemporary doubts about the Epistle to the Hebrews, he "never forgoes the use of this text"; cf. P. W. Skehan, "St. Jerome and the Canon of the Holy Scriptures," MSJ 260 f.

²¹ Cf. Gen. 19.26.

²² Isa. 34.5.

²³ Cf. Gen. 3.18 and 3.14.

²⁴ Eph. 6.12. The Vulgate has: ". . . against principalities and powers, against the rulers of the world of this darkness. . . ."

²⁵ Ps. 90.5 ff.—On the preceding, cf. John 14.30: ". . . For the prince of this world cometh, and in me he hath not any thing."

²⁶ Cf. 4 Kings 6.15 ff.

²⁷ Cf. 4 Kings 2.11.

²⁸ Ps. 123.7.

²⁹ 2 Cor. 4.7.

³⁰ Cf. Gal. 5.17.

[31] Cf. 1 Peter 5.8.

[32] Ps. 103.20 f.

[33] Cf. 1 Cor. 5.12 f.

[34] Cf. Amos 4.2.

[35] Cf. Hab. 1.4 and 16.

[36] Cf. Job 2.1–7.

[37] Cf. Luke 22.31.

[38] Cf. Matt. 10.34.

[39] Cf. Isa. 14.12.

[40] Cf. Gen. 2.15.

[41] Abd. 4. The Vulgate has "and though thou set thy nest among the stars" after "eagle."

[42] Cf. Isa. 14.13 f.

[43] Cf. Gen. 28.12.

[44] Ps. 81.6 f.

[45] Cf. Ps. 81.1.

[46] 1 Cor. 3.3, with some variation from the Vulgate.

[47] Cf. Acts 9.15.

[48] Cf. Eph. 6.15.

[49] Cf. 1 Cor. 9.27.

[50] Cf. Rom. 7.23.

[51] Rom. 7.24.

[52] Amos 5.2. For "has fallen," *cecidit*, the Vulgate has "is cast down upon her land," *projecta est in terram suam*.

[53] Jerome's "audacious" words here are: *Audenter loquor: cum omnia deus possit, suscitare virginem non potest post ruinam. Valet quidem liberare de poena, sed non valet coronare corruptam.*

[54] Cf. Amos 8.13. The Vulgate has *virgines pulchrae*, "the fair virgins," instead of *virgines bonae*, "good virgins."

[55] Matt. 5.28.

[56] Cf. Matt. 25.1–12.

[57] Cf. 1 Cor. 6.15–20.

[58] Isa. 47.1 ff., with some variation from the Vulgate.

[59] Ps. 44.10.

[60] Cf. Ezech. 16.

[61] Cf. Apoc. 17.1 and 15 f.

[62] Cf. Ezech. 16.25.

[63] Cf. Isa. 1.21 "How is the faithful city, that was full of judgment, become a harlot?"

[64] Cf. Isa. 13.21 f.

[65] Ps. 117.6. The principal variation from the Vulgate here is the *caro*, "the flesh," in place of *homo*, "man."

[66] Ps. 41.6 f.

[67] Ps. 136.8 f.

[68] Cf. Vergil, *Aen.* 8.389.

[69] Cf. 1 Cor. 10.4.

[70] *O quotiens in heremo constitutus.* . . . That is, of course, in the desert of Chalcis. Regarding the following account of the temptations of the flesh Jerome suffered in the desert, cf. Letter 125.12, where he mentions them and says that when after frequent fasts his mind still surged with thoughts, he took up the study of Hebrew.

[71] *quia amaritudine repletus eram.* Cf. Ruth 1.20.

[72] Cf. Luke 7.38.

[73] Cant. 1.3.

[74] 1 Tim. 5.6.

[75] 1 Tim. 5.23.

[76] Eph. 5.18.

[77] Rom. 14.21. The Vulgate reads: "It is good not to eat flesh, and not to drink wine, nor any thing whereby thy brother is offended, or scandalized, or made weak."

[78] Cf. Gen. 9.20 f.

[79] Exod. 30.6.

[80] Cf. Gen. 19.

[81] Cf. Gen. 19.36 ff. and Deut. 23.3 (which has "tenth" instead of "fourteenth"); cf. also 2 Esd. 13.1.

[82] Cf. 3 Kings 19.5 f. In the Vulgate it is a juniper tree instead of an oak tree.

[83] 4 Kings 4.40.

[84] Cf. 4 Kings 4.41.

[85] Cf. Exod. 15.25.

[86] 4 Kings 6.22.

[87] Cf. Dan. 14.32–38.

[88] Cf. Dan. 10.3 and 19.

[89] Cf. Gen. 3.

[90] Cf. Ps. 83.7.

[91] Cf. Matt. 4.1–4.

[92] 1 Cor. 6.3.

[93] Phil. 3.19.

[94] Cf. Job 33.3 and 9.

[95] Job 40.11, with some variation from the Vulgate.

[96] Cf. Acts 2.30; Ps. 131.11; 2 Kings 7.12; 3 Kings 8.19.

[97] Cf. Gen. 46.27 and Exod. 1.5, both of which use the figure seventy, not seventy-five.

[98] Cf. Gen. 32.25.

[99] Cf. Exod. 12.11.

[100] Job 38.3.

[101] Cf. Matt. 3.4.

[102] Cf. Eph. 6.14 and 1 Peter 1.13.

[103] Ezech. 16.4.

[104] Cf. Judges 16.4–31.

[105] Cf. 1 Kings 13.14.

[106] Cf. 2 Kings 11.2–27. The "murder," *homicidium,* Jerome refers to consisted in David's sending of instructions for Bethsabee's husband Urias to be put "in the front of the battle, where the fight is strongest; and leave ye him, that he may be wounded and die"—and Urias was killed.

[107] Ps. 50.6.

[108] 3 Kings 4.33.

[109] Cf. 3 Kings 11.4.

[110] Cf. 2 Kings 13.

[111] *Piget dicere, quot cotidie virgines ruant, quantas de suo gremio mater perdat ecclesia. . . .* On the development and treatment of the concept of the Church as mother, cf. esp. J. C. Plumpe, *op. cit.,* where numerous references are given and where note is taken of the present passage in Jerome on p. 91.—On the following clause, cf. Isa. 14.13.

[111a] *. . . et frequenter etiam ipsae commortuae trium criminum reae ad inferos perducuntur, homicidae sui, Christi adulterae, necdum nati filii parricidae.* The *Christi adulterae* as a term for these is in line with the concept of spouses of Christ.—The old Roman law did not directly forbid abortion (although there was recognition of an offense against a husband's rights if a wife defrauded him of a child he had a right to expect), and it was only with the coming of Christianity that the vice was condemned. Cf. in the present series the remarks and references cited by J. H. Crehan, ACW 23 (1956) 167.

[112] Titus 1.15.

[113] Jer. 3.3, with some variation from the Vulgate.

[113a] "little cloak" = *maforte.*

[114] Cf. Jerome's Letter 130.18.

[115] Prov. 6.27 f., with some variation from the Vulgate.

[116] *prima Romanae urbis virgo nobilis esse coepisti.* Many of the noble Roman women who had embraced the religious life earlier were widows.

[117] Furius, the husband of Eustochium's older sister Blesilla, had died several years before this. Blesilla herself was to die in the fall of 384, and Jerome was to come in for criticism and blame from those who felt or claimed to feel that her death was due to her austerities following her conversion.

[118] Cf. Matt. 13.8.

[119] *post cenam dubiam.*   Cf. Terence, *Phormio* 342; Horace, *Sat.* 2.2.77.

[120] Cant. 1.6.   The questions are indirect in the Vulgate: "Show me, O thou whom my soul loveth, where thou feedest. . . ."

[121] Phil. 1.23, with some variation from the Vulgate.

[122] Cf. Luke 2.51.

[123] Cf. Rom. 7.22 f.

[124] Cf. Eph. 6.16.

[125] Cf. Osee 7.4 and 6.

[126] Luke 24.32, with some variation from the Vulgate.   "Burning within us" here = *ardens* (Vulgate: *ardens in nobis*).

[127] Ps. 118.140.   For "exceedingly refined" the text here has simply *ignitum* (Vulgate: *ignitum . . . vehementer*), although Hilberg notes several readings with *vehementer*.

[128] Cant. 3.1.

[129] Col. 3.5.   The text here lacks the "which are" (*quae sunt*) of the Vulgate.

[130] Gal. 2.20.

[131] Ps. 118.83.

[132] Ps. 108.24.

[133] Ps. 101.5 f.

[134] Cf. Ps. 6.7.

[135] Cf. Ps. 101.8.

[136] Cf. 1 Cor. 14.15.

[137] Ps. 102.2 ff., with some variation from the Vulgate.

[138] Ps. 101.10.

[139] Cf. Gen. 3.1–5.

[140] Cf. Gen. 3.21.

[141] Cf. 4 Kings 2.13.

[142] Gen. 3.16.   The Vulgate reads: ". . . in sorrow shalt thou bring forth children, and thou shalt be under thy husband's power, and he shall have dominion over thee."   The text in the present letter for "and thy turning shall be to thy husband" = *et ad virum conversio tua.*   The parenthetical "that law does not apply to me" = *lex ista non mea est,* which might be rendered "that law is not mine [scil., but rather God's]."

[143] Gen. 2.17.

[144] Cf. Gen. 1.28.

[145] Cf. Gen. 3.7.

[146] Cf. Gen. 3.17 ff.

[147] Cf. Matt. 13.8.

[148] Matt. 19.11, with some variation from the Vulgate.

[149] Eccle. 3.5.

[150] Cf. Zach. 9.16.

[151] Cf. John 19.23.

[152] Ps. 114.7.

[153] Isa. 11.1. Jerome follows with *virga mater est domini*, perhaps an intentional play on the words *virgo* and *virga*.

[154] Cant. 2.1.

[155] Cf. Dan. 2.34.

[156] Cant. 2.6.

[157] Cf. Gen. 7.2 f.

[158] Cf. Exod. 3.5 and Jos. 5.16. For "Josue, the son of Nave," Jerome here has *Iesus Nave*, identical, of course, with Josue, the son of Nun (cf., e.g., Jos. 1.1). Such usage apparently dated from the time of Origen, who translated the Hebrew "son of Nun" by υἱὸς Ναυῆ, and many of the Fathers could see the name *Iesus Nave* as typifying Jesus, the Ship (*navis*) wherein the world is saved. Cf. W. Drum, "Josue," *Catholic Encyclopedia* 8 (1910) 524.

[159] Cf. Matt. 10.10; Luke 10.4.

[160] Cf. Matt. 27.35; Mark 15.24; Luke 23.34; John 19.23.

[161] *socrus Dei esse coepisti*. This expression was strongly criticized by Rufinus (*In Hier.* 2.10). Although Jerome's phrase may at first seem flippant, the concept is scarcely more than an extension of the concept of a virgin who dedicates herself to God as a bride of Christ.

[162] 1 Cor. 7.25.

[163] 1 Cor. 7.7.

[164] 1 Cor. 7.8.

[165] 1 Cor. 9.5. The Vulgate reads: "Have we not power to carry about a woman, a sister, as well as the rest of the apostles, and the brethren of the Lord, and Cephas?"

[166] Cf. 1 Cor. 7.25.

[167] . . . *et durissimum erat contra naturam cogere angelorumque vitam ab hominibus extorquere et id quodam modo damnare, quod conditum est.*

[168] Cf. Isa. 31.9 and 54.1; 1 Kings 1.6.

[169] Ps. 127.3.

[170] Ps. 104.37, with some variation from the Vulgate, where the clause is in the past tense, not future.

[171] Cf. Isa. 56.3 ff.

[172] Cf. Luke 16.19–31.

[173] Cf. Gen. 25.1.

[174] Cf. Gen. 30.14 ff.

[175] Cf. Gen. 30.1.

[176] Jer. 16.2. Jerome here has *et tu ne accipias uxorem* instead of the Vulgate's *Non accipies uxorem.*

[177] 1 Cor. 7.26.

[178] 1 Cor. 7.29.

[179] Jer. 4.7. Jerome here has *promovit se* for the Vulgate's *ascendit,* "is come up."

[180] Lam. 4.4. Jerome here actually has *ad faucem,* "to the throat," for the Vulgate's *ad palatam,* "to the roof of the mouth."

[181] Cf. Gen. 3.16.

[182] Cf. Isa. 9.6.

[183] Cf. Judith 13.10.

[184] *suo igne conbustus est.* Actually, Aman "was hanged on the gibbet, which he had prepared for Mardochai" (Esth. 7.10).

[185] Cf. Matt. 4.21 f.; Mark 1.19 f.; Luke 5.10 f.

[186] Matt. 16.24.

[187] Cf. Matt. 8.21 f.; Luke 9.59 f.

[188] Matt. 8.20; Luke 9.58.

[189] 1 Cor. 7.32 ff., with variations from the Vulgate.

[190] Cf. Jerome's *Adversus Helvidium,* written in or about 383, in which he refuted the strictures of Helvidius on virginity and on the Blessed Virgin Mother.

[191] *et, si cui placet, de illo potest haurire fonticulo.* Cf. Horace, *Sat.* 1.1.56.

[192] Cf. 1 Thess. 5.17; also Eph. 6.18.

[193] 1 Cor. 7.28.

[194] This work—to which Jerome also seems to refer in *Adv. Iov.* 1.13— has not survived.

[195] The writings of Damasus referred to here have not survived. The work of Cyprian (cf. above, n. 14 to Letter 10) referred to presumably is his *De habitu virginum.*

[196] The reference is to the *De virginibus* of St. Ambrose, bishop of Milan. The Marcellina mentioned by Jerome in Letter 45.7 may be Ambrose's sister.

[197] *Nobis diverso tramite inceditur: virginitatem non efferimus, sed servamus.*

[198] Matt. 10.22 and 24.13.

[199] Matt. 20.16 and 22.14.

[200] Cf. 2 Kings 66.7; 1 Par. 13.9 ff. (Ozias here = Oza).

[201] *Praecessit umbra, nunc veritas est.* Cf. above, n. 1 to Letter 18A.

[202] Cf. 4 Kings 20.13–18.

[203] Cf. 4 Kings 24.13 and 25.13–17; 2 Par. 36.10 and 18.

[204] Cf. Dan. 5.2 f.

[205] Cf. Ps. 140.4.

[205a] *naturali ducimur malo.*

[206] Cf. Exod. 25.11 and 37.1.

[207] Cf. Ps. 79.2; Heb. 9.5.

[208] Cf. Matt. 21.1–7; Mark 11.1–6; Luke 19.29–35.

[209] Cf. Exod. 1.14 and 5.7 f.

[210] Cf. Exod. 5 ff.

[211] Cf. Matt. 21.12 f.

[212] Cf. Exod. 20.5 and 34.14.

[213] Cf. Matt. 21.13; Mark 11.17; Luke 19.46; also Jer. 7.11.

[214] Cf. Matt. 21.12; Mark 11.15; John 2.14.

[215] Cf. Matt. 27.51.

[216] Matt. 23.38.

[217] Luke 10.41 f. The Vulgate reads: ". . . But one thing is necessary. Mary hath chosen the best part, which. . . ."

[218] Cf. Cant. 3.4.

[219] Cant. 6.8.

[220] Cf. Heb. 12.22.

[221] Cf. Cant. 5.4.

[222] Cant. 5.8. For the Vulgate's *amore langueo,* Jerome here has *vulnerata caritatis ego sum.*

[223] Cant. 4.12.

[224] Cf. Gen. 34.—"Go not out from home" in the foregoing = *cave ne domum exeas.* In view of the *domum* (instead of *domo*), the meaning here would seem to be: "Take care not to go out (of your room or quarters in the palace of Paula) into or to (the rest or other parts of) the house." As for the aptness of such precaution, it appears that on one occasion Eustochium's aunt Praetextata, desiring to reverse the resolution of the young virgin, changed Eustochium's dress and arranged the girl's hair according to the tastes of the world; cf. the account in Jerome's Letter 107.5.

[225] Cant. 3.2.

[226] Cant. 3.3.

[227] Matt. 7.14.

[228] Cant. 5.6.

[229] Cant. 5.7, slightly abbreviated. Jerome here has *theristrum* ("garment," "covering") for the Vulgate's *pallium* (Douai: "veil").

[230] Cant. 5.2.

[231] Cant. 1.12. The Vulgate has "my beloved" instead of "my cousin."

[232] Cf. Matt. 25.10 ff.

[233] Cant. 1.6. The Vulgate has: "Show me . . . lest I begin to wander after the flocks of thy companions."

[234] Cant. 1.7.
[235] Cf. Prov. 4.23.
[236] Cf. Matt. 25.33.
[237] Isa. 26.20, with variation from the Vulgate.
[238] Cf. Matt. 25.10 ff.
[239] Cf. Matt. 6.6.
[240] Apoc. 3.20, slightly abbreviated.
[241] Cant. 5.2, with variation from the Vulgate.
[242] Cant. 5.3.
[243] Cant. 5.6.   Jerome here has *fratuelis*, "cousin," for the Vulgate's *dilectus*, "beloved."
[244] Eccle. 10.4.   Jerome here has *locum ne dederis ei*, where the Vulgate has *locum tuum ne dimiseris*.
[245] Cf. Dan. 6.10.
[246] Jer. 9.21.
[247] John 5.44.
[248] Ps. 3.4.
[249] 1 Cor. 1.31; 2 Cor. 10.17.
[250] Gal. 1.10.
[251] Gal. 6.14.
[252] Ps. 43.9.
[253] Ps. 33.3.
[254] Cf. Matt. 6.2 ff.
[255] Cf. Matt. 6.16 ff.
[256] Cf. Horace, *Odes* 4.3.22.
[257] *frater est mortuus. . . .*   This can be taken in a general sense, with the *frater* here and the *sororis* in the following perhaps referring to any fellow Christians.
[258] Cf. Horace, *Sat.* 1.6.65 ff.
[259] Cf. Jerome's Letter 108.1 and 3 for references to the noble ancestry of Eustochium's mother, Paula.   According to Jerome, Paula's father Rogatus was said to have the blood of Agamemnon in his veins, while her mother Blesilla was a descendant of the Scipios and the Gracchi.
[260] Ps. 130.1.
[261] Cf. Isa. 14.12–15.
[262] Cf. Matt. 6.16.
[263] *. . . venter solus, quia videri non potest, aestuat cibo.*
[264] Ps. 52.6.   Jerome here has *hominum sibi placentium*, "of them that please themselves," for the Vulgate's *eorum qui hominibus placent*, "of them that please men."
[265] Cf. 1 Cor. 11.14.
[266] The two men mentioned are not otherwise known.

[267] 2 Tim. 3.6 f., abbreviated.

[268] *de mei ordinis hominibus,* presumably meaning monks.

[269] *'altilis,' 'γέρων' vulgo 'ποππύζων' nominatur* is the reading given here by Hilberg, who notes, however, a number of variants. Vallarsi *ad loc.* reviews conjectures of scholars on this passage. Cf. also Labourt 1.166 f.

[270] Gen. 3.1, with some variation from the Vulgate. Jerome here has *sapientior* for the Vulgate's *callidior,* "more subtle."

[271] 2 Cor. 2.11.

[272] 2 Cor. 11.2.

[273] Cf. Eccli. 9.20.

[274] *si quae ancillae sunt comites propositi tui, ne erigaris adversus eas, ne infleris ut domina.*

[275] 1 Cor. 7.9.

[276] 1 Cor. 15.33.

[277] 1 Tim. 5.11 f.

[278] 2 Cor. 6.14 f.

[279] Cf. 1 Cor. 8.10.

[280] Titus 1.15.

[281] 1 Tim. 4.4.

[282] Cf. 1 Cor. 10.20.

[283] What follows is the celebrated passage in which Jerome recounts the famous vision or dream (cf. n. 288 below) in which he was accused of being a *Ciceronianus* and not a *Christianus.* Jerome says that he was ill and thought to be near death, *cum subito raptus in spiritu ad tribunal iudicis pertrahor;* when he there described himself as a Christian, he was accused of lying and was beaten; after pleas for mercy, *deiurare coepi,* he writes, *et nomen eius obtestans dicere: 'Domine, si umquam habuero codices saeculares, si legero, te negavi,'* and *in haec sacramenti verba dimissus revertor ad superos et mirantibus cunctis oculos aperio.* How seriously Jerome considered the pledge made in this dream, and how long and how strictly he may have felt himself bound by it, we can only speculate. Sr. M. Jamesetta Kelly, *op. cit.* 61, comments that in view of the great number of authors cited in his works, "we may be tempted to wonder if the Saint kept his promise, even for a short time. . . ." Yet in the preface to his *Comment. in Gal.* 3, Jerome, writing perhaps in 388/389, was to say that for fifteen years he had not had in his hands any author of pagan letters. Monceaux (97–104) says Jerome's "heroic renunciation made no change in his style; he no longer needed to re-read his favorite classics, since he knew them practically by heart"; but Monceaux also allows for a later resumption by Jerome of the reading of pagan authors. Rufinus (*In Hier.* 2) was to accuse Jerome of infidelity to his pledge; Jerome (*Apol. adv. Ruf.* 1.30 ff.)

would point out that he had not promised to forget what he already knew, and assuredly Jerome was a man of great memory. Regarding the dream, cf. also Cavallera 1.29 f. and 2.77 f., Note D, "Le songe de saint Jérôme"; Labourt 1.146 and 167.

In any case, the account of the dream is hardly to be taken as the last word of Jerome on secular letters, and surely not to be considered as a total rejection once and for all by Jerome of what was of value in the old literature. Cf. E. A. Quain, "St. Jerome as a Humanist," MSJ 203–32, where (228) it is stated that Jerome's dream "has won more emphasis than it really deserves from the critics of his inconsistency in both ancient and modern times." Quain (228), citing Jerome's *Apol. adv. Ruf.* 1.30 ff., says that Jerome himself in later years "made very light of the dream, and in view of that, there is no reason why we should hold this temporary aberration, related to us in a moment of undoubted emotional stress, as an epitome of his views on pagan literature."

[284] . . . *et, quod his difficilius est, consuetudine lautioris cibi* (literally, "more elegant food").—In the following, "to be a soldier of Christ" = *militaturus.* Cf. above, n. 5 to Letter 14.

[285] Matt. 6.21.

[286] Ps. 6.6.

[287] Ps. 56.2.

[288] *nec vero sopor ille fuerat aut vana somnia, quibus saepe deludimur.* Cf. n. 283 above.

[289] Luke 16.12.

[290] Prov. 13.8. Jerome here has *redemptio viri propriae divitiae* for the Vulgate's *redemptio animae viri divitiae suae.*

[291] Matt. 6.24; Luke 16.13.

[292] *nam gentili Syrorum lingua mammona 'divitiae' nuncupantur.*

[293] Matt. 6.25 f.; cf. Luke 16.22 ff.

[294] Cf. Matt. 6.28 ff.

[295] Cf. Matt. 5.3 and 6; Luke 6.20 f.

[296] 2 Cor. 12.10.

[297] 2 Cor. 12.7.

[298] Ps. 96.8.

[299] Job 1.21; cf. Eccle. 5.14.

[300] 1 Tim. 6.7.

[301] Cf. James 5.2.

[302] *Inficitur membrana colore purpureo, aurum liquescit in litteras, gemmis codices vestiuntur et nudus ante fores earum Christus emoritur.*

[303] Cf. Matt. 6.2.

[304] *nobilissimam mulierum Romanarum,* with the superlative possibly

to be taken as "a very . . ." instead of "the most. . . ."   Labourt translates: "une très noble parmi les matrones romaines."

[305] 1 Tim. 6.10.

[306] Cf. Eph. 5.5; Col. 3.5.

[307] Matt. 6.33, abbreviated.

[308] Ps. 36.25.

[309] Cf. 3 Kings 17.6.

[310] Cf. 3 Kings 17.8–15.

[311] Acts 3.6.

[312] Cf. 1 Tim. 6.8.

[313] Gen. 28.20.

[314] It was only later, in 385/386, that Jerome himself was to visit Egypt.

[315] Cf. Matt. 26.15.

[316] Cf. the mention of Macarius in Letter 3.2.2, and n. 6 to that letter.   The Isidore mentioned may be the Nitrian monk of that name who accompanied Athanasius when Athanasius, forced into exile the second time, set out for Rome in the year 340.

[317] Acts 8.20.   The Douai reads: "Keep thy money to thyself, to perish with thee. . . ."   (Jerome here and the Vulgate both have *pecunia tua tecum sit in perditionem*.)

[318] *coenobium, quod illi sauhes gentili lingua vocant, nos 'in commune viventes' possumus appellare*.   The word *sauhes* is not found elsewhere.

[319] *tertium genus est, quod dicunt remnuoth, deterrimum atque neglectum et quod in nostra provincia aut solum aut primum est*.   Jerome's low opinion of the *remnuoth* is evident.

[320] Ps. 54.7.

[321] Cf. Philo, *Quod omnis probus liber sit* 12.

[322] Cf. Josephus, *Bell. Iud.* 2.8.2–13.   Note, however, that Jerome refers to Josephus—including a specific reference to *Bell. Iud.* 2—in his *Adv. Iov.* 2.14, but his assertion there that the Essenes abstained from wine and meat and fasted daily is not found in Josephus, and Jerome's source there would seem in fact to have been Porphyry (cf. Porphyry, *De abstinentia* 4.11).   On this question, cf. Courcelle, *op. cit.* 73 f.

[322a] Jerome is referring, of course, to Paul of Thebes and Antony of Egypt.   Cf. Jerome's *Vita Pauli* 1; also nn. 1 and 15 to Letter 10 above.   St. Athanasius' *Life of St. Antony* has appeared in the present series, translated by R. T. Meyer, ACW 10 (1950).

[323] Lam. 3.27 f. and 30 f.

[324] Cf. § 33 above.

[325] Cf. Ps. 72.26.

[326] Cf. Eph. 6.18.

[227] Cf. Ps. 49.20.

[228] Rom. 14.4.

[229] Cf. Isa. 58.5.

[230] Isa. 58.3 f. The Vulgate reads: ". . . Behold in the day of your fast your own will is found, and you exact of all your debtors. Behold you fast for debates and strife, and strike with the fist wickedly. Do not fast as [you have done] until this day, to make your cry to be heard on high."

[231] Cf. Eph. 4.26.

[232] Cf. Rom. 13.14.

[233] Cf. 2 Tim. 1.15; 1 Tim. 1.19 f.

[234] Cf. 1 Kings 16.7.

[235] 1 Cor. 7.34.

[236] Luke 1.28.

[237] Cf. Matt. 12.50: "For whosoever shall do the will of my Father that is in heaven, he is my brother, and sister, and mother."

[238] *ad prophetissam*, as in Isa. 8.3, although one would have expected Jerome here to change "prophetess" to "prophet" in order to make sense in addressing a female. The quotation preceding is, with some variation from the Vulgate, from Isa. 8.1.

[239] Isa. 26.18, with variation from the Vulgate.

[240] Matt. 12.49.

[241] Cf. 3 Kings 4.29.

[242] Cf. Col. 2.14 f.

[242a] *quae quidem universa tunc prosunt, cum in ecclesia fiunt. . . .*

[243] Cf. Gen. 6–8.

[244] Cf. Jos. 6.17 and 25.

[245] *ceterum virgines, quales apud diversas hereses et quales apud inpurissimum Manicheum esse dicuntur. . . .* The Manichean heresy or religion, with its dualistic doctrine of Light and Darkness in constant warfare with each other, was named after its third-century founder, Mani. Started in the East, it spread rapidly in the fourth century in the Christianized West, and in one form or another continued into the Middle Ages. On the Manicheans, cf. F. C. Burkitt, *The Religion of the Manichees* (Cambridge 1924); G. Bardy, "Manichéisme," DTC 9.2 (Paris 1927) 1841–95; H. Ch. Puech, *Le manichéisme, son fondateur, sa doctrine* (Paris 1949).

[246] Cf. Matt. 7.15.

[347] Cf. Phil. 3.8.

[348] Cf. 2 Tim. 2.11; Col. 3.1.

[349] Cf. Gal. 5.24.

[350] Rom. 8.35.

351 Rom. 8.38 f.

352 Cf. Isa. 40.12.—Regarding the "ten months" in the preceding, cf. above, n. 20 to Letter 21.

353 Ps. 115.3(12) f.

354 Ps. 115.6(15) f.

355 Cf. Gen. 4.8.

356 Cf. Gen. 12.11–20 and 20.2–18.

357 Heb. 12.6.

358 *ferre vallum*, like a soldier on the march.

359 Gen. 29.20, with some variation from the Vulgate.

360 Gen. 31.40.

361 Ps. 119.5.   Jerome here has *peregrinatio* for the Vulgate's *incolatus*, "sojourning."

362 Rom. 8.18.   The Vulgate reads: "For I reckon that the sufferings of this time are not worthy. . . ."

363 Rom. 5.3 ff.

364 2 Cor. 11.23–27.

365 2 Tim. 4.7 f.   Jerome here reads: *superest mihi corona iustitiae, quam retribuet mihi dominus;* the Vulgate reads: *In reliquo reposita est mihi corona iustitiae, quam reddet mihi Dominus in illa die iustus iudex.*

366 Hilberg actually punctuates to break the two sentences here differently: *si cibus insulsior fuerit, contristamur et putamus nos deo praestare beneficium; cum aquatius bibimus, calix frangitur, mensa subvertitur, verbera sonant et aqua tepidior sanguine vindicatur.*

367 Matt. 11.12.

368 *Nisi vim feceris, caelorum regna non capies. Nisi pulsaveris inportune, panem non accipies sacramenti.*   Cf. Matt. 7.7 ff.; Luke 11.9–13.

369 1 Cor. 2.9; cf. Isa. 64.4.

370 Exod. 15.1.

371 The story of Thecla, a Greek girl from Iconium who was converted by the preaching of St. Paul, can be found in the so-called Greek *Acta Pauli et Theclae*, which Jerome (*De vir. ill.* 7) calls the *Periodi Pauli et Theclae*.   Although the cult of St. Thecla became very popular, the story cited appears much as fiction, and it is questionable how much historical truth it contains.   Cf. Quasten *Patr.* 1.131 ff.

372 Cant. 2.10 f.   Cf. above, n. 19 to Letter 18B.

373 Cant. 6.9, with variation from the Vulgate.

374 Cf. Cant. 6.8.

375 Cf. Luke 2.36.

376 Paula.

377 Marcella.   Cf. Jerome's Letter 127.5.

[378] Cf. Matt. 21.1–9; Mark 11.1–11; Luke 19.29–38.
[379] Cf. Heb. 12.22.
[380] Isa. 8.18.
[381] Cf. Matt. 21.9; Mark 11.9 f.; Luke 19.38; also Ps. 117.26.
[382] Cf. Apoc. 14.1 ff.
[383] Apoc. 14.4.   Jerome here has *qui se cum mulieribus non coinquina-verunt* for the Vulgate's *qui cum mulieribus non sunt coinquinati.*
[384] Cant. 8.6.
[385] Cant. 8.7.

INDEXES

INDEXES

1. OLD AND NEW TESTAMENT

2. AUTHORS

Rahner, C., 211
Rahner, H., 188
Reticius of Autun, 37
    Adv. Nov., 196; *Comm. in Cant.*
    Cant., 196
Royds, T. F., 190
Rufinus of Aquileia, 6, 7, 18, 30, 31,
    35, 37, 191, 193, 194, 195, 196,
    197, 198
    Comm. in symb. apost., 191;
    Hist. monach. 28: 192; *In Hier.*
    2: 243; 2.5: 233; 2.10: 239
Rush, A., 193

Schade, L., 186
Schmid, J., 186
Skehan, P. W., 219, 234
Sutcliffe, E. F., 219

Terence
    Heaut. 796: 189; *Phormio* 342:
    238

Tertullian, 37, 112, 113, 155, 203,
    225, 226
    Ad amic. philos., 155; *De bapt.*
    1: 198; *De cult. fem.* 2.7.3: 194;
    De pud., 112, 225; 9: 225, 226
Theodoret
    Hist. rel. 10: 190

Vallarsi, D., 9, 184, 190, 201, 243
Vergil, 119, 165, 188
    Aen. 1.37: 224; 1.539 ff.: 213;
    2.677 f.: 207; 3.193: 188, 191;
    3.194: 193; 3.195: 189; 4.366 f.:
    207; 5.9: 191, 193; 5.11: 189;
    7.337 f.: 207; 8.389: 236; 12.59:
    207; 12.611: 189; *Ecl.* 4.61: 225;
    Georg. 2.470: 207; 3.261 f.: 194;
    4.147 f.: 190
Victor, Sextus Aurelius, 51, 203
Victorinus of Pettau, 85, 218
Victorius, M., 9

Wright, F. A., 20, 184, 186, 199

3. GENERAL INDEX

Aaron, 87
abba, 105
Abel, 131, 176
Abercius, Inscription of, 198
abortion, 145, 237; = murder of unborn child, 145
Abraham, 81, 131, 134, 150, 153, 176
absolution, 110
abstinence, 143
Acta Pauli et Theclae, 247
Actium, 224
Acts of the Apostles, 63, 83, 102
Adam, 121, 131, 194; first inhabitant of Paradise, 50
adonai, 105
adoption of the Gentiles, 124
adulterae Christi, 237
adulterer, 110; adulteress, 22
adultery, 18, 23, 144, 164, 187; against Christ, 145
adversary (= devil), 60, 62, 136
Aegyptios confessores, 192, 211
Africa, 14, 15
Agamemnon, 242
Agamestor, 80
Aggeus, 122
Aleppo, 196
Alexander, 174
Alexandria, 17, 191; synod, 211, 212
Alexandrine monk, 30; decree, 71
alleluia, 107
Almighty Jove, 118
alms, 26, 168; when giving, let God alone see, 160
Alps, 22
altar, 57, 65, 67, 79, 84, 90, 92, 98; fire, 63; the forbidden altars of heaven, 115
altilis, 243
Altinum, 6, 192
alumni, 197
Alypius, 13, 190
Aman, 154, 240
Amandus, 11
Ambacum, 192
ambition, 141, 179

amen, 107
Ammonites, 142
Amnon, 145
Amos, 67
Amulius, 80
Anapsychia, 11
Anastasius I, Pope, 18
anathema, 71
anchorites, 28, 170, 172 f., 190; in Nitrian mountains, 192
angel, angels, 54, 68, 72, 73, 82, 86, 99, 112, 123, 125, 128, 131, 132, 135, 142, 144, 153, 154, 156, 176, 178; sin of envy could creep even upon, 131; Gabriel, 174; of Satan, 73, 167; archangel, 55
anger, 57, 126, 129, 205
animal, animals, 46, 114, 116; clean and unclean, 151
Anna, 44, 178
anna, 104, 105, 106, 107; *domine,* 224
anthrax, anthraka, 99
Antichrist, 71, 128, 131, 175
Antimus, 162
Antioch, 6, 18, 19, 38, 73, 187, 188, 189, 190, 191, 196, 206, 208, 210; synod, 211; rival claimants to bishopric of, 11, 210
Antiochus IV, 231
antipope, 212; Ursinus, 190
Antonius, monk of Haemona, 55, 193, 196, 204
Antony of Egypt, 172, 190, 245
Apocalypse, 67, 68, 86, 99
Apollinaris of Laodicea, 17, 210
apostates, 203
apostle, apostles, 32, 33, 35, 40, 48, 53, 57, 62, 63, 65, 69, 70, 71, 77, 81, 85, 87, 91, 100, 101, 102, 118, 125, 126, 131, 132, 137, 141, 143, 144, 148, 149, 152, 153, 155, 162, 163, 164, 167, 168, 173, 174, 175; a spiritual physician, 141; armor of, 33; sin of envy could creep even upon, 131; successor of, 75
Apostles, Acts of the, 63, 83, 102

261

apostolus, 101

Aquila, 87, 97, 98, 99, 100, 101, 105, 106, 218, 219, 221, 223

Aquileia, 6, 39, 46, 48, 187, 188, 191, 192, 195, 197, 198, 200, 201, 202, 205

Aramaic, 222, 223

archangels, 55

archdeacon, 198

Arian, Arians, 71, 72, 76, 210, 212; madness, 75; synod, 210; teaching, poison of the, 44; controversies, 202

Arianism, 202, 212

Aristotle, 69

Arius, 72, 211

ark, Noe's, 71, 151, 175; of the covenant, 156, 157

armor, 144; Apostle's, 33

arms, 176

army, Pharaoh's, 178

Arriana rabies, 213

Arrianorum proles, 211, 212

art, scribe's, 38

arts, world civilized by, 46; liberal, 32

ascetics, ascetic life, asceticism, 3, 4, 6, 8, 10, 19, 198, 206; at Aquileia, 191, 197, 198, 200, 201

Asella, 7, 12

ashes, 35, 77, 81, 136, 149

Asia Minor, 198

aslianna, 105

ass, 44, 157, 179

Assyrian king, 137

Assyrians, 156

Athenians, 80

Attalus, 42

Aurelius, Bishop, 17

Auxentius, 27, 72, 187, 188, 212

avarice, 62, 63, 166–69, 173, 207; comparison of, with idolatry, 63, 207

Aventine, 7, 12

Azarias, 216

Baalbek, 192

babel, 43; i.e., "confusion," 115; tower of, 85

Babylon, 43, 89, 138, 139; daughter of, 139

Baltasar, 156

bands of monks, 30

Banias, 81

banquet, 128; of the King, 121; celebrated daily, 123

baptism, 5, 113, 199, 220; by the Spirit, 90; of Jerome, 5, 210; of Bonosus, 36, 199; Deluge, 50, 202; second, i.e., by fire, 90; receive the garment of Christ, 74; referenced as bath, 36; he who is once washed in God need not wash again, 69; "taken to the water," 42; buried with Christ in, 60

Baptist, John the, *see* John

bark, 46, 201; "bark-users," 46

barrama, 108

baruch, 105

basem, 105

Basilica, St. Peter's, 168

basilisks, 42

baths, 69

battering ram, 62

battle, 60, 154, 237; at Nola, 41, 198; of Cannae, 41, 198

beans, 171

beasts, 48; wild, 77, 140; blood of, 116

Beatitude, Your, 71, 72, 73, 75, 108, 109, 211

bedchamber, bedchambers, 158, 163

beggars, 168

Belial, 116, 165

Bernard of Clairvaux, 196

Beroea, 196

beth, 104

Bethlehem, 4, 7, 14, 16, 17, 233

Bethsabee, 144, 237

betrayal of Judas, 174

betrayer (= Judas), 55

Bible, 3, 7, 15, 38, 135, 172, 195, 220

bird, a fattened, 163

bishop, bishops, 17, 27, 66, 67, 77, 189, 192, 198, 200, 202, 203, 210, 223, 240; clergy of first degree, 208

Cappadocia, 31

Black Sea, 188

blackberries, 67

Blesilla, daughter of Paula, 11, 146, 237

wash again, 69; receive the garment of, 74; vestments of, 70; tunic of, 134; bonds in, 74; always sacrifices Himself for believers, 123; partake of body of, 65

Christi adulterae, 237

Christi vestimenta, 210; *vestem*, 210

Christian, Christians, 20, 38, 48, 56, 62, 63, 64, 65, 76, 77, 113, 118, 119, 163, 166, 186, 188, 193, 197, 199, 206, 223, 242, 243; ecclesiastical rank does not make a, 67; Latin literature, 223

Christianity, 193, 197, 220, 237

Christological heresy of Apollinaris, 210

Chromatius, 6, 41, 46, 195, 196, 198, 200

Chronicles, 217; books of, 80

Chrysocomas, 48, 196, 201

Chrysogonus, 201

Church, 3, 13, 14, 19, 26, 43, 66, 71, 75, 84, 88, 91, 121, 125, 137, 142, 145, 169, 175, 189, 210, 225, 233; ship of, 188; Rachel a symbol of the, 153; bosom of the, 42 f.; as mother, 145, 237

churches, 77, 111

Ciceronian, Jerome accused of being, 20, 166, 189, 229, 243

Cilicia, 31, 190

Cilician goats, 162

circumcision, 112

citizenship, 60; in heaven, 75

cities, towered, 32

city of God, 160

clemency, 111, 112

clergy, 10, 26, 65, 147, 162, 170, 203; of the third degree, 66, 208; three degrees of, 208

cloak, 162, 172

clothes, clothing, 167, 168, 169; of *remnuoth* monks, 170; swaddling, 176; sheep's, 175

coal, 84, 90, 92, 93, 98, 99; coals, 146

coat of mail, 60, 177

coats, 151

coenobium, 245

coin, 129, 168; copper coins, 66; gold coins, 169

colonist, new, of Paradise, 32

colt, ass's, 157

comedies, 118

comic poet, 46

command, 101, 150; God's, 114; God's commands, 127

commander, 60

commandments, 93, 99, 109, 119, 123, 124, 125, 126, 152; of Christ, 44; easy precepts of, 121

Concordia, 19, 191, 196, 201, 202

concubines, 146, 156, 178

confession, 44, 72, 77, 125, 130, 212; house of, 120

confessor, 192

confessors, Egyptian, 30, 71, 192, 211

conscience, 145; a guilty, 145; flame of, 166

consonantia, 124, 231

Constantine, 196, 217

Constantinople, 6, 7, 201, 210, 214, 223; Council of, 7, 210, 212

consubstantialis, 211

continence, 147, 152, 233; virtue of, 154

conversion, 74; of Blesilla, 237

convert, 203, 206, 220, 233

cooks, 142

Corinthians, 129; Paul's second letter to, 177

Cornelius the centurion, 67

Cornelius, Pope, 203

cotidie, 185

Council, of Constantinople, 7, 210, 212; of Nicaea, 211; of Jerusalem, 17; of the Jews, 74

covenant, ark of the, 156, 157; tablets of the, 157

Crassus, 44

creation, plan of, 153; sinners of all, 127

Creator, 115, 120, 122, 173; of universe, 143

creature, 125, 131, 164, 232; creatures, 115

creed, 72; Nicene, 71, 211

cross, 32, 64, 74, 75, 78, 111, 154, 160, 175, 216; disciple of the, 71; standard of the, 60; sign of the, 173

herbs, 142
Hercules, 118
hereses, 246
heresy, 145, 211; Apollinaris' Christological, 210; Manichean, 246; of
the Ophitae, 67; Pelagian, 16;
Sabellian, 76
heretic, heretics, 71, 73, 76, 77, 99;
Sabellian, 212; of Tarsus, 73, 212
heretical sects, 175
hermit, hermits, 53, 77, 191, 196,
206
heterodoxy, 11
heu, 107
Hexapla, compiled by Origen, 222;
of the Psalms, 224
Hibera excetra, 197
Hippo, 4, 14, 15, 16
Holofernes, 154
Holy Ghost, 83, 215, 220; gift of the,
67
Holy Land, 12, 200, 218
Holy of Holies, 87
holy orders, 66
Holy Places, 192
Holy Scripture, 30
Holy See, 203
Holy Spirit, 21, 25, 29, 52, 62, 82,
83, 93, 97, 100, 121, 169, 211;
grace of, 124; temple of, 138
Holy Writ, 143, 215
homicidium, 237
ὁμοούσιος, *homoousion,* 211, 212
honey, 73
horses, 163
hosanna, *osanna,* 11, 13, 19, 103,
104, 105, 106, 107, 108, 179, 223
hostility to God, riotous living is, 115
Hosts, Lord of, 87, 219
household expenses, 174
householder, 113
Humanity, Your, 70
humility, 48, 55, 90, 94, 101, 161
hunger, 143, 148, 168, 177
hungry, blessedness of the, 167
husks, 116, 133
Husband (of virgin Eustochium, i.e.,
the Lord), 147
Hylas, 31, 191, 193
hymn, hymns, 25, 43, 171

hypostasis, hypostases, 11, 71, 72, 73,
210, 211, 212
Hyrcanian tigers, 61

ἰχθύς, fish, symbol of Christ, 198
Iconium, 247
idol, idols, 62, 63, 115, 116, 118;
songs for praises of, 119; of wood,
120; temple of, 119, 165; servant
of, 120
idolaters, 63, 117
idolatry, 62, 63, 126; comparison of
avarice with, 63, 207
Iesus Nave, 239
illnesses of Jerome, 30, 31, 35, 36,
39, 193, 197
Immae, 196
immortality, 69
imperator, 190
incense, 63, 98
income from property, 174
inheritance, 127
iniquity, 127, 132; = Aman, 154
injustice, 115, 132
Innocent I, Pope, 16, 17
Innocent, priest friend of Jerome, 18,
21, 31, 187, 188, 191, 193
insanas feminas, 226
Inscription of Abercius, 198
intercourse, carnal, 146
interpretation, 89, 92, 94, 105, 113,
119, 123, 131, 134, 154; difficulty
of, 84; mystical, 98, 123; of the
Gospels, 103
interpreters, 97, 98, 105; Latin, 124
intrinsecus commorantes, 190
Isaac, 81
Isaias, 80, 81, 82, 83, 86, 89, 90, 91,
92, 93, 94, 95, 96, 98, 100, 121,
122, 159, 173, 179, 217, 221; passion of, 90; vision of, 11, 13, 19,
92, 214
Isidore, 169, 245
Ismael, 89
Israel, 81, 105, 106, 112, 124, 125,
126, 127, 128, 138, 158, 226, 231;
people, 81, 108; sons of, 81, 226;
house of, 89, 113; enemies of, 142
Israelite, 118
Italian people, 46
Italy, 12, 191
ius summum, 189

prison, 22, 33, 68, 140
Procopius of Gaza, 18
prodigal son, 11, 13, 19, 28, 53, 74, 224, 226, 231
Profuturus, 14
property, income from, 174
prophecy, 94, 95, 122, 123, 128, 136, 138, 151; of Christ, 106; of the Psalm, 106
prophet, prophets, 34, 43, 67, 80, 81, 83, 85, 89, 91, 92, 93, 95, 98, 99, 101, 115, 117, 118, 120, 121, 122, 127, 129, 131, 134, 142, 145, 153, 165, 168, 172, 246
prophetess, 175, 246; prophetesses, virgin, 44; of Montanism, 226
proverb, 197
Proverbs of Solomon, 146
Psalm, Psalms, 87, 88, 93, 99, 105, 106, 119, 123, 131, 134, 149, 161, 164, 170; of David, 38; book of, 50; *Hexapla* of, 224; Gradual, 42, 199; prophecy of, 106; superscriptions of, 124, 231
Psalmist, 76, 83, 139
Psalter, 165; New, 219
Ptolemy, 42, 231
publican, publicans, 55, 63, 74, 110, 111, 112, 113, 123, 126, 225

quaestuaria, 209
Quarnero, Gulf of, 194
quinta editio, 223, 224

Rachel, 177; symbol of the Church, 153
rags, 161, 168
Rahab, 175
rank, episcopal, 200; ecclesiastical, does not make a Christian, 67
ravens, 168
reaper, 143, 153
reason, 114
reception of sinners, 129
recruit, 34
Red Sea, 178
Redeemer, 176; of our salvation, 127
redemption, 104, 131
remnuoth, 170, 245
repentance, 53, 110, 111, 112, 113, 120, 123, 134, 225

repentant son, 120, 130
resurrection, 91; to come, 51
rhetoric, 46; rhetorical language, 117; speech, 135; style, 206
Rhine, 6, 34, 197
Rhossus, 190
riches, 130, 167, 173; promise of, 153
right of sanctuary, 127
ring, 109, 121; rings, 162
riotous living, 127; is hostility to God, 115
Riparius, 11
rites, burial, 160
robe, 109; wedding garment, 121
roes, 48
Rogatus, 242
Roman, Romans, 41, 69, 82, 130, 206, 212; synods, 187, 196, 223; empire, 80, 127; law, 237; society, 233; pens, 32; ladies, 7; women, 237
Rome, 4, 5, 13, 14, 19, 27, 34, 71, 74, 146, 162, 165, 168, 188, 190, 191, 192, 195, 196, 203, 210, 214, 223, 233, 245; primacy of, 19, 210; eminence of, 70; delights of, 140
Romulus, 80
root of greed, 167
roses, 152
ruach, 97
rule, rules, of conduct, 209 f., 232
ruler, 44; of that darkness, 116; of the lower world, 145
rust, intellectual, 21
Rusticus, 10

Sabaoth, 87; Lord of, 81, 89, 92
Sabbath day, 112
Sabellian heresy, 76; heretics, 212
Sabinian, 10
sacerdos, 200
sackcloth, 32, 77, 140, 161
sacrament, 5, 135; bread of the, 178; sacraments, 113
sacramentum, 189, 234; *sacramenti, panem*, 247
sacrilege, 63, 72, 145
sailor, sailors, 31, 63, 68
St. Peter's Basilica, 168
saints, 28, 114, 121, 123, 129, 173, 176; merits of, 94; envy may be-